Cosmopolitanism and the Age of School Reform

Cosmopolitanism and the Age of School Reform
Science, Education, and Making Society by Making the Child

Thomas S. Popkewitz

Routledge
Taylor & Francis Group
New York   London

Cover designed by Christine Alfery.

Routledge
Taylor & Francis Group
270 Madison Avenue
New York, NY 10016

Routledge
Taylor & Francis Group
2 Park Square
Milton Park, Abingdon
Oxon OX14 4RN

© 2008 by Taylor & Francis Group, LLC
Routledge is an imprint of Taylor & Francis Group, an Informa business

Printed in the United States of America on acid-free paper
10 9 8 7 6 5 4 3 2 1

International Standard Book Number-13: 978-0-415-95815-8 (Softcover) 978-0-415-95814-1 (Hardcover)

Library of Congress Cataloging-in-Publication Data

Popkewitz, Thomas S.
    Cosmopolitanism and the age of school reform : science, education, and making society by making the child / Thomas S. Popkewitz.
        p. cm.
    Includes bibliographical references and index.
    ISBN 978-0-415-95814-1 (hardback : alk. paper) -- ISBN
    978-0-415-95815-8 (pbk. : alk. paper) 1. Education and state. 2.
Education--Research--Social aspects. 3. Education--Philosophy. 4. Cosmopolitanism.
I. Title.

LC71.P5956 2007
370.1--dc22

2007014025

Visit the Taylor & Francis Web site at
http://www.taylorandfrancis.com

and the Routledge Web site at
http://www.routledge.com

For the Kinder of the Kinder, who are outside the limits of cosmopolitanism: Jake, Gabe, Ryan, Eliot, Jordon, Max, Sammy, Ally, Simon, and Izzy and their parents.

Contents

Preface

As I read contemporary literatures about cosmopolitanism and thought about it in terms of modern schooling, I realized that the idea and aspiration of cosmopolitanism exercised a powerful hold on the pedagogical projects throughout the 19th century to the present. Often traced to the Northern European and North American Enlightenments, faith in cosmopolitanism is the emancipatory potential of human reason and science. The radicalism of that reason is its cultural thesis about modes of living that provide the universal paths that free the individual from provincialism, the boundaries of nationalism, theological dogma, and the irrationalities of mystical faith. The freedom associated with cosmopolitanism enjoins reason and rationality (science) with notions of agency and progress that fill the future with hope.

My interest in cosmopolitanism is not to trace that faith but to consider the politics of knowledge that it inscribes in the practices of schooling, to think about the "reason" of cosmopolitanism as it circulated in issues of contemporary reforms about teaching, teacher education, and research as projects to include "all children" and to leave no child behind. The reforms of pedagogy embody principles about the cosmopolitan child who acts and thinks as a "reasonable person." But what is interesting about this reasonable person who is cosmopolitan is that he or she is not just any person. He or she is someone who is *made* and that is where the schooling and its pedagogy becomes central. That "making" is treated as a unity of "all children learning," and that unity is the crux of cosmopolitanism. It is also the production of differences and fears of those who are not "reasoned" and reasonable.

Cosmopolitanism brings to the surface the importance and limits of a number of important qualities and characteristics of modern life that order what "we" are, what "we" should be, and who is not enabled to be that "we." Let me just briefly state some of these. Cosmopolitanism entails ideas about liberty and freedom, human agency, reason, and rationality (science). But these ideas are not just there for the asking, are not transcendental categories to apply equally across modern life. They are linked to the problem of the social administration of the child so that the child can become the cosmopolitan citizen of the future. The book on cosmopolitanism was ironically to free the individual from local and national attachments through transcendental values of a unified humanity, yet that universalism was historically linked to projects in making the citizen of the republic in the name of cosmopolitan values. As important, the "reason" and rationality of cosmopolitanism instantiated comparative distinctions that differentiated, divided, and abjected groups and individual *not* "civilized" and hence not qualitied for participation. Cosmopolitanism is, then, a strategy to explore historically the intertwining of the problem of social exclusion with the very impulses to include and to "enlighten."

The production of cosmopolitanism and its other aspects do not emerge as one single collection of things to recoup through "rigorous scientific evidence," a trope of contemporary policy and research. The different notions come together and change to order and differentiate images and narratives that fold into cosmopolitanism. The study of schooling requires thinking about how the different historical practices come together and are assembled, and explores their limits in the shaping and fashioning of our notions of humanity and progress.

As I thought about the study of schooling, I also realized that I was getting into the problem of the "reason" that organizes the present and its particular consciousness through which the principles governing schooling are generated. Again, to briefly state some themes that appear throughout the book, the problem of freedom introduces uncertainty. The privileging of reason as a mechanism of change means that we do not know what the consequence of that reason will be. Pedagogy is a strategy that tames that uncertainty by providing the rules and standards by which reason is ordered and change is organized. There is also the introduction of modern conceptions of time that move in a regular fashion from the past to the present and are directed to the future; the latter is embedded in problem solving and concepts of agency and action.

And finally, cosmopolitanism brings into focus the politics of knowledge in the production of the self and the world, with notions of childhood and family as governing practices. That governing is in the partitioning of sensibilities and dispositions in reflection and acts. And that governing is not merely to inscribe transcendental values about the unity of the whole. The inscriptions of cosmopolitanism are processes that qualify and disqualify individuals for participation and action.

The strategy in this book is a history of the present to think about schooling and its double qualities of inclusion and exclusion. I examine the principles assembled at the beginning of the 20th century and those from today, the beginning of the 21st century, through historicizing changes in school knowledge as a cultural theses about who the child is, and should be. I explore the limits of the notions of agency, participation, and community, for example, as they circulate in pedagogical projects. I argue that these very practices to include simultaneously exclude. That is, the practices to democratize and open up the involvement of marginalized groups in society reinscribe their differences.

The focus on the limits of the practices of schooling is not to argue against salvation themes that strive for a more humane and just world, or to argue against participation and the importance of reason in coming to grips with the constraints and restraints that operate on the possibility of the present. It is just the opposite. The strategy is of an optimism that to unthink what seems natural is to open other possibilities of schooling, teaching, and teacher education. To make the naturalness of the present as strange and contingent is a political strategy of change; to make visible the internments and enclosures of the commonsense of schooling is to make them contestable.

This writing of this book is about the politics of schooling and as a political intervention. The politics of schooling is not merely discovering an efficient program or identifying rules. It is diagnosing the very systems of reason that define the problems of social planning, the reforms to rectify human conditions and people, and the expertise of the sciences of planning in the governing of the child and teacher. The history of schooling, from this perspective, is an administrative practice to change society by calculating and inscribing principles of how to think, reason, and act as future citizens of the nation.

The analysis examines the overlapping the practices of policy, education science, teacher education, and curriculum planning through bringing them into contact with broader scholarship. The interdisciplinary qualities of this study bring cultural studies; cultural histories; Foucauldian, postmodern, and postcolonial studies; and feminist theory, among others into a conversation with the phenomena of schooling. What emerges, however, with playing intellectually with these different but intellectually related fields of scholarships interpretative frames that relate to the problem of cosmopolitanism and schooling that underlie this book.

CHAPTER 1

Cosmopolitanism
An Object of Study

Prologue

If I may play with a saying of the times, we live in an age of reform.[1] That age is long in the making and continually expresses the hope of and fears in the cosmopolitan society and child.[2] The thesis of cosmopolitanism was the Enlightenment's hope of the world citizen whose commitments transcended provincial and local concerns with ideal values about humanity. Cosmopolitanism embodied a radical historical thesis about human reason in changing the world and people. The reforms of society were to produce transcendent ethics in the search of progress built on human rights and the hospitality to others. The school pedagogy embodied that optimism of a future that was to be guided by the reason and rationality of cosmopolitanism. But, as I will argue, that optimism is a comparative system of reason that enunciates and divides the child who holds the emancipatory future from those feared as threatening the promise of progress.

The hope and fears of cosmopolitanism are pervasive in the schooling of today's reform society. The aspirations of its transcendental values are seemingly wherever one goes today in the world of school reform. There are efforts to improve something and to emancipate everything, to create a more cosmopolitan society, and, in some cases, to promote the world citizen whose allegiances are to human rights, environmental balances, and hospitality to diversity. The hope for the future embodies fears of degeneration and decay. The fears of the dangers of the future maintain the optimism of finding the right mixtures of reforms and science to produce progress. These different elements of cosmopolitan theses travel as foundation assumptions in U.S. school reforms for curriculum standards for teachers, for children's learning, and for different research practices about finding which reforms work and identifying the pedagogical knowledge and accountability models that will ensure the child's success as the future citizen of the republic. Cosmopolitan aspirations are carried in efforts for collaboration to engage parents, teachers, communities, and administrators in achieving modes of living that enable their self-realization and the collective betterment of all people in the community.

Reforms are planned for everyone in this age of reform. The phrase "all children learn"—signaling the belief of universal equality—is joined with the hope that there will be "no child left behind," the latter phrase capturing the sentiment that every child have the same access to education used to name national legislation. Policy and research seek an inclusive schooling and society where all collaborate to live out the historical dreams of the republic. Neoliberal economic theories of the trickle-down economic model provide one path to the cosmopolitan life. School voucher programs are envisioned by conservatives as enabling children of the poor to emulate the wealthy and share in the cosmopolitan unity where there is no difference. Critical pedagogies draw on the Great Depression's educational reformer George Counts, who wrote "Dare the School Build a New Social Order?" (1932/1980). The essay implores teachers to confront the excesses of capitalism by working towards the reconstruction of society through making schools democratic. The current call to remake society appears in teacher education and critical pedagogy to build the new society, with the emancipatory values of cosmopolitanism also present. Paulo Friere's "pedagogy of the oppressed" is transferred from Brazilian Catholic reforms in a rural setting to American urban schools as a bottoms-up strategy for a cosmopolitan world bound to social justice and equality.

While the phrase "The Age of School Reform" may make it seem as one continuous process from the Enlightenment to the present, that is not my intention. Cosmopolitanism has particular continuities and differences as it travels into the present.

But first we consider today's inscriptions of cosmopolitanism. Reform has promoted the reconstruction of the school, sometimes the society, but always the child and teacher. That reconstruction was part of the 19th-century globalization in which the nation-state was formed (Meyer, Boli, Thomas, & Ramirez, 1997; Meyer, Kamens, Benavot, Cha, & Wong, 1992), and again today with different assemblies and connections about the global citizen and cosmopolitan future. The European Union, for example, declares itself in support of an intercultural and learning society. The Taiwan Ministry of Education quotes George Counts to restructure the school for an information society, combining the new capitalism and environmentalism as a world culture. Professional research associations internationalize education as finding common ground among different nations in the quest for global progress.[3] The seductiveness of reform is its promise of cosmopolitan harmony and consensus.[4]

Today's age of reform leaves no researcher behind. The sciences of schooling, as the progressive educators at the beginning of the 20th century indicated, are to plan for social improvements that will produce an enlightened society. Cosmopolitan notions of empowerment, voice, emancipation, and the mastery of the present through useful knowledge in the name of humanity's future are triggers of that research. The high stakes of research are to reshape the teacher and the child in the hope of reshaping and emancipating society from traditional habits and attitudes.[5] Some research programs align with federal initiatives to identify "what works" so as to fill society with the replications of good reforms. The watchwords are reforms that are proven through "scientific evidence." The "gold standard" of research methods is drug testing.[6] Other research draws on communication theories and constructivist psychologies to make the future child more humane and the world more progressive. That research reincarnates the ideas of early 20th-century Russian Marxist psychologist Lev Vygotsky and the American liberal philosopher-psychologist John Dewey in projects of social psychology about social improvement and useful knowledge. To continue the medical analogy, the potion of this social psychology is to get "what works" but without the drug testing. Change is in the ordering of interactions in and discourses of the classroom (Popkewitz, 1998a). Research designs the conditions of the classroom and people in collaborative processes and feedback loops that are to guarantee the goals of reforms.

This placing of cosmopolitanism into narratives of the school and the nation might seem odd. The Enlightenment is seen as an attitude to transcend the local and provincialism of the nation through its quest for a universal, emancipatory reason of a world citizen. Ideally this may be correct, but historically it is ironic. The universal values of the Enlightenment's cosmopolitan individual were inscribed in the new republics and its citizen as its transcendental values and purposes. This is explored in this text through the discussion of American Exceptionalism, the telling of the nation as a unique human experiment in the progressive development of the ideals of cosmopolitan values.

But there are other elements that go unquestioned about cosmopolitanism in schooling. The cosmopolitan child is not born but made, and schooling is the central site for this production. Theories of and about learning, development, and the problem-solving child in pedagogy are practices to calculate and administer the procedures of "thought" to make the child into the future cosmopolitan citizen.

Equally important, cosmopolitanism embodies a particular mode of organizing difference. That entails comparative installations that differentiate and divide those who are enlightened and civilized from those who do not have those qualities—the backward, the savage, and the barbarian of the 19th century and the at-risk and delinquent child of the present. The universal and inclusive practices of school reforms that speak about inclusion locate difference and incomplete elements, points, and directions in the processes of inclusion and exclusion. School reforms, for example, are to provide an inclusive society where "all children learn" and there is "no child left behind." The gesture is to make all children the same and on equal footing. That gesture of hope overlaps with fears of the child whose characteristics are not cosmopolitan and a threat to the moral unity of the whole. Pedagogical narratives and images of cosmopolitanism simultaneously embody the two gestures of hope and fears of the dangers and dangerous populations.

The double gestures of cosmopolitanism are important to this study for considering how the impulses for an inclusive society produces its opposite. The use of "ism" in cosmopolitanism gives attention to the different assemblies and connections that distinguish reason and "the reasonable person" rather than treating the word as a distinct doctrine. Further, cosmopolitanism is not one thing but historical inscriptions that have different contours in different times and spaces (see Taylor, 1989).

Cosmopolitanism and the Age of School Reform investigates the systems of reason in present schooling, policy, and research as double gestures of inclusion and exclusion. My focus on cosmopolitanism is on its systems of reason in governing who the child is, who the child should be, and who does "fit" in the images and narratives of that child. This interest continues an earlier concern with social epistemology, that is, the politics of reason as historical practices that govern reflection and action (Popkewitz, 1991; Popkewitz, 2004c). The analysis played with politics through Foucault's (1991) notion of governmentality.[7] Pedagogy is political through its inscriptions of rules and standards by which experiences are classified, problems located, and procedures given to order what is seen, thought about, and acted on (also see Rancière, 2004c). The politics involved in the shaping and fashioning of conduct, however, are not only about what "we" should be but also about processes of casting out and excluding what does not fit into the normalized spaces.

The notion of cosmopolitanism was provoked by reading the millennium issue of the *British Journal of Sociology* in the early part of 2000. Many major contemporary figures wrote about cosmopolitanism as the overriding principle for the reconstruction of contemporary world society. Cosmopolitanism was related to European and North American Enlightenments as a set of principles to counter the processes of global genocide and inequalities witnessed as the 21st century started. After this reading, I began to explore a large corpus of literature about, for example, cosmopolitanism and forgiveness (see, e.g. Derrida, 2001) and the need to root its universals in particularities of the nation (see, e.g., Appiah, 2006).[8]

I realized in this reading that what was spoken about as the new 21st-century cosmopolitanism is remarkably similar to the narratives of modern schooling. Although the actual word *cosmopolitanism* is not used much in today's reforms, its foundational assumptions are embedded in theories of learning, development, and curriculum. Cosmopolitanism is embodied in talk about autonomy and self-responsibility, the importance of planning life through principles of reason and rationality (e.g., problem solving), and respect for diversity and difference. These principles are joined with those about participation and collaboration in communities as values that transcend the local and provincial.

The ostensible function of the modern school is to teach children cosmopolitan principles of reason. Education in the early American republic and today is to produce the enlightened individual who acts with self-responsibility that relates to the inscription of universal moral and social values about the good of the community. Interesting to me as I read further, the revision of the modern high school into a comprehensive high school in the first decades of the 20th century was initially called "the cosmopolitan high school" of the future (Drost, 1967).

At this point, it is reasonable to ask about how cosmopolitanism organizes the study of schooling. What does it purchase for interpreting school reforms of teaching, teacher education, and research?

Cosmopolitanism directs attention to sacred notions of the present in school reforms. Cosmopolitanism forms cultural theses about the modes of life organized in pedagogy. To talk of cultural theses is to focus on how different sets of ideas, institutions and authority relations are connected to order the principles of conduct. Teaching the child to problem solve and collaborate in communities of learning, for example, embodies cultural theses about the modes of life of the child. Further, embedded in the cultural theses of cosmopolitanism are certain sacred notions that circulate to order reflection and acts in pedagogy—that is, the role of human agency for the self-realization of the individual, social progress, and community as a site in which the individual accomplishes common values.

The cultural theses of cosmopolitanism do not stand as purely ideals to implement through efficient teaching and planning. The principles that order conduct are double gestures: modes of living given transcendental values, such as living as a problem solver working for a more humane and just world. The transcendal values, however, are paradoxical. The qualities and characteristics of the transcendent subject contains its opposite, the child not guided by reason and science and thus not "fitting" into the spaces of cosmopolitanism.

I focus on the double gestures of pedagogy as processes of abjection. Abjection is the casting out and exclusion of particular qualities of people from the spaces of inclusion.[9] The process of abjection is embodied in the recognition given to excluded groups for inclusion, yet that recognition radically differentiates and circumscribes something else that is both repulsive and fundamentally differentiated from the whole (see Shimakawa, 2002). The category of "immigrant" is illustrative. The immigrant is a category of a group and individuals whose status is somewhere not quite "in"—worthy for inclusion but excluded. The immigrant lives in the in-between spaces between requiring special intervention programs to enable access and equity and at the same time established as different and the Other, outside by virtue of their qualities of life. I argue, for example, that Dewey's pragmatism, Thorndike's behaviorist psychology, and contemporary expressions about empowerment, problem solving, and collaboration are processes of abjection. They function as gestures of the hope for an inclusionary society through the pedagogical reforms, yet the very enunciation of that hope are fears of the dangers and dangerous populations that threaten the envisioned future.

Abjection, then, is a way to think about the complex set of relations of inclusion and exclusion; the casting as outside and placing in an in-between space and excluding in the same phenomenon as the cosmopolitanism of schooling. Pedagogical practices are simultaneously drawing in and yet placing outside certain qualities of life and people. I use the plural cultural theses to talk about changes in time/space in the modes of life as well as the double gestures that differentiate modes of living embodied in cosmopolitanism.

To consider cosmopolitanism as a process of abjection is to think differently about the study of schooling, research, and professional education. It moves from the binary logic of inclusion and exclusion that underlies English empirical-analytical traditions in philosophy and research or Hegelian dialectics of critical studies that differentiates between materiality and knowledge (text and context). This study of schooling is a diagnostic of the systems of reason as practices that simultaneously produce what is inside and outside.

Two questions organize the study of schooling:

> What cultural theses of cosmopolitanism circulate in pedagogy, teacher education, and the sciences of education at the beginning of the 20th and the 21st centuries?

What are the processes of abjection embodied in the cosmopolitan agency, collaboration, and science and how do they change?

The study can be considered as a history of the present (see, e.g., Dean, 1994). This history is not archival in the sense of tracing events and people. Nor is this method to consider the "reason" of cosmopolitanism as a thing of pure logic, something that we do naturally, or the innate qualities of the mind. The history of the present is to explore social epistemological changes that produce the principles governing who the child is, who he or she should be, and who does not fit into those spaces. Its use of primary sources of the past and present is to understand the distinctions, differentiations and divisions through which the objects of schooling are produced, ordered, and classified.

The historicizing of the subject of change is, as the feminist philosopher Butler (1993) argues, to challenge what is uncritically taken as natural to regulate and produce subjects. The study of cosmopolitanism is, to borrow from Foucault, the "matter of shaking this false self-evidence, of demonstrating its precariousness, of making visible not its arbitrariness, but its complex interconnection with a multiplicity of historical processes, many of them of recent date" (Foucault, 1991, p. 75).

The plurality of cultural theses is to recognize another layer of the practices of schooling. The universals of cosmopolitanism were never merely about all humanity but historically particular. The principles of agency, science, and progress emerged in the Protestant Reformation, given secular potency through Enlightenment projects of Northern Europe and North America in which the modern nation and school formed. The principles of the subject of pedagogy are assembled in particular ways in progressive education at the beginning of the 20th century and (re)visioned today in making the lifelong learner and the child recognized as different and left behind.

Outline of the Book and Methodological Note

This and the following chapter from the first section of the book. The chapters focus on reason and cosmopolitanism as historical practices about the function of reason and the making of individuality. I explore briefly the lure of cosmopolitanism in contemporary sociology, philosophy, and education. I then ask about reason itself. Cosmopolitanism is about the individual who uses reason and science to perfect the future, but others before the Enlightenment "reasoned" about existence. What is the distinctive historical quality given to reason in cosmopolitanism? In answering this question, I focus on the notion of human agency, a historically recent idea that people can affect their lives and that of their community through reason and science. The second chapter continues exploring the different qualities through which cosmopolitanism is assembled.

The remainder of the book moves to cosmopolitan principles and its processes of abjection in progressive reforms from the beginning of the 20th century to contemporary reforms about "all children learning" where no child is left behind.

Part 1 examines pedagogy and its sciences at the turn of the 20th century in relation to a particular salvation narrative of American Exceptionalism about the epic of the nation as embodying transcendental cosmopolitan values. The account of the nation as the unique human experiment is found in the psychologies of John Dewey, Edward L. Thorndike, G. Stanley Hall, and early sociology. The reforms and sciences of education gave focus to the urban conditions and people to confront the perceived moral disorder of the city that threatened American Exceptionalism. Progressive education is a response to urban moral disorder that produces processes of abjection in pedagogy. The notion of alchemy is used to consider the transporting and translating of school subjects in the making of the child and establishing difference.

Part 2 examines the changing principles of cosmopolitanism and its processes of abjection in contemporary curriculum and teacher education standards reforms and research. Two cultural theses are explored about modes of living and the processes of abjection in this section. The cultural theses of lifelong learner and the urban, "disadvantaged" child signified in the reforms to ensure that "no child left behind" are placed in relation to each other to simultaneously circumscribe and differentiate the unlivable spaces inside and outside the cosmopolitanism.

The alchemy is again returned to in contemporary standards as forms of mathematics, education is used as an exemplar. A methodological note is in order here. I use the notion of cosmopolitanism over other more familiar words such as Enlightenment and modernity for a number of reasons.

First, histories of the Enlightenment are often social or intellectual histories that do not consider the overlapping of principles generated as cultural theses produced about modes of living.[10] My interest in the cultural theses leads me to emphasize the notion of cosmopolitanism over the notion of the Enlightenment.

Second, I use the word *cosmopolitanism* over the more familiar word *modernity*. Scholarship on modernity typically concerns institutional changes of industrialization and urbanization and leaves questions of social epistemology outside of its purview. In saying why I chose cosmopolitanism in the study, I also recognize the overlaps of these literatures in relation to the arguments that follow.

Third, the United States is an exemplar to explore the double gestures of cosmopolitanism in schooling. That choice is one of familiarity rather than to privilege the nation or to center on the West and its particular systems of reason (see, e.g., Popkewitz, 2005). The United States is a particular site to study the limits of schooling. These limits are related to the sacredness of what is assembled in cosmopolitanism—notions of participation, agency, reason, and science that appear as sacred and natural categories of progress and emancipation. I use the notion of American exceptionalism in the text to provide a specific historicity to the present and not to argue its exceptionalism.

Both in and outside of the West, notions of cosmopolitanism join secularization processes of individual agency and progress with salvation themes of redemption embodied in pedagogical practices of the school. Cosmopolitanism in its European and North American contexts has never been one "thing," as different assembles were brought together in Germany, France, England, and American constructions of "nation-ness" (see, e.g. Elias, 1939/1978; Bell, 2001; Friese & Wagner, 2000; Marx, 2003; Spadafora, 1990). Eastern parts of Europe connected French Enlightenment ideas and German Romanticism in ethnolinguistic belonging in the 19th century and early parts of the 20th century (Sobe, 2006). In postcommunist transitions, national identity was a mosaic of a western European cosmopolitanism and endogenous traditional peasant culture—a liberal enlightenment trend versus an ethnocentric collectivist trend, with sometimes chauvinistic-racist accents (Mincu, 2006).

China visions a modernity that overlaps Confucianism in cultural theses that have cosmopolitanism aspirations (see, e.g., Hayhoe, 2000; Qi, 2005). Japanese modernization processes associated Meiji reforms of the mid-19th century and the post–World War II constructions of the state, and schools incorporated Buddhist qualities of harmonizing through qualities of listening, introspection, sensitivity to nature and natural environments, and a muted sense of the individual that established the particular epic of people, nation, and others in schooling (Shibata, 2005). The secularization and modernization processes of the Kemalist revolution in Turkey during the 20th century cannot be understood adequately without considering the cosmopolitanism that emerged through revisioning of Ottoman Islamic traditions (Kazamias, 2006). I mention these different times and spaces only to further suggest the historical specificity of this study within broader global changes.

The hope of the cosmopolitan future continually has it dissenters. At its extreme were The Nazis who accused the Jews as being rootless cosmopolitanism. Brooks (2007) in an editorial in the New York Times argues that the immigration debate in the U.S. is not between liberal and conservatives that rests on economic or ideological grounds. It is a cultural clash between the cosmopolitan individuals who are university educated and value diversity, global integration and openness verses a rooted nationalism tied to a fear of the destruction of ties to community and social solidarity who favors multiculturalism verses the rooted local. While some see the cosmopolitan as an elite project, what they ignore is how that project was inscribed in modern schooling through its pedagogical projects and linked to notions of democracy and participation, something I focus on in later chapters as it relates to pragmatism and progressive education.

The New Cosmopolitanism: The Seductions of the Global Citizen

With some doubts and cautions, today's cosmopolitanism underpins a faith in the emancipatory potential of human reason in the new millennium (Mehta, 2000). One proponent, Beck (2000), uses cosmopolitanism as a cultural/political counterforce to global capitalism, environmental destructions, and the mass killings that plague the 21st century. Beck offers what he calls a new paradigm of a reflexive cosmopolitanism that intends to eradicate systems of exclusion thwarting human autonomy. Beck considers the Enlightenment's cosmopolitanism as a means to establish a global moral outlook that gives respect to human rights, peaceful relations among nations, pluralism, and diversity. These are coupled with principles of accountability to others. He posits that the present is the first time since the 1648 Treaty of Westphalia, which established the sovereignty of nation that there is a higher regard given for human rights than for national territorial sovereignty.

This elixir of cosmopolitan hope leaches into other fields. As a critique of visual culture, Mirzoeff (2005) calls forth an image of the Enlightenment's cosmopolitanism as the ethics of contemporary life. Mirzoeff argues for the "ethics of hospitality," a notion that "extends and develops the cosmopolitanism of the Enlightenment with reference to the past of the Talmudic tradition, the present crisis and the hope for an ethical future" (p. 15). The universality of cosmopolitanism is given expression locally, "always encountered and enacted in specific circumstances that inevitably put difference into play" (p. 15). The ethics of the cosmopolitan, for Mirzoeff, places the individual in a global community that renews the universal public good and hospitality to difference, removing the fissures of gender, sexuality, and ethnicity.

The aspiration of cosmopolitanism is the purpose of schooling in the new millennium for philosopher Martha Nussbaum (1996). She argues for the ethics of an education that promotes twin allegiances. The first allegiance is to a reasonable and principled cosmopolitanism committed to a community bound by a universal morality that serves all human beings (p. 5). Nussbaum places these universal cosmopolitan commitments in a direct lineage from the Greeks and Diogenes the Cynic, who said, "I am a citizen of the world [*kosmou polités*]."[11] The second allegiance is to the citizen dwelling in the local community of birth through which the commitments to reason and argument form a common source of moral obligations.

Nussbaum's (1996) cosmopolitan thesis envisions the ideal of living as a stranger to oneself and in exile from the provincial and parochial. Communities are sites to enable one to continually be in exile and a stranger to oneself to work to produce moral capacity of the self and others. Educational processes connect students' capacities for reason and problem solving "to fundamental universal values of respect and aspirations for justice and goodness" (p. 8). Students are to understand their own individuality and knowledge, which is bound intricately to the larger world. The deliberative mind is to remake the communities in which one lives. Civic education is teaching students that they are citizens of a world where there is a consensus of shared universal values of reason and moral capacity. Its goal is to enable the child to live as "an exile from the comfort of local truths, from the warm, nestling feeling of patriotism, from the absorbing drama of pride in oneself and one's own" (p. 15).

To make these claims, Nussbaum (1996) deploys a particular analytical history that links the Greeks to the present as a moral lesson for practice. She argues that the twin characteristics of affiliation to a universal moral community and to local practices that work toward a common community resurrect ideas of the Greeks. "Diogenes knew that in the invitation to think as a world citizen was an invitation to be an exile from the comfort of patriotism and its easy sentiments, to see our own ways of life from the point of view of justice and the good" (p. 7). Nussbaum asserts that "We should recognize humanity wherever it occurs, and give its fundamental ingredients, reason and moral capacity, our first allegiance and respect" (p. 7).

Nussbaum's "deliberative mind" is a particular modern consciousness (see, e.g., Berger, Berger, & Kellner, 1974).[12] The "homeless mind" is the process in which one is both an object and subject of reflection. The child is to engage in a mode of living that distances himself or herself from everyday activities through abstract and universal categories that define the just and good as the citizen. That distancing through making one as an object of reflection doubles back on itself to recreate new affiliations, belonging, and "homes." Refusing to be defined by local origins and group membership is to reestablish belonging and a home by ascribing universal moral concepts to personal judgments and experience. The "reflective teacher" embodies this homeless mind, as everyday life is ordered and given significance through ordering principles that have transcendent appeals.

The philosopher Appiah (2006) reasserts this historical construction of cosmopolitanism. It is an analytical set of norms about the universal moral outlook of belonging and home in one's local community. He argues for the rootedness of the cosmopolitan where each individual maintains the home of his or her own cultural particularities but also takes "pleasure from the presence of the other" (Appiah, 1996, p. 21). The engagement in multiculturalism is to give recognition to the diversity of cultures through a dialogue among the diverse groups that develops receptivity to others and a respect for difference.

Perhaps the system of reason about exile, strangers, and receptivity to difference might seem as if there should be no other other way, but it embodies limits as there is nothing "natural" about the notions of progress and emancipation! These arguments elide the double gestures of hope and fear in cosmopolitanism. Mehta (2000), for example, argues European notions of cosmopolitanism are paradoxical. Its images and narratives have been used to commit the violence of colonialization and racism through the transcendent subject who is no subject in particular. Yet at the same time, he continues, the transcendent notions of reason and of humanity have been pivotal as weapons in fights against colonialism.

The Double Times of Reason: The Hope of Progress and Fears of Degeneration

One might ask what is so special about the reason named in the Enlightenment's cosmopolitanism. Did not people always have the facility of reason? And what historically gives the cosmopolitan notion of reason its relation to processes of abjection? This section briefly approaches the questions about the particularity of cosmopolitan reason by locating different ways in which the Greeks and the medieval church considered reason in the ordering of life. I then focus on the notion of progress and the comparative instantiations that emerge as part of the reason of the cosmopolitan.

Reason: Greek Cosmopolis, the Church's Divine Revelation, and the Enlightenment's Secular Perfection

The idea of reason as a principle of governance has a long and varied history in the West that can be traced schematically in the Greek relation of nature and practice, the medieval church's claim to universality, and the secularization of reason is the Enlightenment. What is "new" is the Enlightenment's placement of individuals as agents of change and in inventing possibilities of humans for achieving progress.

If we follow the arguments of Toulmin (1990), classical Greece involved two orders: nature (cosmos, to record the natural order of celestial events) and practical life (activities of human experience and ability in the polis or a community that gave coherence to its organization). In contrast to Nussbaum's account of Greek thought discussed earlier, the Stoic philosophers fused the two notions of order in the word *cosmopolis,* linking practical ideas to the natural order of things (Toulmin, 1990, p. 67).

While the Enlightenment's hope in human reason was to produce a progressive future, the Greeks tied reason to memory and the past. The subject was modified through the acts of memory that liberated one's own being. The primacy of memory was to "sing the hymn of gratitude and recognition to the gods" and "to grasp [the] reality of which we cannot be dispossessed ... [which] makes possible a real sovereignty over ourselves" (Foucault, 2005, p. 468).

To speak of the future indicated hubris and negativity. The future did not exist for people but for the gods. The Greeks saw the search for the future as destroying memory and the person who forgets as "doomed to dispossession and emptiness.... [Individuals] are really no longer anything. They exist in nothingness" (Foucault, 2005, p. 467). Reason, in its modern senses, could not bring agency in the planning of one's life for the future. For the Greeks, one knows oneself through knowing the past. The mind preoccupied with the future is consumed by forgetting, incapable of action, and not free.

The medieval Christian church's claim to universality brought to bear a different notion of reason than the Greek's memory and the Enlightenment's actor who plans for the future. Human reason could not redeem people in their relationship with God (Pocock, 2003). Reason disclosed the eternal, immemorial ordering and hierarchies of nature and events in which people maintained their place in the cosmic of God. Philosophy, the highest form of reason, contemplated the universal categories that rose above temporal knowledge. Reason for St. Augustine and Erasmus, for example, was proof that the individual had a soul and thus could be saved through the church. Reason was given by God and thus distinguished the Christians who, by virtue of the recognition, were civilized and divided from the infidels and nonhumans. Later debates over slavery and colonialization in the Renaissance entailed whether indigenous groups had the faculty to know God's reason and thus could take part in a civic life that recognized the sovereignty of God and his earthly ministries (see, e.g., Fredrickson, 2002).

The shift from the reason used to grasp eternal cosmic laws to secular reason used to plan change was made possible by the assembly of different historical trajectories. These were embodied in the sectarian political and cultural movements of 17th- and 18th-century Europe. Questions of individual freedom, conscience, and the right of individuals to communicate directly with God overlapped secular and religious beliefs of the Moravian brothers, the Puritans, the Wesleyans, and the Pietists. The Puritans, for example, attached the status and attributes of personhood to an inner soul in which the ethical techniques of individual self-monitoring and control—consciousness and self-consciousness—were developed. The Puritan personality formed through the applications of techniques of self-watchfulness in the private pursuit of the "signs of grace" represented in the construction of the self. The early colonial travelogues and the church's ideas of conversion and civilizing "the heathen" embodied this construction of the self (see Hirst, 1994; Todorov, 1984).

The European and North American Enlightenments' cosmopolitanism revisioned and reassembled Stoic ideas with Reformation notions of salvation into secular theses about human intentionality and purpose in designing modes of living that had universal pretensions. Open and free debate in an equitable economy were thought of as ensuring general prosperity and growth by allowing individuals to energetically pursue their own interests as long as they did not impede others (Ganonkar, 2001, p. 8).

Cosmopolitan reason became foundational to the political community of the modern republic, the citizen, and mass schooling. The aspiration of cosmopolitan ideals for individuals to achieve freedom though agency was tied to ideas about a universal set of rights binding a shared polity. Kant's (1796/1939) *Perpetual Peace* maintained a place for a political community of freely acting people guided by cosmopolitan reason and rationality (science). The cosmopolitanism of Kant, however, was an elite project of government to guarantee civil rights and promote the formation of political will. Kant's (1784/1970) "What Is the Enlightenment?" offers the enlightened leader as the guardian who teaches that the duty of all citizens is to think for themselves. The guardian embodied the dual attempt to order and to administer the world through reason.

The location of cosmopolitanism in the nation functions historically to project the reasoning of the citizen as embodying universal principles that only the most advanced civilizations have acquired. The French and American revolutions were premised on the citizen who adhered to cosmopolitan ideals. Further, the freely acting cosmopolitan was bound with recognition of collective obligations and responsibilities that entailed notions of society. Reason did not reside solely in the individual but continually in a field of relations through which consensual norms of the whole were formed. The hope of the consensus and future progress were continually accompanied by fears about degeneration and decay, a theme I return to (McMahan, 2001).

Reason and Science

During the Enlightenment, reason joined with science. Rationality was to correct visual perceptions and the errors of the senses through a scientific mode of thinking based on observation and rationality. Reason was to provide the moral basis in which judgments could be made and progress could be sought. The Enlightenment's cosmopolitan carried a millennial belief in rational knowledge as positive force for action. Many French Enlightenment thinkers, for example, found the answer to the dilemma of progress in knowledge provided by science. Its methods would bring an infinite progress in the natural world and morally righteous and productive lives to the civic world.

The quest for moral improvement left no branch of the sciences or arts unexplored. Reason, it was believed, aided by observation and experience, was efficacious in leading people toward perfection. Comte's (1827/1975) manifesto about "positivism" gave focus to the phrase "order and progress." It captured a generalized belief that science was the new secular religion of progress. The cosmopolitanism of Comte was "the Religion of Humanity, and all true Positivists sought to unite science and religion" (cited in Nisbet, 1979, pp. 172–173). The use of religion in Comte to describe the human sciences is not accidental. The investigations of human affairs were moral sciences. The search for perfection harbored fears of passions and self-interest that needed to be countered to promote the common good. The great French *Encyclopédie* was a monument to the belief that society could be perfected by education, most strongly by those moral sciences through which the somewhat flawed nature of man could be understood and directed toward the common good (Jack, 1989, p. 193).

During the 19th century, science as a practice to master and technologically control nature was brought into the social realm. Science was to "tame" change in a world seen as otherwise as conditional, insecure, ambiguous, and potentially dangerous. The stability given by science was initially based in the belief that scientists would discover God's given unity in the knowledge that crossed physical and social fields into the 19th century. The search for a unity of knowledge was discarded as the sciences, among other things, became more specialized later into the century. The unity of science was now in its methods, and its methods began to distinguish with greater details the worthy from the unworthy. While this gets ahead of the story, the unity of science was tied anew with the logical positivists of the 1920s only to be quickly discarded and then revived in the positivism of defining what constitutes "scientific evidence" through arguments about the unity of all sciences (National Research Council, 2002).

I mention the relation of salvation themes of progress, reason, and science to emphasize that cosmopolitanism is never merely about agency, freedom, and a generalized humanity free from the local and historically particular. Its principles are continual encounters with what is hoped for and feared.

Cosmopolitan Agency and Inventing the Social

Cosmopolitan notions of agency are so much a part of the modern ortho-doxy that a theory of childhood, schooling, and society without signifying the autonomous agent who acts to improve the self and world is almost unthinkable, or at least not politically correct. Similar to the original sin arguments of the church, the *doxa* is that without theories of agency we are left with an antihumanist and deterministic world that would enable the barbarians and the uncivilized to enter and destroy the gates of the republic. What is lost in these arguments about sin and hope is the politics of the particular historical inscriptions of agency.

Agency assumes multiple forms in modernity. It is associated with the individual whose intentions and purposes are brought into the planning of change and bringing of progress. Theories of agency are also expressed in terms of nature, social structures and forces, and institutions. They function as actors in the sense of having capacities to act on others (Meyer & Jepperson, 2000). Theories about capitalism, racism, Mead's (1934) "gen-eralized other," and Dewey's "problem solver" function as agentic entities in rationalizing and ordering responsibilities and obligations.

My interest here is in the principles of human agency generated by cos-mopolitanism as cultural theses that order who the child is and should be as historical practices. The reason and rationality of cosmopolitanism were assembled with the notion of agency.[13] The invention of agency moves rea-son to the function of securing the future in secular time outside of God's wisdom. The Enlightenment pushed to the side the received order given by the grace of God and replaced it with another eternal human purpose: the reason and science of making life (Becker, 1932). One's good works were no longer to prepare for the afterlife. The secular world was organized as *civitas Dei* (city of God), a world organized with certainty about what "man [*sic*] ... ought to be" that was previously shaped by God (Pocock, 2003, p. 37). European religious concepts of the person were revisioned as categories of the human mind whose soul had moral and rational quali-ties for intervening and changing one's life (Mauss, 1938/1979).

Using the language of political theory, agency entails the movement of the objective order of institutions into the realm of subjectivity that is administered in the name of freedom (Pocock, 2003). Theories of agency constituted people as autonomous subjects of motives and perceptions to determine the actions that shape the future (Meyer, 1986). Pedagogy was the site in which to cultivate, develop, and enable the reason necessary for human agency and progress.

The agency of the individual was made into the primordial category of progress as human interventions to bring perfection to the future. Concepts of agency and human interests in Anglo-Saxon–, French–, and German–speaking worlds inscribed an individual who could know and act in the world that allowed for the discovery of an autonomous social order subject to its own laws (Wittrock, 2000, p. 42). Human agency that was enunciated in the Enlightenment brought together the universal and the local that included epistemologies of diversity. Eisenstadt (2000) argues, for example, that first

> there arises the bridging of the transcendental and mundane orders— of realizing through conscious human agency, exercised in social life, major utopian and eschatological visions. A second emphasized a growing recognition of the legitimacy of multiple individual and group goals and interests, [and] as a consequence allowed for multiple interpretations of the common good. (p. 5)

The invention of agency to think about people coincided with the "invention" of society and the social. Varela (2000) argues that the formation of individual personalities, individual subjects, and the idea of society emerges at the precise historical moment when the legitimacy of power was being based on the idea of a general "will." The individual, according to the 18th-century French *philosophe,* for example, was bound to the "discovery of society" in a process of disengagement from the religious representations. While the word *society* is present prior to the Enlightenment, it emerges to provide a way to think about collective human existence instituted as the essential domain of human practices. Prior to the 18th century, society was a notion about associations of people and not about collective "homes" and belonging. Baker (1994) argues, for example, the ideas about progress, civilization, and toleration would be unthinkable without society as their implied reference. They assume the logical priority and moral values of society as the frame of collective human existence.

The agency of cosmopolitan reason and rationality was brought into the construction of the modern nation, but not without certain ironies. Agency was a political concept of society that was fundamental to the modern republics formed through, for example, the American and French revolutions. Republicanism transformed politics from an activity dependent upon a conception of public (as opposed to private) life to a matter of social life and the life of society (Cruikshank, 1999, pp. 99–100; Heideking, 2000). Republican conceptions of agency gave attention to the role of reason and rationality in giving purpose and intention to processes of change. Action was enlightened self-interest bound to the laws of society.

The universal aspirations of cosmopolitan agency embodied in the hopes of the republic contained fears that the masses were not capable of the reason necessary for citizens' participation. Reason, it was thought after the American Revolution, was unequally distributed. Only some possessed reason, and the binding of people was to be organized through common moral sentiments about humanity. Wood (1999) argues, for example, that the making of the citizen in the American republic was to cultivate the sentiments that linked individuals to the nation. The founding fathers, he argues, did not believe that the masses were capable of the reason necessary of a citizen. Government was "to promote happiness negatively by restraining vices, while society was to promote virtues positively by uniting our affections" (Wood, 1999, p. 42). When the leaders of the American Revolution in 1776 claimed "all men" had the same common nature, that claim had particular boundaries about who had instinctive capacity for moral judgments (p. 41).

The fear in the new republic was that if people were not educated, then irrationality and irrational people would rule. It was presumed that the world could be fashioned and made over, if only

> the impressions and sensations that besieged the senses could be controlled. By playing on people's senses and refining and improving their sensibilities, reformers and moralists could turn growing numbers of the people into more loving and more compassionate human beings. (Wood, 1999, p. 42)

Sentimental attachments, benevolence, and compassion among people, it was thought, would create an identity attached to the republican experiment.

Agency is sacred to contemporary life in its different forms of expression.[14] In one scenario, the individual is a purposeful actor who produces change through intentional actions directed to the future. Notions of agency are to bring individual liberty and personal realization, social betterment, and rescue of those who have fallen from the graces of progress. The redemptive projects of the good works of people are central in the thought of Comte and Marx to present theories about "communities of learners." The War on Poverty in the United States during the 1960s was premised on eliminating poverty by creating institutional settings that enabled the poor efficacy for acting on their own lives. Theories of deviancy and failure in schooling focus on the psychology of the individual who has no agency because of a lack of self-esteem or motivation.[15]

Fabricating Human Kinds: Adolescence as an Exemplar of a Cultural Thesis

I have used cosmopolitanism as cultural theses about modes of living to consider its assemblies, connections, and disconnections of multiple historical practices. This section is to provide an exemplar of the historical overlay through the notion of adolescence. Adolescence is a cosmopolitan cultural thesis about a particular mode of life that embodies processes of abjection.

Adolescence is a fabrication in three senses of the word. It is a fiction that responds to something in the world that demands people's attention. G. Stanley Hall (1924a) used the notion of adolescence in child studies to respond to the changing "urban" populations of European immigrants and African American populations that moved from the South to attend schools. The distinction provided a way to think about the child by calculating measures of psychological growth and physical development for the planning of instruction.

Adolescence was also a thing of the world. Theories of children's growth and development, programs of remediation for children who were not learning, self-help books for parents, and medical languages mapped the normal and abnormal child. Discourses of medicine, psychology, and pedagogy were to calculate what was normal and pathological, treating the problems that arose from deviations.

The naturalness of adolescence as a category of childhood is unquestioned today. The subjectivities of the reformed teacher that travel alongside that of the child entail qualities of the professional who investigates, maps, classifies, and works on the territories of the self to order conduct. Few parents, authors of childrearing books, or teachers would argue about the need to pay attention to the adolescence of the child in order to produce a productive and self-responsible adult.

The third quality of adolescence as a fabrication are abjections, the double gestures of hope and fears. To pursue briefly the argument of later chapters, adolescence was given plausibility and intelligibility within a particular historical space. Hall's child studies historically enunciated particular solutions and plans for action about agency and reason that mutated from Northern European Enlightenment into an evolutionary story of the nation. Reform was the narrative of the day to plan urban life to confront *the* Social Question, discussed in chapter 3, the term used by Protestant reformers and social scientists for social planning to undo what was seen as the moral disorder of the city. Progressive social and educational reforms with the new social and education sciences enunciated reforms to include the uncivilized populations. These reforms included projects of abjection, placing particular groups and qualities of living as outside of the spaces of the "American race" and its citizens as "the chosen people"—women not in the home, immigrants from non-Protestant countries, Irish Catholic immigrants, African Americans, and Chinese Americans, to name a few.[16]

Adolescence provides a way to consider the cultural theses of the child that are assembled and connected through historically different practices. Different practices overlap to create a particular fabrication of a cultural thesis about a kind of human—the adolescent (see Hacking, 1986). It is also possible to think of the disadvantaged and the lifelong learner along these lines. These are cultural theses about particular kinds of humans. Each fabrication entails principles of recognition and difference that function to divide and exclude. The task of this book is the historically diagnoses of the double gestures and processes of abjection.

Toward a History of Present Schooling: A Question of Method

Cosmopolitanism is a difficult history to "tell." It moves through multiple registers that change over time and space. I explore the changes in cosmopolitanism through a spiral argument rather than through a deductive logic. The initial discussion, for example, of the double qualities of reason in the fabrications of agency, the temporal dimensions of planning biography, and science in modes of living is continually developed and redeveloped as they intersect in the different sections of the book. The diagnosis is of the shifting boundaries and limits of cosmopolitanism.

The approach used here is "the history of the present." I examine the cultural theses about cosmopolitan modes of living that circulate from the beginning of the 20th century and the present. The history is not of a constructivism that assumes the human agent or the subject that guides history either structurally or through a subjectivism. By saying this, my intent is not to do away with the subject through a focus on cosmopolitanism but to consider how current reforms about the cosmopolitan citizen partition what is sensible, bringing into being objects and subjects through which the self experiences and acts in the world.

The following chapter continues to explore notions of cosmopolitanism through the intersection of multiple historical practices in the constructions of agency, reason, and planning life through science. The next two sections of the book use intellectual tools developed in these first two chapters to examine the progressive sciences of pedagogy in school reforms and today's cultural theses of the lifelong learner and the "left behind child" in curriculum subject standards, teacher education, and urban education reforms. My focus on John Dewey, Edward L. Thorndike, and contemporary curriculum standards reform and research, for example, is not to ask about the author's intent or intellectual formation of ideas. It is to understand the literatures as a historical grid enunciating particular solutions, plans for action, and ordering the reason and the "reasonable person" (Deleuze & Guattari, 1994).

The approach considers broad contours of different practices to diagnosis the emergence of particular systems of reason over time and space and not as a problem of sampling probabilistic or to review the literature. These strategies carry epistemological assumptions not theoretically appropriate for this study, such as in populational and probability theories. My concern is with changes in the systems of reason and the epistemic shifts to explore the limitations of what is given as natural and sacred in the present. It is with this intent that I use cosmopolitanism as a historical notion to guide the inquiry. In following this strategy, a number of pedagogical projects of the past and present are not given attention. This may limit nuances to the arguments made. I recognize this limitation but leave it to others to pursue this as my focus is on the contours of changes in the principles governing who "we" are, should be, and the processes of abjection.

The analysis entails different sources of data that range from the primary and secondary historical texts to ethnographic studies and policy and research texts. This method of analysis combines cultural, social, and philosophical questions in asking about the limits imposed on what is known and acted. The approach brings into a conversation the sociology of knowledge with cultural histories (Popkewitz & Brennan, 1998; Popkewitz, Franklin, & Pereyra, 2001). The actual categories that order this analysis emerged in the constant relating of the different data with the theoretical concerns enunciated. The central concepts of the study about time, agency, science, and abjection, for example, were developed through the interplay of the readings, working with the data, and writing.

CHAPTER 2

The Reason in Question

Cosmopolitanism and Processes of Abjection

David Harvey's (2000) essay "Cosmopolitanism and the Banality of Geographical Evils" discusses broad divisions, nuances, and meanings for thinking about the new millennium. He argues that social divisions negate any unifying ethic in thinking about global economic, ecological, and political changes. Harvey offers a historical-geographical theory about institutional and structural change to radically undo the false separation of the universal and the particular by reconstructing the cosmopolitan outlook. In the end, Harvey's cosmopolitanism renews the normative project of the universal that he suggests others have gotten incorrect.

I start with Harvey to focus on the unquestioned authority given to cosmopolitanism. That is, if only it can be gotten "right" that erases the processes of abjection. The first chapter pursued these erasures by first turning to the construction of the notion of agency and reason. This chapter pursues further the assemblage that joins cosmopolitanism and its abjections. The agency of cosmopolitanism is formed through connections with, for example, a notion of time in which the individual could see one's self as having a past, present, and future. This idea of historical time is captured in the notion of evolution and the psychological concepts of development and growth. The notions of biography and agency are then connected with polysemous qualities of science. Science is, at one layer, an expert knowledge to theorize, calculate, and design social conditions and people. This is where the social and educational sciences play a pivotal role. Science as transforming people brings another quality of science into play. The theories and research about the child and teaching perform as principles through which daily life is planned. This latter notion of science as a method for ordering daily life is not built on the practices of the disciplines of science. It is produced through the overlap of moral, social, and scientific calculations that organize school pedagogy as technologies for governing conduct. While not the overt intent of research or schooling, the distinctions, differentiations, and divisions in pedagogical practices produce processes of abjection.

Agency in the Movement of Time

It is easy to think of time as something always there so that we can organize ourselves and tell our stories as an emergence of successions. Time stands outside history, a silent concept that objectively orders and gives meaning to events. The modern archive symbolizes this stabilizing of time to order the processes of life and biography. Time organizes everything—from the obligations of each day to the psychological and physiological progressions that we undergo from the year of our birth and to differentiate epochs of humanity that make possible our living in the "information age."

But this epistemological view of time as a succession of events has not always been part of organizing society or identity. The Greek worldview of knowing one's self through the past that was linked to a cyclical notion of time rather than a chronological, progressive time of today. Time was a circular vehicle in which things came to be and then passed away. Everything in the present had its place as in the setting of the table. History told of man defined in an indefinite time that did not link the past, present, and future. Herodotus's notion of history, for example, was a chronicle to describe the cycles of truth that had appeared in the past.

Medieval Christianity revisioned that temporality (Pocock, 2003, pp. 5–6). Time in the church's annals chronicled divine intervention and providence. Time was owned by God and the medieval church fought against town merchants who wanted to place secular clocks on its steeples. Truth or reality was grounded in the self-contained quality of timeless propositions. The propositions stood in contrast to circumstantial, accidental, and temporal knowledge. The significance of the events of time was passive and inert, subservient to the eternal paths given by God. Koselleck (1985) argues, for example, that paintings for Renaissance Christian humanists were didactic lessons in which temporal differences were not significant. The time of the painting, the time of its subject matter, and the time of the observer were contemporaneous. History told of expectations related to the constant anticipation of the end of the world and its continual deferment to that end. The human interiority as a project for development of the self was not possible.

The displacement of a transcendent God brought new transcendentals, namely, history, reason, and science (Venn, 2002, p. 68). Agency belonged to the rational, unitary, logocentric subject. The Enlightenment's turn toward secular time replaced the static temporality of the Christian journey. Time was linear and progressive. Reason brought the natural laws of history into the development of the present and the making of the future (Commager, 1950). Its sequence of past, present, and future could be understood and used in planning change.

The sequence of time placed the past as inferior to the present. With much debate, the Enlightenment's cosmopolitanism associated reason and its scientific superiority as the more advanced state of living than that which had been found in antiquity. The quarrel of the Ancients and Moderns in late 17th-century France asked about whether the present stood on the shoulders of the Ancient Greeks or whether contemporary knowledge superseded the past. The answer was resolved in favor of the present. Its "proof" was the extension and consolidation of European power that had extended to the remotest regions of the globe during the "age of discovery" (Porter, 1991, p. 18).

The importance of the modern present and its future was conceptualized in notions of progress and agency. The future was a break with tradition. The veneration of the new and the present traveled across different social and cultural spheres, from architecture, urban planning, and the domestic sciences to the schooling of children. The future was to be without an authoritarian system of religious and aristocratic institutions and without fixed classes. Pragmatism as a particular American philosophy was to shed the Old World's traditions because they prevented progress and salvation. "The old culture is doomed for us because it was built upon an alliance of political and spiritual powers, an equilibrium of governing and leisure classes, which no longer exists" (Dewey, 1916; 1929a, pp. 501–502). The future was to disregard present traditions: There is no turning back "the hands of time" and one needs to plan for the future!

By identifying tradition with dogma and ignorance, theories about agency gave justification to the absorption with the new, and the future brought notions of society tied to the new 19th-century nations. The nation and its citizen were given a history in rational time.

> The modern project itself was the new, the actual, the contemporary. While remembering former modernities, we evoke their pastness to authenticate the newness of "what's new" and yet filter the contemporary through a gauze of the particles of the past. (Jaguaribe, 2001, p. 333)

Present time was used for future rewards, and the past was for comparison. The 19th century produced wholesale awareness of change, the future, and history, with the Faustian notion of becoming rather than being. John Stuart Mills pointed out that "the idea of comparing one's own age with former ages, or with our notion of those which are yet to come, had occurred to philosophers; but it never before was itself the dominant idea of any age" (Eksteins, 1985, p. 3).

The ordering of the self-in-time has its paradoxes. It memorializes cosmopolitanism as a break from traditions to enable the cultivation of things not burdened with past traditions. This theme is central to modern social science. Yet at the same time, the past is to be re-memorialized to "write for a future that the present cannot recognize: to develop, to cultivate the untimely, the out-of-place and the out-of-step" (Grosz, 2004, p. 117).

This disregard of the past in philosophy and social theory focuses on the child and citizen in processes of becoming, privileging the future through concepts of agency and action (Popkewitz, 1997). Kant split the chorographic science preoccupied with the spatial juxtaposition of things and the chronological sciences of sequences (Giddens, 1987). He proposed that the chronological science should be concerned with the sequential development of phenomena. Nineteenth-century science—concerned as it was with process and methods—was an instantiation of the importance of time. Modern sociology and psychology by the beginning of the 20th century defined its subject by functions-in-time in concepts such as socialization, learning, and development. School timetables organized time as a framework for distributing children into prearranged positions.

The "march of time" enunciated the optimism of progress *and* the fears of degeneration and dangers to the future. As Chamberlin and Gilman (1985) suggest, "hope was looked after by progress and seemed as the tenor of the times, but fear was contagious" (p. xiii). The Renaissance equation of degeneracy and diversity led observers increasingly to refine and elaborate symbols of corruption; the Enlightenment projected degeneracy on the lower categories of the taxonomies of humankind rather than, as previously held, on doctrinal opponents in sectarian disputes (Boon, 1985, p. 25). The all-enfolding plenitude of the great chain of being described the comparative morality and physicality of humanity as a qualitatively disparate species in which some were placed as dangerous to the development of civilization (p. 26).

The placement of the self-in-sequential-time was a comparative method in the name of the universal that colluded with the violence of colonialization and racializing. The modern concept of history, Gilroy (2001) argues, presupposes a politics of time whose universality about human emancipation through reason was punctured at the moment of its conception with a "rational irrationalism" in philosophy, anthropology, and geology. The notion of race was raised to an ontological principle of violence. Human time was placed in a sequence as a connection between ontology, nationality, and theories of racial difference. Race was associated not only with the idea of authenticity and national principles but also with the elevation of race to a determining position in theories of history, especially those that spoke of "war and conflict, naturalizing them in the convenient idea of specifically race-based imperial conflict" (p. 64).

Contemporary analyses of time have pointed to the present as a shift from a single universal movement of time, to a time that "moves" as multiple strands with uneven flows.[1] This account of time is taken up with the French historical school of the Annales. Time is thought to go "at a thousand different paces, swift and slow, which bear almost no relation to the day-to-day rhythm of a chronicle or of traditional history" (Braudel, 1980, p. 10). Wittgenstein (1953/1966) spoke about change as having multiple rates developing across different institutions that come together in what can be called a historical conjunction. Notions of discontinuous time are given epistemological spaces in computer gaming (Gee, 2003), architecture (Rajchman, 1997), human geography (Soja, 1989), and social theory (Wagner, 2001a, 2001b).

Progress in the Taming of Agency

Time and agency presents another oddity of joining the opposites of uncertainty with certainty as part of the same phenomenon. Uncertainty is a property of democratization and an element in the Enlightenment to the present. The fall of the authority of the Church in the late Renaissance and the undoing of previous social hierarchies seemed to end certainty. That uncertainty is embodied in notions of human agency and the possibility of progress. Life is embedded in what seems to be a continuous change and historicity in which there seem to be no prior lessons or fixed relations. The very notions of problem solving and participation attest to a world where the future has no guarantees. Paradoxically, the enunciation of reason and agency as calculations of communication in pedagogy are embodied in today's research about learning. These practices of research stabilize and tame contingency by calculating the standards and rules of reason.[2]

Science established consensus to processes of change. It was to identify what was "natural" to humanity through establishing the indisputable facts and thus eliminate the disagreements, debates, and turmoil that accompanied modern life.

The stabilizing and taming of the future are embedded in Darwin's evolutionary theory. Darwin introduced indeterminacy of time into the closed system of the Newtonian universe. Evolution is "the emergence in time of biological innovation and surprise" (Grosz, 2004, p. 19). The Social Darwinism of Galton and Spencer brings that determinacy/indeterminacy into cultural theses that compared, hierarchized, and placed in a continuum of values about civilizations and their individualities. Edward L. Thorndike's behaviorist psychology was also concerned with stability and consensus that simultaneously produced processes of abjection.

How can the opposite of freedom and social administration, and uncertainty and certainty, form part of the same phenomenon? In terms of this discussion, a number of historical trajectories overlap.

First, agency is regulated by placing action in flows of time. Foucault (1984) argues, for example, that a new episteme in the 18th century appears in which there is no longer a transcendental or universal structure of all knowledge but an individuality that emerges "from the contingence that has made us what we are, the possibility of no longer being, doing, or thinking what we are, do or think" (p. 46). The modern republic and democracy embody this conditionality and fluidity of life. What seems to hold back the emancipatory promise of freedom and liberty, concepts of this new uncertainty, is the full development of human reason and rationality. The uncertainty of the future is today given a new life as epistemological underpinnings of the risk society[3] that needs to be tamed so individuals can become productive.

Second, biography in social time enables calculations and administration of reason and the "reasonable person." Reason is both an object of public scrutiny and a private inner mode of conduct to order everyday life. Koselleck (1985) suggests that the idea of progress enables political calculations as a humanist project that marks out the plan for the future (also see Grosz, 2004). The uncertainty of the external world is given stability through the common rules and standards of reason, which enables the individual to act with foresight and to plan for change.

Third, the focus on methods and procedures in science systematizes and regularizes the possibilities for acting and change. As discussed in Chapter 1, the methods of science are to function as procedures that enable a consensus and harmony for the subject to have access to the truth, and to determine the conditions and limits of the subject's access to the truth. The Cartesian notion of method is to fix the certainty of procedures to serve as criteria for truth and the development of statements given as true. Scottish moral or commonsense thinking and Kant's categories of the cosmopolitan, for example, were put forth to counteract the untamed and possibly chaotic implications of political theories such as in Lockean sensationalism. Attention is given in contemporary psychology to the processes and procedures that organize, for example, perceptions, attitudes, social interactions, and behaviors (see e.g., Crary, 1999). The calculations of the interior of individuality map the principles generated for agency in the family, domestic life, and childhood.

Design is, ironically, planning for uncertainty (see chapters 6 & 9). Pedagogy becomes a design project of methods to order thought and actions that bring stability and harmony to the processes of change. The concepts of childhood, for example, place the child in ordered dimensions of time that, if successful, will produce the "reasoned" citizen who acts "sensibly" with self-responsibility and motivation. G. Stanley Hall's early 20th-century studies place the child in a historical progression of stages and development that give consensus and harmony to an ordering of the future. Thorndike's learning studies of mathematics placed thought in sequences to rationally order behaviors to produce future happiness for the individual. The traceable life career is more recently expressed in the notion of the lifelong learner. It is an individuality guided by pedagogical rules for learning from infancy through adulthood and into the geriatric years.

The regularizing and design of life in schools expressed dangers of degeneration and fears of the dangerous. The teacher designs "learning" so the child becomes self-managed and responsible not only for self-development and growth but also for standardized public virtues that enable the conferring of that agency (Rose, 1999). If the development of childhood was not controlled, the fear was that the child would become potentially dangerous to the future of the republic (Krug, 1972).

"The Homeless Mind": Biography as an Object and Subject of Time

The various principles related to reason, agency, science, and planned time in cosmopolitanism embody a particular way of locating one's self in the world, what Berger, Berger, and Kelner (1974) call the "homeless mind." The homeless mind is an individuality that is both an object and a subject of reflection. This quality of the mind is quantified in the modern world (Porter, 1995). Quantification is a technology of social distance from the immediate and the local by providing a common and universal language. That language is to standardize and relocate the local and the personal in abstract systems of knowledge, and functions at the same time to operate in the spaces of daily life as personal knowledge. The homeless mind enables one to think and act in daily life as if belonging to an ethnic population or in judging personal acts by universalizing categories such as in psychologies about self-esteem, efficacy, and personality. The "thinking" through probability theories about populations provides a way of seeing oneself in the universal time of humanity and in the particular time of daily life. The homeless mind is in the consciousness of self that is "to think globally but act locally."

The "homeless mind" placed individuals in a relation to transcendental categories that seem to have no particular historical location or author to establish a home, yet belonging and home are re-inscribed with the anonymous qualities of thought. This reinscription of home through distancing one's self was expressed earlier in Nussbaum's (1996) discussion of cosmopolitanism. Cosmopolitanism was a quality of exile and strangeness to one's self through reflection that (re)makes the sites of affiliation and attachment. The function of the modern expertise of the human sciences from Freud to Thorndike through Vygotsky and Dewey, for example, is to enable the self-reflection in which individuality "lives" in the flows between universals, where the self is an object of reflection and the immediate site of acting and experiencing.

Rancière (2004a) expressed the quality of the homeless mind in the emergence of modern poetry. Rancière argues that Aristotle, Plato, and the Stoics divided the encounter of the poet and the represented others. The representation of people in the poems was "as they should be," which had a double sense. The poems express what was fitting for people to be and how it was fitting to represent them. The art of composing fables represented the conjunction between the ethos of the citizens, which told about "a certain type of individual that should or should not be imitated and a certain place of utterance that is or is not suitable to political experience of the nomoi of the city" (pp. 10–11).

The poem in modernity opens a different space for an individuality that carries the double meanings of the self as an object and subject of the homeless mind. The enunciation of poetry functions as a metaphor of transportation and territorialization that is possible within the new spaces for reflection and action. Modern lyricism is primarily an experience of the self or the discovery of nature or sensibility, which is different from that of the Greeks. It occupies a new political experience of the physical world or the physical experience of politics (Rancière, 2004a, p. 12). Poetry is a method of utterance that enables the individual to create a perceptual space as the act accompanying the individual who is both part of the world written about and distance from it. The "I" of the poem coexists with talking about, for example, wind, clouds, or waves. The "I" is produced in echo with its act and also represents the subjectivity of a traveler who passes through a certain territory to make words coincide with things and utterances with visions (Rancière, 2004a, p. 12).

Biography in Planning Life

The placing of biography as one's career entails that new space of the belonging of the homeless mind that lives simultaneously in exile and through face-to-face interactions. *Career* was a word that literally signified the track that horses ran around in the beginning of the 19th century.

Over time it began to signify middle-class males whose identities belonged in their attachment to an occupation. The idea of an individual having a career signals a broader shift in locating the self in the temporal world (Bledstein, 1976). Career symbolized an identity in which life trajectories and social positions are separated from the family and immediate community. Life was a continuous event of planning through time, shedding the past through the development of the self for the future. Continued calculations organized one's career to assign identity, self-image, and material prospects in an expanding universe (Bledstein, 1976, p. 159).

Life as the planning of a career is articulated in the reflections of Charles Eliot, the president of Harvard University and a leader in secondary school reform in the late 19th century. Eliot expressed a more general optimism of American exceptionalism—that the nation was a unique experiment in producing universal cosmopolitan values. Schooling was a civilizing project through educating children in the systematic use of reason to train them "for the duties of life." Eliot argued that

> I have always believed that the individual child in a democratic society had a right to do his own prophesying about his own career, guided by his own ambitions and his own capacities, and abating his aspirations only under the irresistible pressure of adverse circumstances. (Eliot, 1905, p. 331)

The comment about the child's career expressed a narrative of cosmopolitanism. The child is to become an agent of his future, guided by "his own prophesying" and "his own ambitions and his own capacities." The reason that guides the child's ambitions and aspirations is placed as the universal of humanity, expressed that the "individual child ... had a right" that signified the nation as a personification of the democratic society.

The cosmopolitanism that Eliot assigns to the agency of the child enunciates fears about dangers to civilization from those who do not have the proper modes of reasoning and living. The fears are the irrationality in what Eliot calls "the irresistible pressure of adverse circumstances." I will talk more about the historical grid in which Eliot's concerns with "adverse circumstances" in chapter 3. What I want to draw attention here is schooling as practices that are to replace nonreason or irrationality with the forethought of planning for preparing for the future.

> One is fortified against the acceptance of unreasonable propositions only by skill in determining facts through observation and experience, by practice in comparing facts or groups of facts, and by the unvarying habit of questioning and verifying allegations, and of distinguishing between facts and inferences from facts, and between a true cause and an antecedent event. One must have direct training and practice in

logical speech and writing before he can be quite safe against specious rhetoric and imaginative oratory. (Eliot, 1892–1893, p. 424)

Eliot recognized that such a society was differentiated, but the essential equality of the school was that all students would learn the same logic of reason and thus would ensure the survival of the republic (Eliot, 1892–1893, p. 426). The fact that all children learn systematic modes of argument, he argues, is not a theoretical problem but a practical one of "the study of arguments which have had weight in determining the course of trade, industries, or public affairs, or have made epochs in discovery, inventing, or the progress of science" (p. 428). The use of the word *all* gave a unity and sameness to the nation and its people.

The rational ordering of biography-in-time is so deeply inscribed that it appears as a psychological truism. The modern consciousness of the adult is placed at the foot of childhood. It is a sequence of development in which the excesses, fears, and troubles of the adult are placed in the sins of early years or the consequence of the parental relations with the child. Therapy is premised on such a notion of time and origin because childhood is treated as the root of a healthy or dysfunctional adulthood, a trope that reappears in contemporary reforms.

Science, the Ordering of Change, and Salvation Narratives

Notions of cosmopolitan reason and science emerge as salvation themes in pedagogical practices. The formation of Western schools, for example, cannot be adequately understood without understanding the manner in which Reformation themes of individual salvation were brought into earthly concerns and related to the pursuits of people in daily life (Weber, 1904–1905/1958). The Lasallian school of the 17th century, for example, enjoined secular reason as a complement to faith. Primary schooling was both a method of socialization and individualization (Dussel, 2006; Hamilton, 1989).

Although science is to shed the appeal of magic and the spiritual through its attention to the empirical world, it does not shed themes of salvation and redemption. If I return to the above texts of Charles Eliot, planning the child's career had at least two different qualities of science in pedagogy. Science was to study, theorize, and empirically observe the social world in order to change it. Science is also the mode of living in which individuals observe from experience and order these facts to give coherence and direction to action. Science was the method of the Enlightenment that would enable individuals to pursue happiness. This second view of science is a mode of life that Eliot assigns to the "democratic society." I use quotes around "democratic" to recognize its function as a cultural thesis formed within a grid of practices and not as a universal or transcendental category that stands outside of its historicity. Pedagogy entails the overlapping of the two qualities of science: as the expert knowledge to order, classify, and plan teaching, and as the processes and procedures that order the reflection and acts.

The search for perfection from the Enlightenment to the present functioned as salvation narratives folded into practices to govern the reason and science of the cosmopolitan in 19th-century pedagogy. The first Secretary of Education of the Massachusetts schools and leader in the formation of mass education, Horace Mann (1867a), talked about "the promise of the future" by invoking the pact of the republican government to promote the public good as children acquire knowledge.[4] This pact was embodied in pedagogy. The cosmology of a religious soul was replaced with teaching to instantiate the spiritual/moral life of the republic, shaped and fashioned through the principles generated in pedagogy about the rational, active child.

Although with different foci on the individual and the social, educational research activated a more general Enlightenment assumption that conscious human activity could effect change in one's own life and community. The relation of universalized Protestant reform notions of Christian values about the good works of the individual and democracy was embodied in the pragmatism of John Dewey. Problem solving, experimentalism, and action in pragmatism would produce the ethics that joined Christianity with the democratic mode of living. Dewey thought that since "the future of our civilization depends upon the widening spread and deepening hold of the scientific habit of mind, the problem of problems in our education is therefore to discover how to mature and make effective this scientific habit" (cited in Diggins, 1994, p. 227).

Science had different configurations in ordering the cultural thesis of the cosmopolitan child. Edward L. Thorndike said,

> goodwill to men, useful and happy lives, and mobile enjoyment—are the ultimate aims of school education in particular. Its proximate aims are to give boys and girls health in body and mind, information about the world of nature and men, worthwhile interests in knowledge and action, a multitude of habits of thought, feeling and behavior and ideas of efficiency, honor, duty, love and service. (Thorndike, 1906/1962c, p. 57)

Science, Thorndike argued, enables education to achieve its purposes. To fulfill

> the ultimate purposes of education, we have to measure each study's service in making man's wants better and in making him able to satisfy them. Thus it is expected that the study of literature in schools will increase the student's good will toward men by broadening his

sympathies and inspiring him with emulation of ideas, characters, and will replace selfish sensory pleasures by the impersonal satisfaction of reading, and will also give him an added insight into human nature which will help him to manage himself and other men, so that his and their wants can be better satisfied. (Thorndike, 1912/1962b, p. 142)

Scientific studies in schools were not only about the salvation themes of the cosmopolitan individual and society. Science provided for the paths that would illustrate the nation's triumph over nature and the development of useful knowledge for social development. Progress in government, said Lester Frank Ward (1883), one of the founders of American sociology, was dependent on education. The sciences of schooling were to provide the appropriate methods of intervention to develop an individuality guided by reason and who produces progress. Whereas Thorndike accepted Spencer's Social Darwinist ideas—that the laws of Darwin's natural selection were applicable to society through the laws of civilization and that the unequal distribution of wealth and power was evidence of the laws' validity—Ward looked to intervene in that development.

Science was linked to principles for governing the cosmopolitan society through planning modes of living. The sciences of pedagogy made the interior of the child a site of intervention that would bring consensus and stability to the future, such as ordering life in Dewey's problem solving and Hall's child development and growth. Progressive reformers across different geographical places thought of science as a progressive way of living that undermined the traditions of society and culture (Popkewitz, 2005).

The laws of science helped legitimize a society whose economic system favored growth and man's dominion over inorganic and organic chemistry, and they all promised a practical education that would reveal the working of a beneficial God who always blessed a productive people. (Reese, 1995, p. 108)

Dewey wrote of William James in 1929 that he was "well within the bounds of moderation when he said that looking forward instead of backward, looking to what the world and life might become instead of to what they have been, is an alteration in the 'seat of authority'" (Diggins, 1994, p. 39).

Today, reason and science are used almost interchangeably. People talk about reason and science as synonyms for the ordering and calculating of properties. The reason of science refers to that which mobilizes agency, and is populated with psychological concepts about the inner qualities of the child who works for his or her own improvement, as well as the social progress and fears of those who lack motivation and self-esteem and prevents the agential child from achievement and cognitive development.

Comparative Reasoning and Processes of Abjection

This section explores historically comparative methods that differentiated and divided society through the distinctions that ordered agency, time, and science. The simultaneous inclusion and jettisoning is called "abjection" in feminist and social theories and post-Kantian political theory.[5] The apparatus of abjection is a way to consider how certain cosmopolitan principles produce others designated in unlivable spaces that constitute the moral disorder and threats to the envisioned progress. The latter are unlivable spaces of those who do not enjoy the status of the subject, but whose lives are circumscribed by the cosmopolitan modes of living. The abjection is embodied in narratives of freedom and democracy in 19th-century American literature, as Morrison (1992) argues; such literature inscribed a language that "powerfully evoke[s] and enforce[s] hidden signs of racial superiority, cultural hegemony, and dismissive 'Othering' of people and language" (p. x). Today, that "other" is placed in a space inside but recognized to be included and different.

I pursue cosmopolitanism as comparative instantiations that inscribe difference. Its comparative sets of values produce hierarchies to distinguish civilizations and "civilized" people from others placed in spaces outside the cosmopolitan qualities of the "reasoned person." It is in this comparative "reason" that the historical practices of racializing of "others" are enacted.

The Hope of Civilizing and Fears of the Dangerous

Cosmopolitanism embodies a particular analytic of reason that comparatively orders and differentiates its history and "self" from others. The French Enlightenment's *philosophes* narrated the idea of civilization as a story of the evolution of a universal humanity through the application of reason. The universality given to cosmopolitan theses as transcendent and outside the history functions as a duality that mutually constructs its others. "Man" was placed in a continuum of value and hierarchy to order and divide people, races, and their civilizations. Discourses of war, for example, ordered and classified people to distinguish peace, calm, and stability. Foucault (2003) argues, for example, that in England by the 1630s and at the end of the reign of Louis XIV in France, the idea of war emerges as the uninterrupted frame that underlies the idea of society and history as differences of ethnicity, differences of languages, and differences between savagery and barbarism. And in these differences was a comparative logic that placed civilizations in continuums of "advanced" and "less advanced."

The comparative qualities were embedded in the use of *civilize* and *civilizations* in the English, French, German, and American Enlightenments. The words placed the regulated time of progress in a continuum of values that differentiated people. "To civilize" was to endow what is common to all human beings, or what should be.

> The Enlightenment view of legal codes was less to mirror the distinctive customs and practices of a people than to create a cultural community by codifying and generalizing the most rational of those customs and suppressing the more obscure and barbaric ones. (Scott, 1998, p. 90)

The idea of the civilized also referred to one's manners in bodily relations—how one sits, drinks, greets, shares one's bed, and handles questions of nudity and sexuality. "Civilized" encompassed a politeness, refinement, and new manners and decencies between people (Passavant, 2000).

Civilization was a reformist idea in the modern European nation-state in the 19th century. Broader sections of the population were meant to be liberated from the existing barbaric or irrational conditions through the civilizing project of the state embodied in its written constitution according to natural laws and in accordance with reason, which education was to produce.

Civilization and culture (*Kultur*) in the German Enlightenment were almost interchangeable. They referred to moral and social cultivation associated with urbane and political connotations. The German bourgeoisie separated culture from civilization in the 19th century in its fights with the aristocracy of the old regime (Elias, 1939/1978). The former used culture to promote its position through consecrating the values, ideas, and higher intellectual artistic and moral qualities of society as more important than the outward propriety and etiquette of the aristocracy. Kant, for example, used *kultur* to speak about the values of civil society. He evoked a dichotomy between culture associated with higher goals of moral cultivation and civilization concerned with merely good behavior. Kant's (1784/1970) "Idea for a Universal History With a Cosmopolitan Purpose" placed these distinctions in a temporality that directs the individual to the future and progress. Kant argued that

> We are cultivated to a high degree by art and science. We are civilized to the point of excess in all kinds of social courtesies and proprieties. But we are still a long way from the point where we could consider ourselves morally mature. (p. 49)

The assertion of the homogeneity of values and norms of the nation plays down the national differences of people by emphasizing what is common—or what should be common—to all human beings. Europeans identified the characteristics of their own polite civilization as infinitely superior to others. The travel literatures of the Scottish philosophers, for example, commonly had accounts of savage societies in the New World and Africa. The comparisons judged the other societies in relation to the degree with which they progressed in terms of their approximation of the European models (Jack, 1989, p. 194). Elias (1939/1978) argues that the image of self that I associate here with the cultural thesis of cosmopolitanism is the standard bearer of expanding civilizations in colonial arenas, but it stands also in relation to sexual regulation in the differentiations and distinctions of the citizen of the nation.

The comparative method inscribed in cosmopolitan reason was a particular historical consciousness that made possible the analytical qualities of modern science and medicine. The earlier classifying differentiating of plants in the work of Linnaeus and the biological evolutionary theory of Darwin were made possible by an analytical quality of thought through which parts could be differentiated and placed in a hierarchy of things and events. This comparative installation entailed an analytical consciousness that could see things in its parts that would relate to some unity of the whole; classification and differentiation formed a continuum of value and hierarchy that placed "man" in a continuum of people and civilizations from advanced to less advanced and uncivilized. Nations traced their histories through progressive developments of "civilizations" that started in Ancient Greece or Rome and arrived at the present.

The comparative quality that divides those who reason and are civilized from those not as advanced is embedded in modern philosophy and sociology. Theories made the arbitrariness of differences into necessity and inevitability (Rancière (1983/2004b, p. 205). Plato, Rancière argues, had no propensity for dissimulating inequality. Firm boundaries were maintained about redistributions that refined the chorus (*cicadas*) of the poor that did not deploy any notion of inequality, but which placed the poor in a continuum of values related to others. The dissimulation of inequality stood as a point of difference or unlikeness (p. 206). The new discourses of the Enlightenment, the positivist sciences of Auguste Comte, and the new sociologies, Rancière continues, brought discourses of differences and states of rehabilitation of people that were no longer of an arbitrary order. Social science theories, for example, disclose differences that exclude the ethos that made workers, artisans, and racial groups. The poor of difference in social science were an invention of modernity that were "seen", talked about and acted on as different from the chorus of the poor. The recognition of difference stabilizes the groups as outside normalcy and "incapable of ever acquiring a taste for the philosophers' goods—and even of understanding the language in which their enjoyment is expounded" (p. 204).

Racializing Others

The rationality and reason of cosmopolitanism is not only about the mode of life. They also visualize the civilized through the recognition that demarcates difference. The significance historically in that demarcation is the production of a unity and division that organize notions of "race." Kant's cosmopolitan ideal of agency and participation brought into play the ideal of an international community committed to perpetual peace and discussed as national and racial characteristics of the body, color, and the mind and mental capacity. Kant's cosmopolitanism placed the membership of the Negro, for example, in the lowest position within a nominally inclusive single species in which natural law worked against racial assimilation (Gilroy, 2001, p. 59).

Race through the 19th century in Europe and North America had two different yet overlapping qualities. One referenced the unity of the whole, as "the race of the nation." The nation was signified as a unified "race," a word impregnated with Northern European values about civilization and the civilized people of a presumed human type of shared descent. Society and the state were represented as

> a battle that has to be waged not between races, but by a race that is portrayed as the one true race, the race that holds power and is entitled to define the norms, and against those who deviate from that norm, against those who pose a threat to the biological heritage. (Foucault, 2003, p. 61)

Nation, race and the social/moral/physical qualities of people overlapped. The Northern European and North American cosmopolitanism differentiated certain populations as no longer sharing the same present in the moment of history (Gilroy, 2001). The sailing of the *Beagle* and the collection of data for Darwin's eventual theory of evolution itself embodied the British use of its navy and sciences to classify and order human development that subsequently "proved" the advancement of its civilization over its colonial others (Desmond & Moore, 1991). Across the Atlantic, the "American race" was used in popular literature and political discussion to talk about the nation and its citizens as a unified whole that differentiated its population in a continuum of values that led to peoples and qualities that were classified as "uncivilized" and dangerous to the future of the republic.

The differentiating qualities of people into hierarchies made possible the translation of "things" of the natural biological order into things of comparable moral spaces of societies. Darwin's *On the Origin of Species by Means of Natural Selection, or the Preservation of Favored Races in the Struggle for Life* in 1859 stressed the importance of heartier races and the honing of "moral" qualities through the perfection of natural selection (see, e.g., Glaude, 2000). The Social Darwinism of Sir Francis Galton, Darwin's cousin, stressed the inheritance of moral and mental traits assumed in the character of individual members. The traits entailed, for example, sobriety and genius. Galton's hope was for better human breeding to ensure the civilized and nobler qualities to prevail over those that were feebler. Spencer spoke about education for "complete living" that embraced notions of the natural differentiation of people's abilities. The eugenics movement gave biological and physiological qualities to social differences among groups.

The comparative spaces of the cosmopolitan citizen entailed the racializing of populations. This was not necessarily the intent of policy or practice but, rather are consequences of the system of reason generated through assemblages and connections formed in cosmopolitanism. Inclusion/exclusion was simultaneously recognition of children as future citizens and yet different and outside the boundaries of normalcy that shaped the characteristics of "the American race" (Popkewitz, 1987, 2001; Ferguson, 1997).[6] To paraphrase curriculum writers of the 19th century, the hope of schooling was preserving the American race and its civilization by preventing "the barbarians" from knocking at the door of the nation. The arguments about schooling in Horace Mann's (1867b) school reports to the Massachusetts Board of Education said that schooling was concerned not with the external qualities of people but with the inner self of the child. Education is to develop in the child

> a general amelioration of habits, and those purer pleasures which flow from a cultivation of the higher sentiments, which constitute the spirit of human welfare, and enhance a thousand fold the worth of all temporal possessions, these have been comparatively neglected. (Mann, 1867a, p. 7)

If education did not succeed in its transcendental image of humanity, then Mann asserted that the barbarians would be let in the gate and destroy the republic.

The hope and fears travel as part of the same phenomenon of schooling to distinguish, differentiate, and divide. The categories of childhood are morally charged cultural theses that differentiate the spaces of the civilized and civilizations from those called savages and barbarians in the 19th century and today the "at-risk" or disadvantaged child.

Toward the Study of the Reason of Cosmopolitanism and Schooling

These first two chapters focused on cosmopolitanism as a system of reason. The focus on cosmopolitanism is done using cultural theses about a universal humanity through the invention of individuals "endowed" with agency that enabled self-improvement and progress. Agency was ordered through "reason," science, and new epistemological spaces of time in planning mode(s) of living. The particular qualities of this reason embodies the homeless mind, living as a stranger and as acting to affect the design of one's life. The universalizing was particular, and its sanctification elided the processes of abjection in the phenomenon of cosmopolitanism: the universal as particular, comparative instantiations that circulate to differentiate civilizations and the civilized, and in comparative inscriptions that racialized people that is a particular modern characteristic of reason itself.

Cosmopolitanism entails double gestures of hope and fears that are continually assembled, connected, and disconnected in different times and spaces in the formation of modern schooling. Although my historical attention is to the United States, there were other notions of cosmopolitanism that were assembled, for example, in the secularization and modernization processes of the Kemalist revolution in Turkey during the 20th century that connected and disconnected the Islamic traditions of the Ottoman Empire (Kazamias, 2006). The Japanese modernization processes associated Meiji reforms of the mid-19th century to the post–World War II constructions of the state and schools as well, which generated different sets of principles to cosmopolitanism (Shibata, 2005). I pose different historical settings here to suggest that cosmopolitanism is not a single set of practices, nor does it necessarily center on European societies.

The following chapters explore the double gestures in the cultural theses of cosmopolitan modes of life. The beginning of the 20th and 21st centuries are examined to explore the changes in the social epistemology and the processes of abjection. I will continually return to the inside and outside of cosmopolitanism through the principles that order agency, reason, and science in the planning of the self in different historical contours.[7]

PART 1

Twentieth-Century Reforms, the Unfinished Cosmopolitan, and Sciences of Education

In chapter 1, I posed two questions about pedagogy, teacher education, and research in the beginning of the 20th century:

> What cultural theses of cosmopolitanism circulate and change to order the problems and solutions of reform and change in pedagogy, teacher education, and the sciences of education?
>
> What are the processes of abjection and how do they change in the ordering of cosmopolitan agency, collaboration, and science?

This section examines the long 19th century as it reaches into the start of the 20th century. I use the term *long 19th century* to give attention to uneven historical processes that move from the 18th into the 20th century to order the cultural theses about cosmopolitan modes of living. The interweaving of different historical processes is to recognize the cosmopolitanism is merely one discourse about salvation but overlapped different social and cultural practices that leached into the pedagogical psychologies and sociology associated with progressive education. It is the assembly and connection of these different practices that I explore as generating principles of agency and reason in planning who the child is and should be as the future cosmopolitan citizen.

I begin with chapter 3 with Puritan notions of the New World as it was transmogrified into notions of the nation as American exceptionalism, the unique human experiment that would provide direction for the development of a universal cosmopolitan society. I pursue this salvation theme in national belonging as it connects with principles generated in the construction of agency, community, and nation as they connect in pedagogy.

As I argued previously, the hope of an inclusive society that circulated in the cosmopolitanism given to the nation and its citizen simultaneously produced principles about those outside of cosmopolitanism: those in need of rescue and the fears of the qualities of the child and family that threatened the future of humanity in the narratives of American exceptionalism. The hope was for the child to be a future cosmopolitan citizen, and with the hope were fears were given expression through the Social Question. The Social Question was historically related to Protestant social movements concerned with reforming the urban conditions classified as producing moral disorder. American progressive education is located in these Protestant social movement and social sciences as a different register about the formation of schooling than that found in institutional and intellectual histories. Theories of community, social interaction, and communication in pedagogy and sciences of family, for example, are argued as giving recognition to urban populations, which circumscribed and differentiated the unlivable spaces outside cosmopolitanism. The history explored in this section serves as an epistemological *platform* to consider the changes in the cultural theses generated in today's school reforms.

Chapter 3 examines American exceptionalism as the epic of the nation as it was assembled in the cultural thesis of cosmopolitanism in pedagogy. I explore narratives about the early American republic as they overlap with the emerging social sciences and pedagogical sciences in designing the principles of reason as guiding human agency. Processes of abjection in American exceptionalism, its cosmopolitanism, and schooling are also explored. The imagined unity of the "nation-ness" of the citizen differentiates and divides the urban immigrant, poor, and racialized populations in need of rescue, as they lie outside the moral and ethical qualities of the reasoned individual.

Chapter 4 focuses on the polysemous qualities of the education sciences. Science is a practice to order, classify, and differentiate the world through its theories and methodologies of investigation. Science is also brought into everyday life as a set of principles of ordering and classifying experience and acts. The two different meanings of science, however, overlap but are not the same in the practices of pedagogy. The sciences of pedagogy generate principles about children's learning and development that are in turn brought into the procedures through which child is to think and act with the intentionality of agency and freedom. The discussion draws on icons of American pedagogical sciences—Edward L. Thorndike,

G. Stanley Hall, and John Dewey—as well as early sociologists influential in the construction of the sciences of education. The different authors are treated as conceptual personae, to draw on Deleuze and Guattari (1994), enunciating particular solutions and plans for action that go beyond their specific scientific projects. As such, the different texts about science, school reforms, and pedagogy provide vantage points to understand the principles generated about the cultural theses of pedagogy.

Chapter 5 pursues more closely the cultural theses of cosmopolitanism and its double gestures in sociology and psychology. Notions of community and the psychological qualities about child development, behavior, and problem solving relate cosmopolitanism to the Social Question about the moral disorder of the city. Notions of learning and community, for example, are examined as formulating a reordering of modes of life for the immigrant family and child as well as for African Americans who moved to the cities.

Chapter 6 focuses on the process of abjection. Pedagogical reforms and science differentiated and divided the qualities of those "civilized" from those who were cast out of that space. I play here with the the Enlightenment's phrase of "the pursuit of happiness," placed in the American Constitution, as transmogrified into a focus on those different from the cosmopolitanism visions in the national exceptionalism. I use the metaphor of "unhappy" populations to consider the sociological focus of the sciences of schooling on the danger of urban populations cast in an in-between space—recognized in need of rescue and inclusion and simultaneously cast out. The formations of school subjects of literacy, mathematics, and music at the beginning of the century are explored as processes of abjection that inscribe distinctions and divisions of who the "civilized" child is, should be, and is not.

CHAPTER 3

Cosmopolitanism, American Exceptionalism, and the Making of Schooling

This chapter is the first of four to examine the cultural theses about cosmopolitanism and its double gestures in American pedagogy at the beginning of the 20th century. This chapter explores the assembly of notions of agency, time, and science as they connect to the narratives of collective belonging and home with regard to an American exceptionalism—that is, the telling of the nation as an epic account of a unique human experiment in the progressive development of the highest ideals of cosmopolitan human values and progress.[1] Pedagogical projects, I argue, are cultural theses about the child as the future cosmopolitan citizen that embody this sublime of American exceptionalism.

This chapter explores American exceptionalism. First, the uniqueness of the nation as bringing human happiness through the inscription of the cultural thesis of cosmopolitanism. Second, the emergence of social and education sciences within the narratives of American exceptionalism is discussed. These sciences entail a set of practices to design the agency and progress of cosmopolitanism within the spaces of the nation. The final section considers processes of abjection in American exceptionalism, its cosmopolitanism, and its schooling. The imagined unity of the "nation-ness" of the citizen differentiates and divides the citizen from its "others"—the urban immigrant, poor, and racialized populations in need of rescue—because they lie outside the moral and ethical qualities of the "reasoned" individual.

Cosmopolitanism, National Exceptionalism, and Its Pastoral Images

Most studies of the nation are related to the formal legal-administrative institutions, with more recent scholarship focusing on the cultural production of the citizen. The latter studies of the nation argue that the cultural unity has little to do with geographical or linguistic unity and natural cohesion (see, e.g., Bell, 2001; Hunter, 1994). The construction of a European, an American, or a German "identity," for example, is not the outgrowth of some natural "home" where one belongs but is produced through an amalgamation of technologies, ideas, and social practices (see, e.g., Balibar & Wallerstein, 1991). Anderson (1991) has called the institution of an imaginary unity as an "imagined community," one in which cultural representations are historically fabricated to produce a "nation-ness."

The focus on cosmopolitanism provides a different strategy to consider the cultural production of the citizen and nation than Anderson's "an imagined community." It does this through focusing Anderson's cosmopolitanism as a cultural theses about modes of life produced through the assembly and amalgamation of different historical trajectories. Further the individuality and collective belonging and home produces double gestures central to that production. The American republic assembled Enlightenment notions of cosmopolitanism with Protestant salvation narratives expressed as the New World and Promised Land, and territorial expansions as manifest destiny. The secular promise was that the nation and its citizens would escape the burden of historical time by fabricating a future cosmopolitan citizen who would truly be universal and a model to the world. The self-reliance and self-motivation of the child was to produce the cosmopolitan citizen who acted with liberty and freedom.

"The Light of the World"

One might argue that religion and cosmopolitanism do not "fit" together as the Enlightenment was to supersede the authority of magic and superstition through its reliance of reason and science. Further, the narratives of the Enlightenment's cosmopolitanism were to transcend the parochialism of the nation through inserting a grand narrative about humanity and progress. Yet the narratives of the Enlightenment's cosmopolitanism embodied salvation narratives of the soul transmogrified as redemptive themes of the secular republican of the American and French revolutions (Gorski, 1999; Ferguson, 1997; Marx, 2003). The Puritans, a religious group that came to America in the 17th century to escape persecution, recognized the site of their colony as the New World.[2] It was God's chosen place, with the Puritans serving as God's elect to make possible "the day of God's judgment and the new reign of Christ on earth" and thus reverse the corruption of Europe (McKnight, 2003, p. 17).

The nation and education were placed in salvation themes as "the city on the hill" and "errand in the wilderness" fulfilling the role of New Israel with individuals creating the greater corporate mission. The Reformation's faith in Enlightenment reason was brought to schooling (McKnight, 2003, p. 25). The errand into the wilderness required the education of children, which extended to those children beyond the Puritan community (p. 11). Drawing on John Calvin's notion of curriculum vitæ or "a course of life," education was the persistent preparation for a conversion experience that gave the individual moral behavior. Pedagogy was the "converting ordinance," written with an evangelizing and calculated design on the souls of their readers, and later rewritten as the "soul" translated into theories of the actor and agency, and given expression in the notions of community. The method of reason was to build revelatory, spiritual fulfillment. Community was part of this course of life or one's curriculum vitæ. The individual's freedom was indivisible from the shared cultural world that gave unity to all of human kind (p. 44).

The narratives leading to the American Revolution connected and disconnected Puritan salvation themes with the universal reason of the Enlightenment ideas, which were different from those in British and French contexts. The cultural thesis about republican modes of living moved from a Christian millennial belief that the proper object of study was God to an Enlightenment cosmopolitanism that rejected, at one level, religion as the basis for a morality common to mankind (Schlereth, 1977, p. 56). The republic joined "the health of the soul and the regeneration of the Christian and the virtuous citizen, exultation of the divine and the celebration of design" (Ferguson, 1997, p. 43) with the planning of human improvement and "happiness." A paradoxical insertion of Puritan notions of "good works" into notions of the republican citizen was embodied in the writings of John Adams, one of the signers of the American Declaration of Independence. He said that the settlement of America was "the opening of a grand scene and design in Providence for the illumination of the ignorant, and the emancipation of the slavish part of mankind all over the earth" (Wood, 1991, p. 191). The redemptive salvation stories of the nation told of "boundless sources of energy through which individuals discovered who they were: personality flourished only through exploration and growth" (Wiebe, 1995, p. 186).

The rational and moral order in American exceptionalism embodied the universalism of the Enlightenment's cosmopolitan reason joined with Unitarian Protestantism in what Bellah (1975) calls "civil religion" (also see Bercovitch, 1978). The nation inscribed salvation and redemption in its collective being and in its citizens. The Puritans' biblical interpretation of America as "the light of the world" was brought into political, social, and economic narratives, written into the formulations of the Declaration of Independence and the Constitution (McKnight, 2003, p. 19). The Puritans' saga of "events to lead to a Utopian moral grace on earth" was transmogrified into the saga of the nation told with an evangelical purity and political goodness in its land and its people. The epic of the nation was of a reclaimed utopian past lost in the corruptions and traditions of the Old World, Europe.

The exceptional redemptive nature of the nation was given in the phrases assigned to the nation. The nation was the New World, given the providential character of religious conceptions of a Garden of Eden that had escaped the evils and disfigurements of Old World traditions (Jehlen, 1986; Ross, 1991). America, as the home of the chosen people, was a radical "otherness" in which the nation's citizens were the "racially elect" (Glaude, 2000).[3] The concept of manifest destiny appeared in the 1837 journal *Democratic Review* and explained the national expansion to the Pacific that captured the Puritan rhetoric of divine sanction in the view of diverse European peoples populating the new continent and receiving the divine principles of liberty and equality (Wald, 1995, pp. 106–111). The literature of the nation told of heroes who had evangelical qualities endowed within their worldly pursuits (Furstenberg, 2006).

The struggle of American exceptionalism was cast in a mixture of Enlightenment and religious images. The great effort of the nation was between darkness and light; "the civilizing mission" of the nation was to spread the ideals of a unified enlightened humanity. John Adams, evoking a biological metaphor of growth and decay that juxtaposed the hope and fears of the Enlightenment, said, "The mind could be cultivated like a garden, with barbarous weeds eliminated and enlightened fruits raised." The cultivation of the mind would destroy "the savage" in the individual (Wood, 1991, p. 191). The enlightened, virtuous citizen of the American republic was labeled civilized by the inner characteristics of being reasonable, tolerant, honest, virtuous, and candid (p. 195). The civilizing mission placed the individual in the worldly, secular transcendent values of cosmopolitanism and judged the development of others by "civilized" standards and rules of conduct.

Particular groups and individualities whose manners, dispositions, and cultural practices were not cosmopolitan were recognized as not civilized— former African American slaves after the American Civil War, Asians legally excluded and then internally segregated in schools, the Native Americans, and different Europeans, among others, during the 19th century and into the 20th century. The "others" were outside of reason and of being reasonable people. The position of such exclusions, however, was not fixed or stable. The public rhetoric about Chinese Americans, for example, were classified as a race of a previously advanced civilization but one that had declined and, as an inferior race, now carried disease, was unchristian, and "deemed a social disease infecting the American body politic" (Wong & Chang, 1998, p. 7; also see Low, 1982).[4]

The history of American exceptionalism as finding moral grace in the nation was told in the narrative of the school. The U.S. Department of Interior's Bureau of Education report on American education for a conference in Vienna (U.S. Government Printing Office, 1874) was entitled "Statement of the Relation of Free School to the American Commonwealth." The public school was spoken of as part of the idyllic evolutionary movement of the national destiny.[5] The history of the United States was "the founding [of] a civilization" that expresses the "peculiar phase of character in the American people" (p. 13). That history was narrated as the development of the nation in three evolutionary stages: (a) the settlement of new territory by pioneers and the reduction of the wilderness to an agricultural country; (b) the rise of commercial towns and the creation of transit facilities in the new regions; and (c) the development of manufacturing centers and the ascendancy of domestic commerce (p. 13).

The design of the child as the future republican citizen embodied fears of darkness and the backwardness of the others. Thomas Paine told of throwing off the Old World prejudices and adopting new liberal, enlightened, and rational ideas. "The mind once enlightened cannot again become dark" (cited in Wood, 1991, p. 191). The cosmopolitan citizen was placed in the American epic of a civilization whose moral universalism differentiated those not as reasoned or without reason; slaves and First World people as well provided the providential purposes for territorial expansions, and more recently in the 21st century, to assert the role of the nation and its particular ways of life in global affairs.

The "founding of a civilization" in the Bureau of Education's report embodies, as I will discuss later, a central tenet of cosmopolitanism as a comparative instantiation to differentiate the qualities of reason and rationality from others who are not as advanced. Natural history and Social Darwinism told the story of an evolutionary movement from the savage and the deviant to the modern American. The story of the advance of civilization was a "great chain of being" that established as a hierarchy of an evolutionary racial history (Lesko, 2001). The chain of being is composed of a great number of hierarchal links, from the most basic and foundational elements up through the very highest perfection seen as given by God. The tale of American exceptionalism as the most advanced civilization—differentiated from others, who had fallen from moral grace—was told in the school textbooks of the 19th century (see, e.g., Kaestle, Damon-Moore, Stedman, & Tinsley, 1991).

Transforming the Wilderness and the Technological Sublime

For many Americans, the epic of regaining a lost utopian past was no longer sustainable by the close of the 19th century. The crises of unbridled capitalism, the perceived breakdown of moral order in the city, and the brutality of modern warfare coupled with the struggle over slavery of the American Civil War, among others, cast doubt on the American exceptionalism as the idyllic reincarnation of a biblical Garden of Eden (see, e.g., Menand, 2001). The special place of the nation in heralding redemption and salvation for humanity was in the future rather than recapturing the biblical garden in the incarnation of the nation.

The moral grace of the New World was revisioned as the millennial potential of the future. The new beginning was told in the frontier thesis of Frederick Jackson Turner, an early 20th-century historian. The religious idea of manifest destiny was assembled in the cultural and political epic of the nation in its westward expansion to the Pacific. "Turner wove the tale of an exceptional nation removed from the corrupting influences of Europe, a country where the frontier produced the perfect mix of abundance, individualism and equality" (Oshinsky, 2000, p. A19). Turner (1893/1994) argued that the existence of the nation's frontier of free land and the American westward settlement explained American democracy and the particular character of its national "soul" that served as the enactment of New Israel's divine principles whose model of advancements could be brought to all humanity.

At the conclusion of Turner's career, he decried the closing of the frontier because of the uncertain consequences it posed for the American future. In contrast to Europe, America had no history, which made it possible to fulfill its promise to provide the universalist cosmopolitan history (Turner, 1893/1994, p. 38). The future agrarian and pastoral image of society was now placed in the urban nation and an expanded educational system that substituted for the mobility of the frontier west (Faragher, 1994, p. 8). The New World that Turner saw replacing the frontier was a homogeneous world. It had no violence, no African slaves, no Indians, and no women to unsettle the story.

The new epic tale of the nation that replaced Turner's frontier was told through the technological sublime: narratives of beauty, aesthetics, awe, and fear. The technological marvels of the railroad, electricity, bridges, and skyscrapers were placed in a cultural dialogue about the national manifest destiny (Nye, 1999). The natural power of Niagara Falls, the Grand Canyon, and technologies represented in the railroad, bridge, and city skyscrapers were viewed as triumphs of art and science in the liberation of the human spirit realized by the young republic. The technological changes were made into the apotheosis of cosmopolitan reason and science in the making of the nation. The technologies of the canal and the railroad were narrated as a causal chain of events of an inevitable developmental process. Foundation stories were told about Americans transforming a wilderness into "a prosperous and egalitarian" cosmopolitan society whose landscape and people had a transcendent presence through its technological achievements (Nye, 2003, p. 5). The exceptionalism was of the technological promise of the future in which individuals would overcome the evils of modernization that inhibited progress.

The new social sciences embodied the universal history of cosmopolitanism as the inevitable developmental process of a prosperous and equalitarian society. The sociologist Charles Horton Cooley (1909), who wrote about education, saw the United States as "nearer, perhaps, to the spirit of the coming order" (p. 167) that would be totally different from anything before it. Evoking exceptionalism, Cooley wrote that "the new industrial modernity" of America was close to being the first real democracy that is "totally different from anything before it because it places a greater emphasis on individuality and innovation" and "does not inherit the class culture of Europe" (cited in Ross, 1972, p. 245).

While the Old Country was decried as outdated and bound to harmful traditions, counter stories were told about the backwardness of the nation and its need to look to Europe. The prevailing narratives, however, were about the New World. During the American Revolution, the idea of democracy was viewed as the "sister spirit of Christianity" (Wald, 1995, p. 119). The Puritan notions of the Kingdom of God on Earth were brought into and revisioned to confront the dangers of the unchecked capitalism and the urban social conditions in industrialization (Tröhler, 2006).

Inclusion and Casting Out: Urban Populations, The Urbane, and the Social Question

The redemptive themes of American exceptionalism as "the apotheosis of reason" and the hope of the future were given expression in the narratives of the nation and its progressive hope. The poetry of the European immigrant Emma Lazarus, placed on plaque at the foot of the Statue of Liberty, epitomizes what was seen by many immigrants as the hope of the new land and nation. Lazarus wrote of the United States:

> Give me your tired, your poor,
> your huddled masses yearning to breathe free,
> The wretched refuse of your teeming shore,
> Send these, the homeless, tempest-tossed, to me:
> I lift my lamp beside the golden door.

The exceptionalism inscribed in Lazarus's poem was not only about the hope of the New Land and its inclusion of immigrants. Lazarus, although a Jew, embodied the Protestant redemptive hope of the new nation in which the constituted "wretched" of the Old World would be reborn to develop and "breathe free" of the Enlightenment "lamp." The Old World's "tired" traditions would be shed as the New World opened "the golden door." The redemption embodies a cosmopolitanism as the "lamp" of freedom that overcomes provinciality and exclusion.

The promise of enlightenment recognized and inscribed difference. The "wretched refuse" of the immigrant also embodied the "poor" as a marker of the late 19th century, the "cause" of poverty had shifted focus from individual sinfulness and idleness to the environmental conditions in which the poor lived and worked. The solution to the problem of poverty in the early 19th century was also individual: "Man [sic] to suffer the evils of penury and idleness in the manner of the English workhouse tradition" (Reese, 1995, p. 120). By the later part of the century, the focus was on changes in the circumstances that would prevent sinfulness and enable the poor to succeed. The muckraking traditions in American newspapers to uncover the evils produced in the new city landscape and the settlement houses' work with immigrants and racial groups in the large urban areas were linked to redemptive themes associated with cosmopolitan images and narratives of progress, enlightenment, and inclusion.

Science as the Hope of the Republic and Protection Against Its Dangers

Science was to bring efficiency to society and its schools in the movement towards the progressive evolution of society. This faith in science was not only in North America. Crossing the North Atlantic and ranging from the Fabian Society to the German Evangelical Social Congress, the French Musée Social, and the Settlement House movements in many countries (Rodgers, 1998), reforms directed attention to the "Social Question." That question concerned the loss of moral order produced by urban conditions. The Social Question was embedded in American Progressivism, a varied set of reforms to change the conditions and people in urban settings.

Earlier 19th-century populism of Jacksonian democracy was anti-city, anti-business, anti-government, and anti-intellectual. Progressivism urbanized that populism into reforms organized by businessman, civic leaders, and intellectuals. Central to the reforms were the search for scientific principles to plan the reorganization of the city and its urban populations. Although the advent of central heating and building improvements, modernization of sanitary and firefighting facilities, truck gardens, and advances of food processing pointed to progress in city conditions, these changes were continually placed against the unplanned growth and squalid conditions of the slums. Doubt arose about the immigrants who stayed in the city rather than being absorbed in rural areas: the Irish were viewed as troublesome, and the Italians, Greeks, and Galician Jews produced alarm regarding their customs and manners, and sometimes their religious beliefs (Joncich, 1968, p. 43).

Reforms addressed questions of poverty, inequality, racial tensions, urban conditions, and schools, among other isues. The programs were to eliminate the social evils of the city by active intervention in the life and conditions of the city. The poor and immigrants were to develop their skills and talents in modes of living that would undo what was seen as moral disorder.

The struggle was "the civilizing mission" that contrasted darkness with the light of the nation. The social gospel movement to which many Progressive reformers belonged sought to incorporate Christian ethics into government and civic life. The evangelistic hope of exceptionalism was to bring the Christian gospel to non-Christians—that is, the heathen. That gospel mixed religious notions of salvation of a generalized Protestant Christianity into missionary work directed at immigrants and sometimes former Black slaves that had moved into the city. "How long will American Christianity allow this process of degeneracy to go on, before realizing the peril of it, and providing the counteracting agencies of good?" asked a missionary book printed in New York City (Grose, 1906, p. 224). The Christian society feared that the lack of enforcement of laws (p. 66) and the intolerance of some native groups who "brutally abuse the immigrants" (p. 10) would lead to less equitable conditions.

The immigrant was placed in the flow of time that established a hierarchy of value about those who belonged to "advanced" and "less advanced" civilizations. Protestant missionaries in New York (Grose, 1906), for example, wrote about the problem of "unguarded gates":

Wide open and unguarded stand our gates,
And through them presses a wild, motley throng
The fear of unguarded gates.

The narrative evokes a military language of defense against the invasion of uncivilized hordes who crossed over from Europe. The differences of the great chain of being had been discarded as an explanatory device about difference but principles of difference were reinscribed in natural histories that ordered civilizations in a continuum. The comparative distinctions and the hierarchies of qualities of people provided a grid in which movements such as eugenics were made intelligible. Eugenics drew on the symbolic forms of rationality to produce a quasi-science that combined moral and spiritual narratives with ideas about progress and degeneration to rank individuals, groups, and societies.

The Redemption of the Urban Populations

Science was key to the civilizing process. Diagnosing the impediments to progress meant pushing back the boundaries of darkness and barbarism, and spreading light and knowledge. The American Enlightenment was to resist "Gothic barbarism." The Gothic barbarism was to be defeated through

> the struggle of natural science in understanding of nature, the tempering of superstition in religion in the politics of new free government— not only in the spread of science, liberty or republican government but in the spread of civilization. The civilizing was to calculate happiness. (Wood, 1991, pp. 191–192)

Missionary work entailed close interaction between city reforms, the settlement house movement work, and the social sciences that were institutionalized in universities. The Hull House and the University of Chicago's Department of Sociology, and professors such as George Herbert Mead and John Dewey, gave attention to the modes of living of the family and the upbringing of the child through the Social Question concerned with the loss of moral order.[6] Protestant redemptive themes in the progressive urban reforms were to produce the self-motivated and responsible cosmopolitan individual who would actively intervene in his or her own development and thus guarantee the progress of the nation.

The sciences had different paths to change the conditions and the populations of the city although the principles in social planning crossed the different disciplines. One approach entailed the purification of Old World cultures by resocializing and integrating "the best" of the immigrant culture. Others intellectuals spoke about "race suicide" as a national problem produced by immigration but understood and represented the threat as a challenge, literally and metaphorically, to the American family (Wald, 1995). Massachusetts Institute of Technology (MIT) President Francis Amasa Walker, a statistician involved in the censuses in 1870 and 1880, saw the outcome of immigration as the destruction of the American family.

John R. Commons, a prominent economist in the Progressive era, raised the question of race suicide through the analogy of the family and gender, heeding Theodore Roosevelt's warning that

> if the men of the nation are not anxious … to be fathers of families, and if the women do not recognize that the greatest thing for any woman is to be a good wife and mother … that nation has cause to be alarmed about its future. (cited in Wald, 1995, p. 245)

The domestic science movements embodied the task of rescuing the family which did not embody the cultural thesis of the cosmopolitanism. Linked to the settlement house movement, it entailed deference to medical and scientific expertise to influence the infant- and child-care practices of mothers (Apple, 2006). Although there were self-help books written for the gentry earlier, the late 19th-century family (mother) was to learn how to organize the house and to provide child rearing through interiorizing medical and scientific information about growth and development. Principles of the sciences of hygiene, moral economy, and child rearing were to construct ways of thinking and organizing life through rational planning directed to the future.

The sciences associated with pedagogy and the urban family inscribed qualities of the homeless mind into the practices of the home. Empirical and theoretical distinctions overlapped those of morality to order and rationalize the home. The new discoveries about disease and bacteria were placed in systems of family interaction, child rearing, and the moral economy of the household. The scientifically managed home, for example, entailed regulating eating habits to obtain rational planning of diets for health. The proper running of a household entailed scientific management, such as hygiene measures related to washing hands before handling food, but hygiene was more than scientific practices. Diets, for example, entailed restrictions on consumptive goods and immoral habits such as drinking or gambling. The calculated order of the urban home carried into the gendered images of the bourgeois home and its family relationships.

The Double Gestures of Schooling

Education was a "civilizing mission" to secure the future of the civilized society. The school was intended to connect the scope and aspirations embodied in American exceptionalism with the rescue and redemption of those feared as dangerous to the promise of progress. Charles Eliot, president of Harvard University and a leading school reformer, argued that democratic institutions required that children be educated in the systematic use of reason in order to train them "for the duties of life." The school guaranteed the future of society! Teaching was to produce the democratic society though principles assembled in American exceptionalism. The enlightened, virtuous citizen of the American republic was marked as civilized by the inner characteristics of being reasonable, tolerant, honest, virtuous, and candid (Wood, 1991, p. 195).

The school organized around "prophesies about ultimate destination of child" should be replaced with the general cosmopolitan education "for power and general cultivation as distinguished from training in special means of obtaining a predestined sort of livelihood" (Eliot, 1892–1893, p. 421). The optimism of American exceptionalism led to the theory that the school would create the civilized society necessary to fulfill the dream of the nation. Education was to teach children the how to reason and a general rationality that would enable the wise conduct of life.

The reason and rationality that constituted "wise conduct" was central to The Committee of Ten's report that Eliot chaired. It recommended the integration and standardization of the high school curriculum for college admission, embodied the principles of agency and science as the fulfillment of the national destiny. Developing the child's "reason" would train all children "in the duties of life and that such training could work almost a revolution in human society in two or three generations if wisely and faithfully conducted" (Eliot, 1892–1893, pp. 416–417).

The power of reason was associated with a general sense of science as a practice in ordering everyday life. To practice science was to be reasonable, and reason was what science provided. The individual was to act through the "process or operations of observation" that would include "alert, intent, and accurate use of all the senses" (p. 417).

School was integral to and the guarantee of the development and future of the republic. The school was "crystallized in our American notion of patriotism, five hundred years of passionate struggles for liberty, of breaking chains and abolishing formulas" (Eliot, 1892–93, p.418).

A speech given at the National Educational Association, an organization of school leaders, asserted that our history, a global history, is told of the American nation as expressed in its national anthem:

> America is a sweet land of liberty; land where our fathers died; Columbia's heroes fought and bled in freedom's cause; in the rocket's red glare, and with bombs bursting in air, the star-spangled banner waves o'er the land of the free and the home of the brave. (Martin, 1895, p. 134)

Martin continues:

> Our heroes are global and not limited to the American Revolution: from William Tell, Cromwell, Lafayette, and Touissant L'Ouverture

to Bolivar, Garibaldi, and finally Washington. The legend of America is the fulfillment of the universal enlightenment of humanity as expressed in Thomas Paine's *The Rights of Man.*

The new patriotism is not contained in the old theology, Martin (1895) argues, of building monuments and hanging flags at school, nor is it an unyielding obedience to authority and social inequities. The new patriotism is in the inscription of the character and dispositions that tell the good from the evil. The child-as-the-future-citizen is "to learn the essential and underlying principles of today" so as to identify who "today's enemies are" (p. 135). Education is the march of the republic toward the promise of the harmony of humanity, and its progressive history is

> to develop common standards and "a common weld" in which personal interest[s] are set aside for public ends. The civilizing of the child is to combine social and personal obligation. The past, present and future are joined as education civilizes by bringing back new patriotism … to penetrate this system and bring back personal responsibility and social harmony that combines social and personal obligations. (Martin, 1895, p. 138)

Pedagogical projects were to reduce or eliminate the dangers of those who challenged the search for order and harmony. Jane Addams, founder of the Hull House in Chicago, and John Dewey, for example, searched for ways "to transform social relations and establish patterns of thinking so that increasing numbers of people, from increasing numbers of cultural traditions, could live together in crowded, urban conditions and still maintain a sense of harmony, order, beauty, and progress" (Lagemann, 2000, p. 55). Addams thought that the influx of foreigners were "densely ignorant" of American customs and institutions (cited in Lybarger, 1987, p. 181).

Pedagogy and the Hopes and Fears of the Urban Child and Family

The school pedagogy embodied double theses. Early 19th-century Jacksonian populist school reforms argued that there was a strong consensus of public elementary schooling as "necessary to the moral, political, and economic health of the republic" that served to "open a school and close a jail" (Joncich, 1968, p. 46). The fears of decay and degeneration of the "American race" gave the school a different redemptive task by the end of the century—one that was related to the city which served as the source of innovation and progress (Nye, 2003, p. 35) and the threat of the moral degeneration. The fears of "foreign" radical ideas and anarchy were highlighted near the end of the century in the 1886 Chicago labor protest, called the Haymarket Riot. Schools were to protect children from foreign notions (Joncich, 1968, p. 46).

The promise of the future of the republic was to promote the public good through school pedagogies. School pedagogy engaged the Social Question through changes in the conceptions of the child and school subjects. The education setting shifted from a severe and formal environment of instruction and moralization to one that joined intellectual and academic teaching with moral or character development, social-emotional aspects, and health education. Schools were designed as urban institutions to teach American moral behavior and conduct and to aid society by preventing disease, vice, or future crime (Bloch, 1987, pp. 52–55). The progress of humanity, to use a phrase of the American neo-Hegelians of the 1880s, could be recapitulated in the growth of the child, and this concept became a central form of planning the principles of agency, reason, and rationality in different strands of progressive education. The pedagogical planning of the child was placed in a flow of time that could be calculated, ordered, and administered as the growth, development, and problem-solving abilities of the child.

The Social Question of changing urban populations was critical in curriculum and instructional designs. Horace Mann (1867a, 1867b), discusssed earlier, talked about the republican government's mission to give the child the habits of mind of the cosmopolitan citizen. The key to these habits of mind was reason directed toward the social good. In the name of that good, Mann addressed the problem of physical appearance and disease in the city in his 1842 and 1844 annual reports of the state of education in Massachusetts (cited in Gustafson, 2005). The threat entailed overlapping discourses of science, medicine, and morality. The spread of disease (specifically the epidemic of tuberculosis) was connected to the socializing habits of a large proportion of Irish Catholics and the growing Black population in Boston. Mann's curriculum reform, summarized in his sixth annual report to the state legislature, was to incorporate the study of physiology, a science at that time that combined the new theories of disease with aspects of phrenology or health regimens. In the eighth report, the music curriculum provided children with opportunities to sing to make the lungs healthier, improve comportment, and have positive outcomes for the general outlook on social life. The curriculum would provide for the moral development of character and personality traits through a complex system of exercise and diet.

The registers of hope and fear were articulated in the formation of school subjects. The formation of social studies as a school subject emerges, for example, in relation to Protestant reformism's concern with the Social Question. The writing of Thomas Jesse Jones provides an exemplar of the double gestures in school reform. Jones was the future chair of the Committee on Social Studies and had worked at the Columbia University Settlement House before assuming an academic position. He was interested in the transformation (social evolution) of the immigrant to embody "the Anglo-Saxon ideal" (Lybarger, 1987, p. 185). Different populations of immigrants were compared to differentiate "educational needs." The Italians, for example, were differentiated as less impulsive and more cautious and deliberate compared to the "need" of educational experiences for Jewish children (p. 187). The notion of "need" was "the social judgment ... about what ideals and traits ought to be inculcated in the weak by the strong through instruction in the social studies" (p. 187).

While I will not examine the curriculum writers of the Depression, I want to briefly examine the redemptive and comparative distinctions in George Counts's (1932/1980) book about the responsibility of teachers for the social reconstruction of society. Written during the Great Depression, it embodies narratives of American exceptionalism, moral disorder and order, and the use of pedagogy to bring consensus to society as a response to the fears located in the debilitating conditions of capitalism. The focus is on changing society by changing people and the view of the teacher as the shepherd in social reconstruction. The schools were the site of the struggle between totalitarianism and democracy. Evoking an American exceptionalism, Counts argued that teachers needed "to assume unprecedented social responsibilities" as "we live in a difficult and dangerous time" (p. 106). The schools had an obligation to bring back the morality of the previous pastoral society in which democracy had developed in the 19th century. The hope of a cosmopolitan reason as a spiritual obligation of saving civilization through the school moves through the text.

> Until recently the very word American has been synonymous throughout the world with democracy and symbolic to the oppressed classes of all lands of hope and opportunity. Child of the revolutionary ideas and impulses of the eighteenth century, the American nation became the embodiment of a bold social experimentation and a champion of the power of environment to develop the capacities and redeem the souls of common men and women. And as her stature grew, her lengthening shadow reached to the four corners of the earth and everywhere impelled the human will to rebel against ancient wrongs. Here undoubtedly is the finest jewel in our heritage and the thing that is most worth of preservation. (Counts, 1932/1980, p. 99)

The principles ordering the reconstruction of society are cosmopolitanism through the nation's "revolutionary temper" and its devotion to democracy. These stand in the text as exemplars of humanity's hope for all classes excluded previously in world society. A revitalized and revisioned America is more than the nation's formal institutions but

> it is a sentiment with respect to the moral quality of men: it is an aspiration towards a society in which this sentiment will find complete fulfillment. A society fashioned in harmony with the American democratic tradition would combat all forces tending to produce social distinctions and classes; repress every form of privilege and economic parasitism; manifest a tender regard for the weak, the ignorant, and the unfortunate; place the heavier and more onerous social burdens on the backs of the strong; glory in very triumph of man in his timeless urge to express himself and to make the world more habitable; exalt human labor of hand and brain as the creator of all wealth and culture. (Counts, 1932/1980, pp. 199–200)

Teachers were to design the progressive "vision of American destiny." They were to give children a better "legacy of spiritual values" so our children were "enabled to find their place in the world, be lifted out of the present morass of moral indifference, be liberated from the senseless struggle for material success, and be challenged to high endeavor and achievement" (Counts, 1932/1980, p. 107).

Governing as Schooling: Some Concluding Thoughts

Although the world of cosmopolitan reason and rationality sounds ideal— reason and science in the pursuit of human progress and happiness—it had its difficulties. This chapter explored the reason and rationality of cosmopolitanism as assembled through the Social Question and American exceptionalism. The "chosen people" were not elected, and those not chosen were identified as the people who could not be or were not civilized enough to partake in the future of American exceptionalism. The recognition to include others was embodied in fears of differences that cast out some from the spaces given as normalcy in the constituted civilization and the civilized.

The social sciences were to bring moral order through two overlapping projects that ordered modes of living. One was the studying of behavior, the mind, and social interaction to render the characteristics of the child and teacher visible and amenable to government. The other characteristic of science concerned its theories and methods that generated cultural theses of modes of living that functioned as principles in daily life. The agentive individual was to live as a planned biography ordered by the calculated rules and standards of reflection and action.

The converting ordinances of pedagogy did not leave these principles that ordered life to mere chance. The problem of pedagogy was one of design, a word that continually appeared in the chapter and again in contemporary school reforms discussed in chapter 9. Design was a word that spoke of what God gave to human affairs in the first coming of Puritan theology. It moved from the "Heavenly Paradise to the City of Man," which allowed for the earthly progress of the 18th-century philosophers (see, e.g., Becker, 1932). Each individual has a design given by nature, itself a thing ordered by heavenly intervention. Design proved the existence of God, which was based on evidence of intelligence or purposefulness in nature, and was considered one of the most convincing illustrations of supreme intelligence (Reuben, 1996, p. 31). Later in the 19th century, debate about evolution questioned the design in natural selection. Some liberal theologies, for example, used the notion of design to show the harmony between evolution and Christianity and the possibility of divine intervention through human planning.

CHAPTER 4

The Sciences of Pedagogy in Designing the Future

During the 19th century, science became a central strategy in planning the changes of societal conditions that would transform people. The practices of science were sanctified in public life. Science had polysemous qualities, and provided practices to order, classify, and differentiate the world through its theories and methodologies of investigation. A different notion of science, powerful as well, was that life should be ordered in a rational way. This notion of science had less to do with the theories and empirical findings of science. Rationality associated with science was re-visioned and assembled as processes of reflection and acts in daily life. This latter function of science is best captured in the school curriculum in which the child was a learner and problem solver who acts towards future goals. The two different meanings of science, however, overlap in practice. The sciences of pedagogy generate principles scaffolded into the cultural theses of how the child lives as a "reasonable person." These principles connect notions of agency and freedom embodied in cosmopolitanism with, as I argue below, a collective home shaped and fashioned with the narratives of American Exceptionalism.

To consider science as practices ordering everyday living, I focus first on the notion of planning that emerges in the long 19th century. The idea emerges relatively late that sciences provides "useful knowledge" that mutates into today's distinctions between theory and practice, and policy-oriented education sciences. The next section pursues the social and psychological sciences as double gestures of cosmopolitanism that differentiate who the child is and should be. Science in the governing of the family and the child is discussed in the third section. The final section takes up the secularization of the soul as the object of planning and intervention. Targeting the soul is spoken of in instructional design and research today as learning and shaping the dispositions and sensitivities of the child, which is a different "soul" from previous religious cosmologies about the life hereafter, but a soul just the same.

I discuss icons of American pedagogical sciences, Edward L. Thorndike, G. Stanley Hall, and John Dewey. I also consider some of the early sociologists who were influential in the construction of the sciences of education, Lester Frank Ward and Albion Small of the Department of Sociology at the University of Chicago, Charles Horton Cooley of the University of Michigan, and Edward A. Ross of the University of Wisconsin. They are treated as *conceptual personae,* to draw on Deleuze and Guattari (1994), enunciating particular solutions and plans for action within a historical assembly of ideas, institutions, and technologies. As such, they provide vantage points to understand the principles generated about the cultural theses of pedagogy.

Social Science as Planning People

The search for truth through science expressed an almost millennialist faith in rational knowledge as the most potent force shaping the world during the 19th century. Notions of science were transported from realms of investigating and controlling the natural world into social realms to plan society and individuality. The hope was that human institutions could be brought into the scope of scientific control through the use of reason and rationality. "People and nature were thought of as subjects to the same inexorable laws that governed the movement of heavenly bodies or the circulation of blood" (Commager, 1950, p. 201). The science of society needed only to find those laws and it could then take its place among the other disciplines, such as chemistry and physics. This control was expressed by Adam Smith. Science was to discover "the hidden forces that moved and held people together in the moral world, forces that could match the great 18th-century scientific discoveries of the hidden forces of gravity, magnetism, electricity, and energy" (Wood, 1999, p. 42).

The shift in what constituted science in the 19th century contained connections to later pedagogical sciences. At the beginning of the century, science was viewed as a method by which one could find the unity of knowledge. That unity of knowledge combined the natural world with the social through the belief that both embodied the providential rules of God on Earth (Reuben, 1996). The idea of a unity of knowledge no longer held sway by the end of the century. Specialization, continual changes in what constituted scientific knowledge, as well as philosophical theories of knowledge, among others, challenged the very notion that such a unity was possible. Science was defined by its unity of methods and a focus on processes. Applied to human beings, theories of behavior, problem solving, and development gave attention to processes in ordering conduct in the name of progress.

Although science as an activity to plan social life and individuality was expressed at the time of the American and French revolutions (Wagner, 2001a), social planning and amelioration were made central in its theories and methods in the 19th century. The self-regulated process of laissez-faire liberalism was no longer considered workable (Eisenstadt, 2000; Wittrock, 2000).

Science provided technologies for artificially intervening in society. European and U.S. social reformers viewed science as calculating and organizing the development of the self and society. Central to the planning of the social and education sciences was a belief in the self-endowed reason of individuals. That reason needed to be specifically constructed and not left to the devices of the unregulated liberal society.

Science was an attitude as well as a set of practices for undermining established traditions and the harmful effects of modernity. It carried the spirit of the Puritan promise of the New Jerusalem in the optimism of American exceptionalism about opening up of a more progressive and democratic society. Dewey's pedagogical creed was to install methods of science into daily life to shed the traditions that prevented progress and salvation. Dewey wrote of William James in 1929 that he was "well within the bounds of moderation when he said that looking forward instead of backward, looking to what the world and life might become instead of to what they have been, is an alteration in the 'seat of authority'" (cited in Diggins, 1994, p. 39). Action directs thought and participation in a future unencumbered by the past. That future was to be without an authoritarian system of religion, as well as without fixed classes and ancient institutions. "The old culture is doomed for us because it was built upon an alliance of political and spiritual powers, an equilibrium of governing and leisure classes, which no longer exists" (Dewey, 1927/1929d, pp. 501–502). Arthur Childs, Dewey's colleague and sometime collaborator, quoted Dewey: "Our life has no background of sanctified categories upon which we may fall back; we rely upon precedent as authority only to our own undoing" (Childs, 1956, p. 7).

Thorndike, as well, sought to remove any teleological or supernatural causes in psychology (Thorndike, 1923a, 1923b). The science of psychology, he asserted, was to develop systematic empirical knowledge so as to repudiate "the caprices of persons—of gods, goddesses, fairies, and elves—as explanations of one physical event after another." (Thorndike, 1909/1962a, p. 44) Psychology modeled Darwinism by studying the concrete particulars of intellect and character in individual men to classify continuous scales of learning. The scales are analogous to "how the physical sciences consider length, temperature, weight, or density" (Thorndike, 1909/1962a, p. 43). Such scales place individuals in time by empirically observing individuals in their "natural world." The observation of behavior makes possible its regulation and planning.

> No excuse is left for hoping and fearing instead of thinking—for teasing and bribing instead of working. Our intellects and characters are no more subject for magic, crude or refined, then the ebb and flow of the tides or the sequence of day and night. (Thorndike, 1909/1962a, p. 45)

Planning, in the anthropological psychology of Dewey and behaviorist psychology of Thorndike, was spoken about in the cosmopolitan hope of democracy and the republic. The sciences of pedagogy would enable children to have the reasoning skills to participate in and effect change. The theories of the child and family in the sciences told of the apotheosis of cosmopolitan reason brought into children's modes of living. The social sciences were the engineers to bring the new order, a task reasserted in contemporary sciences of school reforms.

Science, in the planning of the child, spread internationally in the new school movement, variously called the "new education fellowship," "active pedagogy," "The New School," and "progressive education" (see, e.g., Cremin, 1962; Depaepe, M., et al. 2000a). The heterogeneous associations promoted school reforms in the first decades of the 20th century as necessary for industrial and cultural changes (Brickman, 1949). The scientific study of childhood and pedagogy was to efficiently and effectively organize the school, although these words had diverse frames of reference and relations to authority. American progressive education reforms placed its sciences in the service of creating a democratic society that enunciated principles of agency and freedom related to the nation's exceptionalism.

The planning agenda of the social and education sciences was not planned, nor was it a foregone conclusion. The early psychology of Wundt or Titchener in Germany or that of William James did not think of psychology as providing explanations of everyday conduct or as a force in the planning of the future and progress. But with the overlapping of various progressive social, political and educational reforms with changes to an organized capitalism, this hesitation about the scientific planning was, by and large, no longer present. Phrases such as "social engineering" and making the "new man and woman" become more commonplace. The interest in early American psychology, for example, was to remove a child's "fatigue" in learning by calculating and influencing the child's will, motives, interests, needs, and desire.

Bringing Out the Latent Design in People

The social and pedagogical interventions were design projects to plan society and individuality. In 19th-century Sweden, for example, the educator Rudenschöld placed the notion of design in the *Ståndscirkulation,* the outer technological side of an evolutionary process that would inaugurate Christian values and life forms on Earth (Hultqvist, 2006). The evolutionary process embodied Sweden as exceptional from other nations. That exceptionalism of the nation was embodied in the individual's heritage of certain virtues such as modesty or freedom from vanity and overlapped with the Lutheran heritage of individualism and self-practices. G. Stanley Hall's child study was to complete the latent design of God within each child, the family, and the citizen.

Design in the social sciences embodied themes of salvation and redemption related to secularization of life. The rationality that Weber (1904–1905/1958) put forward about social science brought to bear particular Calvinist notions of salvation into a secular world. Weber theorized a psychology that underlaid a Protestant theological epistemology about the inner qualities of the individual that would bring about a life of good works. Weber's theology-driven rationalization of the world was directed by the individual who would exert active self-control over the state of nature. The cultural thesis of individual self-control was envisioned in the idea of the republic and its citizens (Tröhler, 2006). When it came to the republic and its American exceptionalism, I will argue later that some of the early sociologists and psychologies saw no difference between the ethos and salvation themes of Christianity and democracy (Popkewitz, 2006).

The notion of design assumed particular configurations in the cultural theses of cosmopolitanism. Design was a word that did not fully reject early religious notions about pedagogy as "converting ordinances" but redesigned the project of design as enunciating values about human agency and community. Design implied flexibility and openness in the future and accompanied broader tenets associated with democracy. It suggested intent and purpose to what was planned and thus, to human agency and uncertainty. The task of science, it seemed, was only laying out the directions and outlines of what was possible for people who made their own future. That direction, however, was not left to chance but inscribed through the rules and standards to calculate what constituted the problems of "problem solving" and the spaces through which "reasonable" acts and outcomes were imagined. Design thus carried the qualities of openness and responsiveness to changing environments through new ideas of human agency. The concept of "design" gave rules and standards of reason that shaped and fashioned the options possible.

The problem of design in the social sciences was linked to the planning of social welfare in progressive reforms. The design of the city in urban planning overlapped with calculations of the characteristics and capabilities of the interior of the child who was to become the future citizen. Pragmatism was one device of intervention and planning that responded to the conditions of the city. John Dewey's writing, for example, can be interpreted as expressing concerns with the moral conditions of the city and the optimism of making its populations cosmopolitan.

The sciences of designing the city and people were associated with the problem of social engineering. Social engineering was not only to develop institutions responsive to modern urban and industrial life. Science was also to be in "the service of the democratic ideal," to use a phrase from progressive movements concerned with rectifying the changing social conditions and people of the city. The new educational sociologies and psychologies focused on the problem of design to shape and fashion the will to act. Progress in government, said Lester Frank Ward in *Dynamic Sociology* (1883), was not simply an education to accommodate society but "must be in the direction of acquainting every member of society more thoroughly with the special nature of the institution, and awakening him to a more vivid conception of his personal interest in its management" (p. 243). Science, Ward continued, orders and modifies the contemplative "man" by allowing for the artificial construction of evolution. Education was to open knowledge to all members of society, and such knowledge was to be directed toward social ends that embodied cosmopolitan hopes of agency, freedom, and progress.

Designing the interior of the child entailed a new materiality of time. The child was located in the history of development, growth, and learning. During the Victorian Age, for example, there was no difference between age and gender when talking about the child. The young girl was sometimes 5 or 15 and still called a "baby" or infant, as there was a lack of interest in actual chronological ages (Steedman, 1995, p. 8). The modern school placed the child into dual sets of distinctions that related experience and growth with time. Childhood was given chronological ages and developmental stages (p. 7). The idea of individual differences and changes in body and mind gave the child a progression that could be mapped and administered through purposeful, orderly, and goal-directed actions, whether that progression was ordained by the "nature" of the child or socially produced (p. 53).

Science as a process of enacting life entered into curriculum theory. The "methods of science" in curriculum were not merely of rationally organizing life through, for example, problem solving and community participation. The individual was linked to norms and values of collective belonging. The distinctions of scientific thinking and acting were associated with a "Christian

Democracy," as Dewey called it in his early writing, emphasizing that that the rationality of science, the qualities of the democratic citizen, and a generalized Protestant notion of salvation were synonymous in defining moral characteristics in the construction of desire and the will of self (see, e.g., Childs, 1956; also Westbrook, 1991). Agency is a universal assigned to a transcendental good that associated the ethics of Reform Christianity of Congregational Calvinism with secular life and as a solution for its issues and problems.

Designing the interior of the modern individual was spoken of as the great panacea for equality. The new psychologies of the child envisioned the empirical building blocks of selfhood as the tasks of deliberate design rather than as something related to a static, metaphysical soul (Sklansky, 2002, pp. 148–149). For the progressives, such as Dewey, the problem of design embodied the triumph of cooperation over competition as the natural destiny of human progress (p. 161). William James's notion of a pragmatic psychology placed a premium on habit formation as the main means of acting in accord with one's designs (p. 146).

If I stay with Dewey's pragmatism as an important symbol of progressive education and today's reform, the agentive individual is linked to a particular grid of planning. The model of democracy was a mode for achieving individual happiness embodied in an American exceptionalism that brought Calvinist reform notions of salvation into the vision of the nation and its chosen people. Action was designed as temporal sequences geared to the future. Life became a planned series of events, for example, through problem solving to calculate and order experience.

> [T]hinking enables us to direct our activities with foresight and to plan according to ends-in-view, or purposes of which we are aware. It enables us to act in deliberate and intentional fashion to attain future objects or to come into command of what is now distant and lacking. (Dewey, 1933/1998, p. 16)

The focus on action affirmed principles of progress in the revisioned myth of America as the cultural frontier. The school was a site where experience reinscribed the life of the pioneer as "literally instruments of adjustment and the test of consequences" (Nisbet, 1979, p. 182). Pragmatism was a new frontier mentality of "American civilization" as a "process of continual expansion and reconstruction." Dewey's individual was a "pioneer American" who opened the universe "in which uncertainty, choice, hypotheses, novelties and possibilities are naturalized [and] that come from experience of a pioneer America" (Childs, 1956, p. 11). Participation in community and problem solving were particular strategies that would produce enlightened reason for the common good shaped in the narratives of the exceptionalism of the nation.

The Domestication of Virtue

I turn now to the family and the child in the sciences associated with pedagogy. As a central site to constitute and shape the moral agency associated with cosmopolitanism, the family assumed a special position in the planning of the education sciences. The innovation of modern pedagogy in the 19th century was to develop the inner qualities of the mind of the child and the cultural organization of the family as sites of intervention and of change. The intellectual tools of pedagogy produced types of maps about the conduct of conduct. Science was a governing practice that provided a method for individuals to navigate and give a moral quality to uncertainty and change.

The Family as the Cradle of Civilization

The family embodied the redemptive metaphor of the home and salvation narrative linked to the nation. The family was visualized as the cradle of civilization where a child learns to be civilized and of civilization. Puritans called the family the "little commonwealth." It was the fundamental source of community and continuity, the place where most work was done, and the primary institution for teaching the young, disciplining the wayward, and caring for the poor and insane. The family was the basic institution in society in which all rights and obligations were centered (see, e.g., Foucault, 1991).

Whereas children formerly mixed freely in adult society, the child in pedagogy was seen as a person with distinctive attributes—impressionability, vulnerability, innocence—that required a new pattern of governing to protect and prolong the period of nurturing and to regulate development (Steedman, 1995; also see Ariès, 1962). Parents, under the guidance of new social and psychological theories of health, were to develop altruistic instincts of obligation and responsibility in their children.

The family constituted the organization that shaped moral agency. Children were thought of as moral beings who needed to be cared for to enable proper moral development. Previous views saw the child as a small adult who was not in need of the special administration as there was no notion of child rearing or development. The Enlightenment injunction of the mother observing the unfolding of the human mind through recording changes in the language and the moral sentiments of her children (Steedman, 1995, p. 68). The family ceased to be simply an institution for the transmission of a name and an estate. Parents were criticized in the late 18th century literature for placing family pride and wealth ahead of the desires and integrity of their children. A literature spoke of mothers giving attention to their child's body and to the signs and symptoms of sickness. Wood (1991) argues, for example, that history and literature dwelled on issues of familial responsibility. Parents were "warned against the evils of parental tyranny and harsh and arbitrary modes of child-rearing of an older, more savage age" (p. 148).

Philosophy, sociology, and psychology, with increasingly different disciplinary foci, took up the tasks of artificially interfering with children's growth and the family in the name of the development of democratic values and a cosmopolitan outlook. The social sciences and psychologies connected the child, family, and community in social policy, health, social science, and schooling with the metaphorical "American family" of the nation (Wald, 1995). The focus of research concerned itself with the social relations, patterns of communication, and the personal and psychological characteristics of the child and family. The child was to develop a cosmopolitan sense of self-reliance and control to act with liberty and freedom. Theories of growth, development, and progress embodied the moral, social, and economic qualities of an industrious people who would bring progress to humanity (see Ross, 1991).

The invention of a range of technologies in the social and education sciences inscribed norms of public duty and vigilance in the life of the family while not destroying its authority. The government of freedom may be analyzed in terms of the deployment of technologies of "responsibilization."

> The home was to be transformed into a purified, cleansed, moralized, and domestic space. It was to undertake the moral training of its children. It was to domesticate and familiarize the dangerous passions of adults, tearing them away from public vice, the gin palace, and the gambling hall, and imposing a duty of responsibility to each other, to home, and to children, and a wish to better their own condition. The family, from then on, has a key role in strategies for the government of freedom. It links public objectives for good health and good order of the social body with the desire of individuals for personal health and well-being. A "private" ethic of good health and morality can thus be articulated onto a "public" ethic of social order and public hygiene, yet without destroying the autonomy of the family—indeed, by promising to enhance it (Rose, 1999, p. 74).

The enlightened family would counter the threat to the moral order. The family and community were transformed into particular spaces of intervention that would move the adult away from public vices and impose a duty of responsibility to the home, the child, and the desire for bettering one's own condition.

The school had a particular place in this governing. The school was to replace the family and the community as the primary influence in socializing children to act as free and self-motivated individuals through the laws of reason. This assumption about the social administration of the child did not mean, however, that there was one notion of the child or agency. The school, in the pragmatism of Dewey, was to open up society by engaging the child in effective self-reflection and actions. The sociology of Edward Ross and the psychology of Edward L. Thorndike placed the notion of agency (and the citizen) in a curriculum that differentiated the place of the child in society as agency was bound to the individual adapting to his or her lot in life intelligently and efficiently.

The discourses of the classroom were narrated through categories connected with the family, yet superseded the family's norms and cultural values in order to produce the citizen who would guarantee the future of American progress. The American superintendent of schools (U.S. Government Printing Office, 1874), for example, wrote that "The existence of a republic, unless all its citizens are educated, is an admitted impossibility." The school, continued the superintendent, was differentiated as

> lying between the earliest period of family-nurture, which was still a concomitant and powerful auxiliary, on the one hand, and the necessary initiation into the specialties of a vocation in practical life, on the other. The peculiarities of American civil society and its political organization drew the child out of the influence of family-nurture earlier than was common in other countries. The frequent separation of the younger branches of the family from the old stock renders family influence less powerful in molding character. The consequence of this is the increased importance of the school as an ethical point of view. (U.S. Government Printing Office, 1874, p. 13)

The "American Race", Teachers, and the Social Question

The sciences, I have argued, embodied cultural theses about the mode of life that carried narratives of American exceptionalism. G. Stanley Hall (1924a) inscribed a notion of civilization in child study to judge the way children grew. That development was associated with the "American race," its double qualities discussed in chapter 3. G. Stanley Hall believed in ontogeny (the development of the individual organism) that recapitulated phylogeny (the evolution of the race). Psychical life and individual behavior developed in a series of stages that corresponded more or less to the stages through which the race was supposed to have passed from pre-savagery to civilization. Education was to provide the opportunity to live through each of the stages of the normal growth of the mind since it was believed that the development of any one stage was the moral stimulus for the emergence of the next.

The sciences of the child were to recoup the race's history and reveal its nature, which would bring the child a higher unity of the soul. The nation, Hall argues, was coming to lead in energy and intense industrial and other activities; our vast and complex business organization that has long since outgrown the comprehension of professional economists, absorbs ever more the earlier and best talent and muscle of youth. (Hall, 1924a, p. xi)

This development of civilization embodied spiritual and humanist values that articulated a moral code. The most important time of child growth, Hall continues, is what he calls adolescence. Adolescence is a point in tracing this development of the race in the transition point between childhood and adulthood and the site in which to reconstruct the cosmopolitanism necessary for morality and citizenship. Hall combined the importance of human development and race to speak about the fears of the future of civilization in which child study would serve as the safeguard against moral decay.

Along with the sense of the immense importance of further coordinating childhood and youth with the development of race, grew the conviction that only here can we hope to find true norms against the tendencies of precocity in home, school, church, and civilization generally, and also to establish criteria by which to both diagnose and measure arrest and retardation in the individual and the race. While individuals differ widely in not only the age but the sequence of stages of repetition of racial history, knowledge of nascent stages and aggregate interests of different ages of life is the best safeguard against very many of the prevalent errors of education and of life (Hall, 1924a, p. viii).

The worry of not reforming pedagogy through science was that immigrants from eastern and southern Europe would overtake and destroy the civilization. Hall spoke of an American exceptionalism in which "our very Constitution had a Minerva birth, and was not the slow growth of precedent" whose "conquering nature, achieving a magnificent material civilization, leading the world in applications "of science." In contrast to this hope of the future, Hall inscribed narratives of the Social Question that directed attention to the moral disorder of the city. Hall spoke of the "urban hothouse" whose "modern conditions have kidnapped and transported" the child through its moral and social diseases and temptations (Hall, 1924a, p. xi). The sciences of pedagogy, Hall continued, will undo these conditions that bring "degeneration" to "the American race."

The Social Question was embodied in sociology as preserving the promise of American exceptionalism as an epic vision of the future of humankind. The early sociological theories of Lester Frank Ward, Albion Small, and Charles Horton Cooley, for example, accepted the uncertainties of a democracy but sought to tame change by fabricating the rules and standards of action and participation. Small, a former Baptist minister hired by John D. Rockefeller to start the Department of Sociology at the University of Chicago, combined social and psychological notions of agentive actors with an interest in pedagogy. For Small, and later for his colleague John Dewey, the social significance of the curriculum was in its promise of social progress through producing the child as the agentive actor. Education was related to the evolution of the inner dispositions and sensitivities of the child that was not merely his or her intelligence. Pedagogical science was "the science of assisting youth to organize their contacts with reality" by ordering "both thought and action" (p. 178).

The teacher held the key to the future of society by remaking the inner qualities of the child:

> Sociology knows no means for the amelioration or reform of society more radical than those of which teachers hold the leverage. The teacher ... will read his success only in the record of men and women who go from the school eager to explore wider and deeper these social relations, and zealous to do their part in making a better future. (Small, 1896, p. 184)

Teachers were analogous to the parent but their tasks were to generate the principles by which the child would act in disregard of the familiar traditions and provincialism that worked against the universalistic collective norms and values of cosmopolitanism. Teacher education, for example, was to select self-motivated and morally devoted candidates who would shape the character of the child. "The real end of all education is to produce morally trained men and women," an educator wrote in 1898,

> rather than, except in special cases, "scholars," a term previously used for pupils. Unless this point is kept in mind by the teacher throughout his school-life experience, the professional element of his chosen vocation fails utterly of its chief end, and the pedagogue places himself in the same class as the mechanic, producing things instead of creating characters. (cited in Mattingly, 1977, p. 44)

Professionalization projects embodied a dual problem in the relationship of cosmopolitanism and American exceptionalism. At one level, the incorporation of teacher education into the university was to create a teacher whose allegiances were cosmopolitan in orientation and thus free from local, provincial, and communal attachments. Higher education was a "civilizing" process. Professionalization was a set of practices "to reshape the lines of authority in school administration and to weed out those of less desirable ethnic and social values through requirements for higher education, and to instill a sense of loyalty not to the community but to the school principal, superintendent, and educational professorate" (Murphy, 1990,

p. 23). Teaching the new pedagogical methods and theories of the child related to this moral ordering. The teacher was to organize the classroom using theories of development and growth, learning, and achievement that were effectively distancing processes from local ethnic affiliations. The ensuing self-conscious monitoring functioned to differentiate, and actions to cast out those not cosmopolitan and different—the feebleminded and backward child who often were of working-class, immigrant families, and when allowed in schools, American Blacks, Native Americans, and Asians.

The design of the professional teacher and developed child entailed the particular self-consciousness and reflectivity of the "homeless mind." Experiences are reflected on through practices of distancing and self-objectification through the categories of behavior, learning, and community. The homeless mind, ironically, placed the self in the trajectory of universal history which advances the civilization underwritten through American exceptionalism. That universal history entailed contingencies of an untold future, yet calculations and standards of reason to stabilize and give a consensus to the processes and procedures made that future less unpredictable.

Science and Governing the Pedagogical "Soul"

Putting the soul in the pedagogy assembled in cosmopolitanism might seem a little out of the ordinary since the trio of reason, psychology, and pedagogy are historical processes of secularization and rationalization. Intellectual histories of sociology and psychology, for example, are celebrations of the triumph of science over mysticism and the movement from "the soul" to the more scientific categories of the mind and habits (Reed, 1997). That history ignores how the soul is transmogrified into the theories and concepts of research if the soul is thought about in salvation narratives of the future as the life of progress. The characterizations of the subject of the state and social class concerned with the outer adornments of manners is replaced with inner directed modes of living—a soul in conception, if not in the name of formal religious cosmologies. The soul is expressed through secular terms of teaching, taking into account and working to improve personality, attitudes, motivation, and esteem. The inner qualities of the individual are connected with cosmopolitan qualities of reason, science, and the planning of biography.

To understand the scope of this soul entails a seemingly simple proposition. From the beginning of modern schooling, pedagogy and its sciences of education, do Ó (2003) argues, were designed to act on the spirit and the body of children and the young in the name of the soul. Examining French and Portuguese pedagogy at the beginning of the 20th century, do

Ó explores the pedagogical sciences as a method of observing and making visible the inner psychical and moral life of man, the spirituality of the educated subject ("the human soul"). The pedagogical purpose was, however, not to find God. The sciences of education were written in the spirit of the Enlightenment to provide knowledge that would free people to follow the path of reason. The French pedagogue Gabriel Compayré asserted in 1885 that pedagogy is an applied psychology. He said "psychology is the source of all applied sciences that are related to the moral faculties of man; pedagogy contains all the parts of the soul and must use always psychology" (cited in do Ó, 2003, p. 106).

Across the Atlantic were similar discourses that linked universal notions of reason and the inner qualities of the individual that transfigured into notions of the soul. Discourses of a "nation-ness," reason, science, and religion, for example, overlapped in child study. There was a romantic desire to build organic values into an increasingly specialized and mechanized urban, industrial, and scientific civilization (Ross, 1972, pp. 335–337). Hall's (1924a) view of psychology, for example, was to reform the soul. Psychology and the moral scriptures of the Bible overlapped in the cultural thesis of development in the life of the child. Psychology was to replace an outdated philosophy that looked to the afterlife. Psychology was to make "new contact with life at as many points as possible" (Hall, 1924a, p. vi), to look at psychic activities of childhood and youth and of the common average man as "worthy of all scientific honor" (Hall, 1924a, pp. vi–viii). School pedagogy was inescapable from the higher pedagogy. "Psychology and the higher pedagogy are one and inseparable. Not only the beautiful and the good, but the true, can have no other test of validity than they appeal to and satisfy certain deep needs; and these are many" (Hall, 1924a, p. ix).

The sciences of the child were to spread the "gospel of child study" (Depaepe, 1997, p. 73). Francis Cravens, a proponent of child study, deployed principles of a cosmopolitanism bound to child study. He said that

> in a few years, more will be done toward raising the standard of morality, toward uplifting humanity, toward ridding asylums of their inmates, the Keely cures of their inebriates, the prisons of their law breakers than has been accomplished in several centuries.... Whenever the ministers, teachers, law makers, mothers feel that through Child-Study Round Table a great mission can be accomplished the work will go speedily on, and perhaps more fathers will die with these words on their lips, "duty, man, God." (cited in Depaepe, 1987, p. 283)

The new disciplines of psychology and child study, for example, would replace moral philosophy in the challenge put forth by the materialism of Darwin. Hall spoke of the soul in describing the focus of psychology and the relation of psychology to pedagogy, as did other social scientists. Psychology replaced moral philosophy in reconciling faith and reason, Christian belief, and "Enlightenment empiricism" in the making of an American society. "The Bible is being slowly re-revealed as man's great text-book in psychology" (cited in O'Donnell, 1985, p. 119; Bloch, 1987). Hall asserted that scientific psychology brought a new method that from the standpoint of philosophy

> is, I believe, Christian to its root and centre; and its final mission in the world is not merely to trace petty harmonies and small adjustments between science and religion, but to flood and transfuse the new and vaster conceptions of the universe and of man's place in it … with the old Scriptural sense of unity, rationality, and love beneath and above all, with all its wide consequences. (cited in Ross, 1972, p. 140)

The concept of adolescence and the natural education of children that Hall expressed were first worked in "the context of religious feeling, and … to describe the newer experience of intellectual doubt and return, a confirmation of one's place not in a religious universe but in the natural world (Ross, 1972, pp. 334–335). The study of the child was to intervene in the child without "the soul is still in the making" and that the "truth about things of the soul, in a unique sense, is never complete or certain till it has been applied to education" (Hall, 1924a, pp. viii–ix). Hall's synthetic "soul" was a double gesture about the threats to modernization and the cosmopolitanism inscribed in the nation.

The domestication of virtue in the thought of the child and family differentiates and comparatively inscribes its opposite, the nonvirtuous. Charles Eliot argues, for example, that it is not enough to put into place modern schools with rethinking the project of education. The school is to provide the child without "the habits of observation and recording to prevent the child from reverting to the habits of the savage who does not use the rules of observation and the correct methods of recording to collaborate and verify one's observations" (Eliot, 1892–1893, p. 418). Without such rethinking, the school can produce despots as well as enlightened citizens.

Designing the Interior of the Child

Cosmopolitanism embodied the cultural theses in which the agency of the child formed a narrative that would ensure that the pursuit of happiness, liberty, and freedom as national achievements. Biography was the planning of self-responsibility and self-motivation, which were organized through psychologies of development, growth, and problem solving. Pedagogical practices were to generate principles about the "habits of mind" that would navigate the webs of uncertainty. The contingencies of an untold future were stabilized and harmonized through the rules and standards of reason. Further, the model of the future democracy embodied an American exceptionalism that brought Calvinist reform notions of salvation into the vision of the nation and its chosen people.

When the practices of pedagogy are examined as a system of reason, the differences between Hall's, Thorndike's, and Dewey's child are differences within particular ordering principles related to cosmopolitanism and the sciences of pedagogy. Designing through calculating and comparing the interior of the individual was spoken of as the great panacea for equality. Psychology and sociology provided the technologies in which to calculate those principles by which an individual reasoned about and planned for the future of progress and self-realization (Popkewitz, 1991). The sciences were to give direction and classification to what constituted the practices of daily life as planned events in regulated time and with the past discarded as a hindrance to the progress of the future.

The urban space was the site in which hopes and fears were met. The cosmopolitan hope feared the moral disorders of the "urban hothouse" and its temptations that would produce the degeneration of "the American race." The social sciences in the service of the democratic ideal planned through differentiating those who embodied the civilized qualities from those different and cast out of its spaces.

It is to these sciences of education that I now turn my attention, to focus on the principles generated about who the child is, who he or she should be, and who does not fit in its spaces.

CHAPTER 5

Educational Sociology and Psychology
Calculating Agency and Ordering Community

This chapter pursues sociology and psychology more closely as cultural theses of cosmopolitanism and its double gestures at the beginning of the 20th century. These social and psychological studies leached into pedagogy as "converting ordinances." Individual self-realization was not only about the individual but linked to collective belonging in order to develop the common good. The converting ordinances also related to the Social Question of poverty and populations of the city discussed in chapters 3 and 4.

The first section of this chapter focuses on the theories of sociology and social psychology as urbanizing the former pastoral image of community into a mode of life for the immigrant and the racialized family and child. The new sociological conceptual apparatus about individuals' interactions functioned as domains of remaking the moral community that was thought to have been lost in urbanization and industrialization. The issues of the city and its moral disorganization were embodied in Thorndike's behaviorist psychology. The last section of this chapter considers the behaviorist psychology and corresponding notions of agency and planning of biography. Chapter 6 focuses on the processes of abjection in the sciences through the principles generated about the hope of cosmopolitanism and the fears of those populations whose qualities are different.

Sociology and Social Psychology: Urbanizing the Pastoral Community

The city signified the cosmopolitan urbanity of the individual who could reflect on and plan for the advancement of civilization through science, "high" culture, commerce, and progressive politics. This city of the urbane was juxtaposed with the "urban-ness" of the city as the site of corruption and moral decay expressed in the Social Question. The images of the urban setting as pure and as dangerous overlapped in various political and social reforms of progressive movements and the emergence of social sciences.

The social and psychological sciences were projects to identify the conditions that produced moral decay and to plan for effective reforms to eliminate the evils of the city and purify its citizens of moral transgressions. Studies done at the Department of Sociology at the University of Chicago, for example, were associated to the work of the Hull Settlement House led by Jane Addams.

The social scientists engaged the Social Question through surveys of urban conditions and studies of immigrant life. From city government reforms to studies of the family, child, and urban housing, progressive reforms sought to improve the modes of living for the immigrants and the poor of the city. The studies of the physical conditions of tenements, health, and labor were given to more empirical methods of surveys, social mapping of neighborhoods, and qualitative studies in the early sociology. The social theories and empirical studies focused on producing the "social likeminded and universal values for social cohesion" in which participation and cooperation would create a united nation (Franklin, 1986a, p. 52).

The family was a place of nostalgia for something lost but also the place to find a home (Steedman, 1995, p. 78). Connections between the family, marriage, urban conditions, and, in some instances, women's issues were studied to consider the new problems of socialization and identity formation (see, e.g., Franklin, 1986a; Lindner, 1996). The urban family was the site that would bring stability and consensus to the future and the hope of a cosmopolitan society whose progress enabled the pursuit of happiness.

In this section, I explore the relation of community and family in the new sociological and social-psychological theories. Community was to inscribe and remake Protestant pastoral images in the new urban contexts that threatened the moral order. The cultural theses of sociology and social psychology were to manage conduct and mold character for social ends that would embody the divine sanction given to the nation. Pragmatism was a specific social-psychological approach about cosmopolitanism modes of living in remaking urban populations.

Urbanizing the Pastoral Images of Community in Progressive Movements

The new community-oriented sociology and social psychology embodied a systematic knowledge that pinpointed the individual citizen as the normative figure in social, civic, moral, and economic relations (Hennon, 2000). Community and family were the intermediary sites to establish a home that connected collective obligations and intimate relations. Newer and finer distinctions of the mind, social interaction, and community emerged to direct attention to processes mediated through a social-psychological language (Ross, 1991, pp. 230–239).

German social theories about the fall and resurrection of the city as a center of culture, belonging, and home were translated and reassembled in the Social Question about the American urban context. The pastoral world of community (*Gemeinschaft*) was where God would be found and where neighbors prior to modernity would come closest to nature. The moral and spiritual conditions of community were contrasted with modernity expressed in the notion of society (*Gesellschaft*) by German sociologist Tönnies (1887/1957). *Gesellschaft* embodied the laws, conventions, and rule of public opinion that were without the moral or ethical grounding of the memorialized pastoral past envisioned in Christianity. In a variation of contemporary debates about alienation in modern society, the moral order of the pastoral community was viewed as lost through the abstract and impersonal systems of communications and social relations produced by urbanization and industrialization. The soullessness of society was represented by unbridled capitalism and by robber barons such as Rockefeller, Carnegie, and Mellon.

The Chicago sociology urbanized the pastoral of community (*Gemeinschaft*) in its theories of society and community. Theories about changing the conditions and populations of the city joined Protestant pastoral images of community with the foundation stories of American technology transforming the wilderness into a prosperous and egalitarian cosmopolitan society.[1]

The notion of community embodied spiritual and religious traditions in the processes of secularization (Cronon, 1996). Community articulated a liberalism shaped by national exceptionalism in which the American spirit was an embodiment of "a more general spirit of human nature" (Ross, 1991, p. 245). Community mediated and created collective belonging in the abstract and impersonal relations of modern *Gesellschaft*. Charles Horton Cooley, a founder with George Herbert Mead of what later was called "symbolic interactionism," directed attention to the remaking of urban moral order by the linking of the self to community. The center for the development of social organization, social consensus, and order was the urban family and its environment. The family was no longer a hindrance to developing a universal reason and a reasonable person but one that linked the family/community and interpersonal (*Gemeinschaft*) with the conditions of modern society (*Gesellschaft*). The family was an administrative practice that brought love and sympathy into the industrial world. Its interactions and communications were central to placing America at the forefront of progress.

The cathedral of community in the city landscape embodied a face-to-face relation with God's creations of nature through the authenticity given by the networks of interactions found in urban communities. The pastoral image of *Gemeinschaft* was revisioned so that it was no longer irreconcilably divided from *Gesellschaft* in governing the urban poor and immigrant family. Community was a fabrication to change the modes of living of the urban family and thus ensure the future of the American experience in democracy. America, Cooley (1909) said, was like a family, in which "there was never before a great nation in which the people … had so kindly and cheerful a sense of a common life" (p. 168).

Gemeinschaft coupled community with the concept of primary groups to focus on the social relations and networks of the family and child (see, e.g., Franklin, 1986a; Popkewitz & Bloch, 2001). Cooley (1909) saw the family as a *primary group* where a child learns of civilization through face–to face interaction—an assumption that persists in various forms in contemporary social and psychological thought (Greek, 1992). The focus was on the processes of intersubjective mediation for the self-realization of the individual in social or communal patterns (see, e.g., Franklin, 1986a; Kliebard, 1986). The communication systems of the family would, for Cooley, establish Christian principles in the family that stressed a moral imperative to life and self-sacrifice for the good of the group. Cooley thought that proper socialization of the child by the family and the neighborhood would enable the child to lose the greed, lust, and pride of power that was innate to the infant, and thus the child would become fit for civilized society.

The concepts of community and primary group were conceptually inscribed in social psychologies of John Dewey and his colleague George Hebert Mead, first at the University of Michigan and then at the University of Chicago. Mead's social interactionism, for example, revisioned the imagined *Gemeinschaft* as an urban idea of community "without doing violence to liberal democratic values" (Franklin, 1986a, p. 8). Mead linked "the general social attitudes" that made possible the organization of the self in community to broader social-institutional practices as habitual in one's life. The reciprocal interaction was concerned with the social administration of the self through the ordering of language and communication (see, e.g., Franklin, 1986a, p. 61).

> It is the ability of the person to put himself in other people's places that gives him his cues as to what he is to do under a specific situation. It is this that gives to man what we term his character as a member of the community; his citizenship, from a political standpoint; his membership from any one of the different standpoints in which he

belongs to the community. It makes him a part of the community, and he recognizes himself as a member of it just because he does take the attitude of those concerned, and does control his own conduct in terms of common attitudes. (Mead, 1934, p. 270)

There is, looking back at this argument, an irony. The cultural theses embedded in social interactionism and pragmatism to produce belonging among the city's urban populations requires the homeless mind to effect the loss of belonging. The connection of self and family through the distinctions of community and primary group involved a particular self-reflexivity. Thought was simultaneously distanced from and reattached to the immediate through ordering what constitutes experience. It became possible, for example, to think of one's conduct through notions of problem solving, socialization, personality, attitudes, motivation, and learning—words of sociology and psychology. The categories enabled daily life to become an object of one's reflection through universalized distinctions that at the same time were brought to daily life as principles to classify experience, purpose, and intentionality.

Pragmatism: Agency, Community, and Planning Biography

The particular innovation of the pragmatism that circulates in Dewey's writing was to take an elite notion of the Enlightenment's cosmopolitanism and provide technologies for its ordering of everyday life. Arthur Childs (1956), a colleague at Teachers College, Columbia University, argued that pragmatism was "a system in which ordinary people are to reshape the conditions that mold his own experience within the context of their own ongoing activities, all necessary institutions, and regulative principles and standards" (pp. 3–4).

The social psychology circulating in pragmatism embodied a particular cultural thesis about a mode of life. It expressed the belief in a new liberal social order that would produce the "New Man" and "New Woman," terms that circulated in intellectual and political arenas in the 19th and early 20th centuries to focus on the future by changing people. Dewey argued that human agency, if properly directed, could respond effectively to the injustices and ineffectiveness of modern life by focusing on continual processes of change and innovation. The school was to make the individual into a central actor of change and progress by providing the dispositions and style of living that enabled human agency.

Pragmatism generated characteristics of the cosmopolitan individual related to Enlightenment principles about universal humanity that transcended national boundaries, yet the transcendence of agency was bound to New World exceptionalism. In a statement that followed closely the end of the frontier thesis of Frederick Jackson Turner, Dewey argued that the conditionality of the world and thus the importance of human agency and freedom impelled new conditions for the progress of humanity. Dewey stated that central to the new individuality was

> the idea of a universe which is not all closed and settled which is still in some respects the indeterminate and in the making, which is adventurous and which implicates all who share in it, whether by acting or believing, in its own perils. (Dewey, 1927/1929d, p. 439)

The psychology of the child was to replace older values that were no longer seen as sufficient for the future. Pragmatism

> denotes faith in individuality, in uniquely distinctive qualities in each normal human being; faith in corresponding unique modes of activity that create new ends, with willing acceptance of the modification of the established order entailed by the release of individualized capacities. (Dewey, 1927/1929b, p. 489)

The science of pedagogy had two foci: to calculate and order participation, and to produce principles of a mode of life reasonably and sensibly planned. Dewey spoke of agency and science as important to citizen participation and democracy that exuded the optimism of American exceptionalism. Dewey talked about "the future of our civilizing" as dependent on the inscription of a "scientific habit of mind" (cited in Diggins, 1994, p. 227; also see Dewey, 1916/1929a; 1916/1929c). These "habits of thinking" were to "create attitudes favorable to effective thought" (cited in Boyer, 1978, pp. 73, 79).

Action was a central concept that does not merely describe what someone does. It entailed an assembly of different ideas and institutional patterns that are inscribed in social-psychological theories (Ross, 1991, pp. 230–239). Action entails a set of *plans of operation* to enable people to transform a given situation through resolute action in a world that is continually in the making. Acts and reflection were to model the experimental method of the natural sciences. The formulating of hypotheses to test theories was thought to be the best method for resolving conflicts about beliefs and revising ideas in response to experience. Dewey's pragmatism emphasized the individual who participated in communities to act on an environment of continual processes of change. Problem solving and community, for example, connect thought and action as intrinsically linked; theories and doctrines became working hypotheses tested by the consequences in actual life situations.

The idea of foresight, notions of an end in view, and intelligent action that Dewey spoke about were to bring the sensitivities of science into a mode of organizing daily life and constituting community. Action was given creative power through science. Its notion of humanity was historically particular, linked to the rational ordering of the world in which the individual sought "to gain control of the future" (Rockefeller, 1991, p. 3). Dewey, for example, saw science as a continual pursuit or method that gave agency through its procedures and acceptance of change and difference. "Command of scientific methods and systematized subject-matter liberates individuals; it enables them to see new problems, devise new procedures, and, in general, makes for diversification rather than for set uniformity" (Dewey, 1916/1929e, p. 2). The application of science would bring the possibility of intentionality and purpose to action.

The new system of reason was a philosophy that "could examine how change served specific purposes, how individual intelligences shaped things, how scientific administration might beget increments of justice and happiness" (Kuklick, 1985, pp. 247–248). The connection of science and action (agency) was believed to be the essence of democracy and the means or instrument for securing the common good (Reuben, 1996, p. 74). Dewey urged his readers, for example, to stop thinking of democracy as something institutional and external but as a mode of living that embodied a moral ideal.

The cosmopolitanism in Dewey's pragmatism embodied a Protestant notion of hard work, a commitment to science as a problem-solving approach for a democracy, and an Emersonian notion of citizen "volunteerism" in social affairs. The habits of science that made democracy possible were not different from the universalized notion of Christian values about the good works of the individual. Dewey, for example, thought that all that was wrong with the nation was that the Christian ideal of fraternity had not yet been achieved in the nation, that society had not yet become pervasively democratic.[2]

The Psychology of Connectionism as a Cultural Thesis

Psychology, as sociology, embodied responses to a perceived breakdown of social order and stability. The cosmopolitan principles of reason and rationality tamed the seeming uncertainties of urbanization and industrialization in everyday life (Franklin, 1986a, p. 48). This section focuses on the connectionist psychology of Edward L. Thorndike. Histories of education have tended to differentiate Hall, Thorndike, and Dewey. Hall's psychology, discussed earlier, was a recapitulation theory that connected the history of the race with the development and growth of the child. Thorndike worked for social efficiency in progressive educational reforms, and Dewey considered action as directed toward the future. If Thorndike, like Dewey, is to be viewed as a conceptual persona, the often-stated belief of historians that Thorndike's behaviorist psychology won over Dewey in influencing American pedagogy would have to be revised (see, e.g., Lagemann, 2000). It was not a winning or losing.

The different pedagogical psychologies embodied homologous terrains as calculi that connected individuality with norms of collective "homes." The different psychological projects were to intervene in the child's soul by calculating and ordering modes of living in which (1) time (past, present, and future) was regularized; (2) principles of agency tamed change by ordering thought in the flow of time and progress; and (3) biography was the individual planning for future agency. Science was to study and order social and individual life to make it more efficient and effective in the new political and social conditions.

The different psychologies had different loci in designing the child as the future citizen. Hall's child study, Dewey's pragmatism, and Thorndike's connectionist psychology embodied cultural theses about cosmopolitanism in which the individual was an actor whose behavior, development, or action needed governing to guarantee the future of the republic. The pedagogical psychology of Dewey gave focus to a plastic quality of the individual formed through social networks and communication patterns. Hall and Thorndike, in contrast, sought to develop that which was innate to the child. Thorndike's "connectionism" or stimulus-response psychology, for example, was to make the school a more useful and vital social institution by revealing more facts about how human nature rules behavior (Joncich, 1962, p. 9). The model of education science was the researcher who sought truth; the practitioner was merely the person concerned with application. This interest in behavior was to eliminate consideration of consciousness by focusing on human actions as responses to stimuli (Lagemann, 2000, pp. 60–62, 69).

In this section, the connectionist psychology of Thorndike is discussed as a cultural thesis of cosmopolitanism. First I focus on its principles of reforming the child in the name of reforming society. Second, the science of learning is discussed as an ordering everyday experience.

Psychology and Reforming Society

Psychological theories of learning provide a different strand for ordering the child as the rational, cosmopolitanism citizen than that of child study and pragmatism. Although one can find the use of the word learner in the texts of John Locke, that usage was in the common sense rather than scientific psychological use of the word. At the beginning of the 20th century, the word was used as part of the study and rationalization of processes associated with the mind. Learning was something with which to order life through the ordering of thought, action, and behavior.

Science had a dual quality: to reform the city in a complex industrial society, and to study and order social and individual lives in order to make them more efficient for a conditional life associated with democracy. That democracy in Thorndike's psychology was expressed through the scientific efficiency that matched the abilities of individual students with different mental requirements to a vast array of occupational roles in a complex industrial society (Labaree, 2004, p. 146).

The science of learning interiorized time as the development of reason and the making of agency. If Edward L. Thorndike is viewed as a conceptual persona, the sciences of pedagogy were to identify connections, in that if "*a given response is connected with certain situations, the more likely it is to be made in that situation in the future*" (Thorndike, 1912/1962b, p. 79; italics in original). *Connectionism* enunciated agency as calculating and organizing the processes of the mind that would produce efficient behaviors (see, e.g., Thorndike, 1935). The conception of, if the not the word, *agency* was a functional notion about what could be developed efficiently in the nature of the child in order to have a more productive and happy life (see, e.g., Thorndike, 1923a, 1923b). Agency was embedded in finding the laws of how the mind responded or acted (Thorndike & Woodworth, 1901/1962). The laws of psychology were to bring efficiency to the techniques of teaching by enabling the students to develop and increase the desirable qualities of their natures.

Thorndike's psychology measured behaviors in order to make visible the nature of the mind that could be experimentally developed. The school was the laboratory in which experiments had two functions. First, it was to identify the laws of behavior. The law of exercise, for example, focused on the frequency or repetition needed to make a connection between a situation and response. The strength of connection increased with increasing practice or exercise. Thorndike's law of effect spoke about a modifiable connection between a situation and response, followed by a satisfying state of affairs in which that connection's strength was increased. Agency was framed as the disciplining of the mind so that people could be successful in their lives and prescribed positions. Psychology was to organize processes associated with the mind as it responded to behavioral performances.

Second, psychology was to function to reveal more facts about human nature to make the school more socially useful and vital (Joncich, 1962, p. 9). Psychology's incorporation of rigorous approaches was to mirror the physical sciences in verification and objectivity in the study of particular intellectual and characteristics of individuals (Joncich, 1962, p. 2). Thorndike saw the focus on behaviors as central to schooling in making the pupil "to be an effective organization of abilities, cooperating in useful ways to meet the quantitative problems life offers" (Thorndike, 1922/1962d, p. 89).

The development of testing and measurement as well as the observing, subdividing, and mapping of the child's behaviors were to make more efficient processes of selection and division in society.

The problem of education was posed in Enlightenment principles about reason and the particular development of the nature of the individual. Invoking Darwinism, education was to produce the citizen who advanced the common good.

> The best citizen is one who advances most the common good. The surest, perhaps the only sure, means of advance is increase in truth. To the search for the truth Darwin gave an intellect of wonderful fairness and care, and a life of perfect devotion. (Thorndike, 1909/1967a, p. 47)

In contrast to Dewey and Hall, who spoke about the relation of science and spirituality, Thorndike's psychology rejected overt qualities of philosophy and spirituality. Science focused on heredity as a major factor in variation between individuals, in the innate and inherited inequalities in capacities to learn. The child was not a *tabula rasa* as in Lockean thought. Every child possessed a legacy of possibilities; experience realized these possibilities. Schools should build intelligence in the society by making available and enriching functional learning for *all* (Joncich, 1962, p. 22). The "all" was a unity of the whole in which functional differences gave society its stability and consensus.

The studies of human variations embodied the frontier thesis of the nation associated with American historian Fredrick Jackson Turner, discussed in chapter 3 (see Joncich, 1968). The principles of agency in learning theory were also a cultural narrative. It was to restore the lost pastoral community in the new urban settings. A primary characteristic of the free and individual who engaged in the pursuit of happiness was a rugged individualism.

Studies of behaviors provided the expertise to guide and organize the sequences and outcomes of the experiments. The administrator and psychologist provided the expert knowledge from which the classroom teacher acted. Reason in problem solving is functional, to seek "to order how best to get to reason to getting to a solution through associative habits" (Thorndike et al., 1923, pp. 458–459). Yet, as I will argue below, the classifications of the nature of the child entailed a particular sublime in the assembly of the cosmopolitanism.

Science in Everyday Life

Pedagogy was to be scientific because it adopted the more rigorous objective and verifiable scientific methods drawn from the physical sciences (Joncich, 1962, p. 2; Thorndike, 1923a, 1923b). The connectionist psychology was to aid schooling by setting statements of objectives (goals) as exact changes in behavior that education was to bring about (Joncich, 1962, p. 8). Psychology was to expunge teleological or supernatural causes—"gods, goddesses, fairies, and elves—as explanations of one physical event after another" (Thorndike, 1909/1962a, p. 44).

> No excuse is left for hoping and fearing instead of thinking—for teasing and bribing instead of working. Our intellects and characters are no more subject for magic, crude or refined, than the ebb and flow of the tides or the sequence of day and night. (Thorndike, 1909/1962a, p. 45)

Laws of analysis, for example, gave stability and consistency by identifying responses in a variety of contexts of "like elements in very different situations" (Thorndike, 1912 /1962a, p. 81).

While science expunged "gods, goddesses, fairies, and elves," it did not expunge the images and narratives of the good, the desirable, and the moral of cosmopolitanism. Progress through science was "to demand rationality and morality" (Thorndike, 1912/1962a, p. 78) in the ordering of life. The optimism of change traveled with fears of those qualities of people that threatened the unspoken qualities "desired." As Thorndike said, the scientific basis of teaching was "to produce and to prevent changes in human beings; to preserve and increase the desirable qualities of body, intellect and character and to get rid of the undesirable"; and subsequently, "to control human nature, the teacher needs to know it" (Thorndike, 1906/1962c, p. 60).

The notion of problem solving appeared in different strands of the psychology of education. Whereas problem solving in pragmatism was tied to action in planning of one's life in which foresight and purpose was brought through designing a series of ordered experiences, problem solving in connectionism was concerned with identifying the specific skills needed to learn specific subject content of the school curriculum (Thorndike, Cobb, Orleans, Symonds, Wald, & Woodyard, 1923). It was a particular technique related to the psychological demands that the solution of problems—in algebra, for example—made on the student.

The techniques of problem solving were differentiated in relation to what was assumed as the natural abilities of the child. Teaching algebra, for example, was for those students who would go to college because it was a "tool for scientific work for thinking about general relations" that was rarely used by workers except those who used the sciences (Thorndike et al., 1923, p. 47).

The psychology of problem solving assumes that what is selected as the content of the curriculum by focusing on identifying applications of, for example, algebraic technique to the solution of problems (Thorndike et al., 1923, p. 132). Research is to determine the psychological demands that the algebra makes on the pupil. Two types of problems are studied: Type I is the problem to answer for which no explicit equation or formula is needed or supposed to be used, and Type II is the problem to answer for which an equation or formula is supposed to be used (p. 133). The problem of science is to break down the problem solving to identify what techniques should be applied and how far problems are to be worked on as original and as routine procedures. Different natures of problems require different techniques, such as those requiring general solutions and those that are problems of puzzle or mystery. Problem solving was further broken down into subsets to identify the criteria used for selecting problems, the criteria for isolating and grouping problems, and the mechanisms required in the selection of data and organization of data (Thorndike et al., 1928, pp. 137–165).

The idea of "habits of the mind" that Dewey expressed was visioned differently and with different functions. Psychology "finds that the mind is rule[d] by habit throughout, the correction or opposition being of certain more simple, thoughtless and coarse habits, by others which are more elaborate, selective, and abstract." Reason is the outcome of "the organization and cooperation of habits rather than as a special activity above their level; and expects to find 'reasoning' and habit or association working together in almost every act of thought" (Thorndike et al., 1923, p. 458). The ability to attend can "properly mean only the sum total of all the particular abilities and inabilities, each of which may have an efficiency largely irrespective of the efficiencies of the rest" (Thorndike & Woodworth, 1901/1962, p. 50).

The psychology of learning was not only for the child; it was also to remake the teacher. Teaching methods, according to Thorndike, should follow children's nature and the laws of learning that psychology provides. Further, the results of learning, such as arithmetic, could be used to evaluate the efficiency of a particular teaching method (Joncich, 1962, p. 6). Teaching is rationalized to *rationalize thought*. Teaching arithmetic, for example, was the development of a hierarchy of intellectual habits that gave learning a clear sequence of development and assessment. The science of teaching was to identify the proper sequence and ordering of knowledge for learning the content. The problem of teaching and learning is "in large measure a problem of the choice of the bonds to be formed and of the discovery of the best order in which to form them and the best means of forming each in that order" (Thorndike, 1909/1962d, pp. 83–84; also see Thorndike, 1921).

Thorndike compared teachers' knowledge of psychology to the gardener's need to know the laws of how plants grow, the architect's need to know of mechanics to plan stresses and strains of a bridge, and the physician's need to know of disease. "[T]he teacher must act in accordance with the laws of the sciences of human nature" (Thorndike, 1906/1962c, p. 60). In this way,

Thorndike likens schooling to the building of a house's foundation. The teacher is like the builder:

> how to erect a frame, how to lay a floor and the like with reference to what is to be built; the teacher should often study how to utilize inborn tendencies, how to form habits, how to develop interests and the like with reference to what changes in intellect and character are to be made. (Thorndike, 1906/1962c, p. 57)

Taking out of teleological causes did not remove the processes of abjection in Thorndike's connectionism. The law of exercise and law of effect were not only filled by the rules of science. Thorndike incorporated a hereditary view of intelligence that was moral in character and not merely technological. The notion of intelligence and moral character embodied a belief, for example, that Black Americans were less intelligent than White Americans. Thorndike conducted comparative intelligence levels of White and Black students in high schools in 1922. With a grant from a philanthropic organization, Thorndike administered Army Alpha, Army Beta, and the Stanford-Binet tests of selective and rational thinking, generalizing, and organizing (Krug, 1972, p. 109). The test scores had fewer than 4% of the Black students passing the median White scores for the corresponding grades, supporting the claim for lower capacity of Black students (Thorndike et al., 1928). This "nature," identified by research, differentiated students, and the new immigrants were seen as weakening the overall intellectual pool of students.

The Homeless Mind, Community, and Biography

The distinctions of the educational psychologies and social psychologies were shaped and fashioned through cosmopolitan principles of the child. The differences among the psychologies related to the problem of designing the child as the future cosmopolitan citizen. Hall's child study (discussed in previous chapters), Dewey's pragmatism, and Thorndike's connectionist psychology embodied cultural theses about cosmopolitanism in which the individual was an actor whose behavior, development, or action needed governing to guarantee the future of the republic. Hall saw psychology as replacing the Bible in the development of a spirituality that joined science with a moral philosophy related to theology. Dewey's science in the administration of the self, in contrast, focused on the ways in which community ordered the consciousness of the individual and gave direction to action, with the teacher as a central actor who ordered daily life by scientific approaches to problem solving in communities.

The distinctions and categories of the mind, behavior, social interaction, and community placed the child or individual as a central actor of change and progress, and hence his or her school experience was key to this future. Pragmatism focused on reason formed through the relation of community, problem solving, and primary group to plan the child's biography in the name of the future. Problem solving and community were intrinsically linked with action, and would be working hypotheses to be tested by the consequences in actual life situations. Science was a set of plans of operation to enable the child to transform a given situation through resolute action in a world that is continually in the making.

The use of psychology as a method to order life through reason functioned in connectionism. Problem solving was also a principle of planning who the child is and who the child should be. Problem solving was to find solutions through associative habits related to specific subject content of the school curriculum. Reason was the habit of thought that was to organize the child's behavior and cooperation in the future to find the child's place in society that would be determined by his or her "nature."

The child across the different pedagogical projects was concerned with generating principles about modes of living which could be calculated and designed. That design was about the interior of the child who would "reason" and become a reasonable citizen. The design projects to calculate "reason" and reasonableness seemingly introduces qualities of stability and consensus to the future. The various psychological categories of learning, development, problem solving and the social concepts of community placed one's biography in the sequences of ordered time whose processes, if not outcomes, had a regularity and order. The regularity implanted a sense of rationality through which life was to be organized by processes of, for example, formulating hypotheses and testing by observations. The processes of problem solving, while different in the psychologies, generated principles to judge and evaluate the design of the child and society.

The distinctions and divisions of pedagogy inscribed qualities of "the homeless mind" as a method of organizing and identifying experience. Experience was not something naturally there to recoup, but fabricated through particular forms of knowledge. Cosmopolitanism embodied "reason" as a method of detachment that was to transcend the provincialism of daily life through the acts of reflection. The interpretative systems removed the individual from his or her immediate experiences through concepts about childhood, development, and child rearing. The concepts looped back to immediate practices of everyday life to bring universalized sets of ideas about moral development and collective belonging into problem solving, learning, and community in every day life. The rules and standards for introspection of one's own mental state was given a common and universal language through which one could self-consciously monitor one's own actions or describe one's own character traits.

The assemble of agency as a cosmopolitan mode of living can be understood within these processes that provide order and classifications to experience. Pragmatism and connectionism articulated, for example, a particular time/space relation through which the child was to be the agent of his or her own future. The child was someone no longer related to conceptions of time and space bounded in his or her community but to an universal, regulated time of the clock, year, and ordered career of life. The distinctions of the social and educational sciences functioned as tools to reposition immediate and practical activities through abstract systems of ideas such as community and children's problem solving.

The self-objectification (detachment and reattachment) in theories of childhood ordered the interventions of pedagogy. The knowledge through which the child was known and knew himself or herself was recognized as a set of particular universal qualities and characteristics which were irrespective of the child's geographical place. These qualities were embedded in notions of stages of development, personality, achievement, cognition, and so on. Each of these categories of learning was a distinction applied everywhere to the child, whether he or she lived in Boston or London. Yet the categories were resituated in daily life that was not only external to the child but also as internal feelings and ways of talking about satisfaction, success, self-realization, commitment, and affiliation.

The distancing and attachment of self-objectification produced subjectivities that were not previously available. There is an absence of references to internal states of characters and no words for the self, mind, or consciousness in Homeric texts (Danziger, 1997, p. 23). Classical ideas of knowing, as well, did not make the writer as capable of the reason in which individuality is an object of self-reflection. Keeping a diary and writing letters involved a degree of self-disclosure, but this writing stressed what you did and not what you thought.

The broader, universal principles about the self are not only interpretive schema. As Giddens (1987) argues more generally, they produce subjectivities that are continually repositioned as immediate practices within abstract systems of ideas. The abstract systems of thought about childhood (adolescence, attitudes and motivation, child rearing and parenting, and learning) circulated as principles through which individuals could establish a sense of belonging and affiliation with communities, and gave intelligibility to the planning of life itself. From Freud's ego and id to Marx's class and Dewey's intelligent action, the navigation of the self in everyday life is given sets of distinctions and relations that enable reflection about one's life through interpretive grids that enable "seeing" and give meaning to events and its possibilities.

[T]here is no science without abstraction, and abstraction means fundamentally that certain occurrences are removed from the dimension of familiar experience to that of reflective or theoretical inquiry. To be able to get away for the time being from entanglement in the urgencies and needs of immediate practical concerns is a condition of the origin of scientific treatment in any field. (Reuben, 1996, p. 16)

I now move to the "habits of thought" of cosmopolitanism in pedagogical projects as processes of abjection, inserting differences as outside the normalized space of childhood.

CHAPTER 6

The Alchemy of School Subjects

The Hope of Rescue and Fears of Difference

This chapter focuses on the process of abjection. The twin elements of hope and fear in Enlightenment thought, I have argued, traveled and mutated as comparative methods that differentiated and divided the qualities of those "civilized" from those who were cast out of that space. The cosmopolitan hope of universal understanding of diversity and an inclusive society with rights for all (or at least to extend the boundaries of inclusion downward from the aristocracy in the 18th century) inscribed that society's reason as different from "others" classified as "the less civilized."

This chapter focuses first on the transmogrification of the idea of the "pursuit of happiness" into fears of populations cast as "unhappy" in pedagogy. I use the idea of "unhappy" metaphorically to capture shifts in public discourses to those populations recognized as unable or prevented from participating and thus not free "to pursue happiness." The term is used sociologically and not to talk about psychological states. The second part of the chapter considers the alchemy of school subjects as an analogy for thinking about the translation "tools" of pedagogy as disciplinary knowledge (e.g., physics, biology, literature, sociology), which are made into problems of teaching and learning.

Schools require translation and transportation models, as children are not scientists or historians. My concern in the alchemy is with the particular translation tools of school subjects and their processes of abjection. The rules and standards of reflection and participation in school subjects have little to do with the disciplinary fields in which they are labeled. Pedagogy is directed to the planning of biography that links the self and society.

I discuss the formation of literacy, mathematics, and music as school subjects at the beginning of the 20th century as psychological inscriptions that generate principles about who is, should be, is not the "civilized" child.

Planning for the Pursuit of Happiness to Planning for the Unhappy: Processes of Abjection

The notion of the pursuit of happiness and the rescue and redemption of those who had fallen outside the "civilized" spaces in the educational psychologies and sociologies were discussed in previous chapters. Pedagogy entailed double gestures. They were directed to the child's soul in the pursuit of happiness. There was a growing optimism about the "eternal promise" of childhood in which the pragmatism of Dewey and the scientific pedagogy of Hall and Thorndike competed (Monaghan & Saul, 1987, p. 96). That optimism was not only about the child as the future citizen in the promised land. The positive hope of planning was also a process of abjection. Recognition was given to children and families in need of rescue but cast out as different and oppositional—the child who was called backward, feebleminded, and today as the disadvantaged and at risk (see Franklin, 1986b).

The political doctrine expressed as "the pursuit of happiness" is written into the U.S. Declaration of Independence. The pursuit of happiness is an "unalienable right" of people, a phrase that gives greater emphasis to individualism than, for example, the tripartite French expression of "liberty, equality, fraternity."[1] Some historians have said that the Enlightenment translated the ultimate question of "How can I be saved?" into the pragmatic one of "How can I be happy?" (see, e.g., McMahon, 2006). Pleasure was no longer seen as a distraction in the pursuit of virtue, but virtue itself. With respect to the notion of the pursuit of happiness, its positive focus was reversed in the 19th century to focus on those populations constituted as "unhappy," that is, those who were not able or did not embody the qualities and characteristics of the cosmopolitan who could pursue happiness.

The salvation themes in the later part of the 19th century epistemologically shifted from the object of government to enable individuals to pursue happiness to those populations signified as not able or capable of freedom and liberty. The early republican ideas of American exceptionalism, for example, folded the Enlightenment ideas about the notion of life, liberty, and the pursuit of happiness into a government that enables liberty and freedom (at least for those recognized as citizens). This idea of laissez faire ended in the mid-19th century as illustrated in the urban reforms related to the Social Question. Brought to the fore were ideas of planning and science to reduce or eliminate the conditions that prevented the individual's pursuit of happiness, in what today might be seen as the construction of the subject that made possible the welfare state.[2] Personal psychological characteristics of the child and family were cast in theories about the populations cast as outside the normal. The plan to intervene in populations constituted as morally deviant produced a class of people outside the space of the citizen. Although the rhetoric of government noninterference in "markets" is prevalent in contemporary neoliberal policies and its ideological critiques, the analyses lose sight of the historical end of free markets in the 19th century when the new planning or welfare state emerged and continues today, something turned to in the final part of this book.

If I use connectionism psychology in this context of intervention that differentiate the happy and unhappy populations, Thorndike accepted Bentham's notion of seeking the greatest pleasure for the greatest numbers (Joncich, 1968). Educational psychology was to prepare children for "the serious business of life as well as for the refined enjoyment of its leisure" (Thorndike & Woodworth, 1901/1962, p. 58). The science of psychology was to identify the nature of the individual, which pedagogy could develop to bring greater happiness. Thorndike sought correlations between those actions that give pleasure and those that promote survival. The Spencerian question of "What Knowledge Is of Most Worth?" (Thorndike, 1912/1962b, p. 144) was transferred into the criterion of *happiness* identified through calculating individual wants: "We judge the relative value of different sorts of knowledge by the extent to which each helps toward the ultimate end of education—the improvement and satisfaction of wants" (p. 144). The idea of worth is "worth more to most people" (p. 145).

The agency of the individual was described as a series of acts guided toward the future that were framed, in certain ways, with the idea that individual freedom was the right to pursue happiness as a social as well as a personal goal. Education was to change the individual so that the individual could effect change in the world in what Thorndike thought of as part of the democratic processes of the republic, the pursuit of individual "happiness" (see, e.g., Thorndike, 1906/1962c, p. 56–57; 1912/1962b, p. 77).

Included with the ordering of the curriculum and the psychology of the child was the planning of biography in the name of freedom and the future. The sciences of pedagogical psychology were to serve as social engineering. It was to produce a like-minded American community populated by urbane, capable, and virtuous individuals—the cosmopolitan in which "able and good 'men of affairs' would direct American society" (Franklin, 1986a, pp. 52, 55). The pursuit of happiness was also the pursuit of those populations whose qualities and characteristics did not enable or embody the capacity of that pursuit. In chapter 9 I come back to social engineering as it is reassembled in the research of contemporary school reforms.

Studies of arithmetic assume, for example, that learning will further individual wants in the pursuit of happiness. Thorndike argued that what differentiated people was their original nature (ability) to reason (Thorndike, 1912/1962b, pp. 75–76). The learning of the relation of the words one, two, three, four, and the meaning of adding and the numerical equal, for example, placed concepts of arithmetic in a system of ordering and classifying by which the child could develop an understanding of and give relevance to the world through the logic of mathematical relations (see, e.g., Thorndike, 1923b, p. 1333; also see Thorndike, 1923a; Thorndike et al., 1923).

The psychology of Thorndike assembled the more general cultural premise about producing the self-motivated and self-responsible individual who participates in processes necessary for the working of the republic. Here, we can think about Thorndike's learning theory as the means to effect wants that were believed to further the cosmopolitan goals of freedom. The utilitarian purpose about learning was to most efficiently pursue happiness through learning to reason. That reason was what Thorndike took as natural to the individual.

To effect individual happiness is to reach into the soul. The modern soul, for Thorndike, was given efficiency by educational sciences that shape and fashion "the mind and the spirit of man [*sic*]" so individuals could be responsible for their progress or entrusted with their future (Thorndike, 1909/1962a, pp. 46–47). He argued, for example; reason is what differentiates humans from nonhuman (Thorndike, 1912/1962b, pp. 75–77). The role of education is to move the individual from mere instinctual habits "to more complex capacity, predispositions that grow into thought, speech, music" that embody "the capacity for reasoning," so as to satisfy one's wants (p. 76). But these wants are not merely natural to the child but are what enables society and people to progress. And the role of education is both the production and the prevention of change.

> The art of human life is to change the world for the better—to make things, animals, plants, men, and oneself more serviceable for life's ends … man tries to change their original natures into forms which serve his needs … education is grouped with government, hygiene, medicine, business administration, and the like, as one of the arts busied with the production and prevention of changes in *human beings*. (Thorndike, 1912/1962b, p. 70; italics in original).

Thorndike's aims of education were a double gesture of finding happiness and decreasing human discomfort.

> Education as a whole should make human beings wish each other well, should increase the sum of human energy and happiness and

decrease the sum of discomfort of the human beings that are or will be, and should foster the higher, impersonal pleasures. (Thorndike, 1906/1962c, p. 57)

Research finds the "facts and laws" that would reduce discomfort, with the notion of discomfort related to questions of moral qualities. The innate qualities of "the good will of men," Thorndike argues, can be created and intensified by identifying "facts and laws." Those "facts and laws" inscribe the normal and the pathological. They establish the consensus from which difference is constituted. The efficient practices to satisfy wants establish the "urge for children [to study] those subjects by ... which they may get health, escape poverty, enjoy their leisure hours, and otherwise have more of what a decent, but not very idealist, person wants" (Thorndike, 1912/1962b, pp. 142–143). Thorndike (1912/1962b) considers tradeoffs in the choices made about what is taught to produce happiness: "[O]ther things being equal, ... knowledge of the real is better than knowledge of the non-existent" (p. 145) and "Knowledge is of value in proportion to the number of situations to which it applies" (p. 146).

Making a more precise and accurate knowledge about individual behaviors was to improve the nation's human resources by enabling the fittest to profit the most from schooling. Thorndike's references to the range of abilities among children and to equal practice opportunities gave scientific sanction to the liberal theories about individual freedom and self-actualization through the teacher's discovering "where each child stands and lead him from there" (Joncich, 1962, p. 20). At the same time, it embodied fears of the dangers posed in immigration questions that evoked divisions between the urban immigrants and Catholics and the rural pastoral images of the reform, urbane Protestantism. The disinterest of science in psychology embodied both a sublime that overlapped Protestant reformism and American exceptionalism in the "reason" that generates principles of reflection and action.

Recognition of "Unhappy" Populations and Their Rescue

Salvation narratives about the good life gave recognition to those who had not secured the benefits of the good life, but were recognized for inclusion yet different. The Social Question was turned into a reformist science of psychology. Science was the "only cure" for the nation's ills and the foundation of progress directed "toward the good will of men" (Thorndike, 1909/1962a, pp. 46–47). That good, however, is positioned against those who do not embrace its cosmopolitan principles. If the good will of men can be created and intensified, Thorndike continued, by identifying "the facts and laws" for the "treatment of subject races, in legislation for criminals and dependents, in the care for public health, and in the new view of the family, we may see the influence of Darwinism beginning to spread to statesmanship and social control" (pp. 46–47).

The urban order or disorder differentiated the civilized from the deviant. The narratives of civilization were woven into the theories of the child that divided the characteristics and sensibilities of the civilized child from the uncivilized child, who was not reasonable and who was not capable. G. Stanley Hall's (1924a) merging of child studies with pedagogy was a strategy to confront the moral disorder of urban life and its uncivilized modes of living (p. viii). Hall considered this civilizing mission within a continuum of values that placed the American race as the most advanced civilization. His "recapitulation" theory saw the child moving through an evolutionary history via the development and growth to that advanced stage.

They hope of development embodied fears of the future. It was the fear of not providing the right strategies to change and rescue the targeted populations. And there was the fear about those characteristics of people that would not enable them to live morally and satisfyingly. Thorndike's laws of psychology were to undo the irrational, emotional, and unlettered qualities of immigrant populations in industrial, urban America.

> To change men's wants for the better, we must heed what conditions originally satisfy and annoy them since the only way to create an interest is by grafting it onto one of the original satisfiers. To enable men to satisfy their wants more fully, the crude curiosity, manipulation, experimentation and irrational interplay of fear, anger, rivalry, mastery, submission, cruelty and kindliness must be modified into useful, verified thought and equitable acts. (Thorndike, 1912/1962b, p. 76)

The fear was of those not schooled to embrace the cosmopolitan mode of life. This fear was in the narratives of sociology as well as psychology. Edward Ross, one of the founders of American sociology, took the notion of social control to argue for inscribing habits that would bring moral order. In *Principles of Sociology* (1920), Ross suggested that there were various instruments of social control to contain the threat of the growing diversity of the population but that none was as important as the school. The nationalizing of different peoples with different cultures, languages, and norms required schooling to unite the whole by disseminating the ideas and ideals of American exceptionalism: "The Tsars relied on the blue-domed Orthodox Church in every peasant village to Russify their heterogeneous subjects, while we Americans rely for unity on the 'little red school house'" (p. 409).

Ross's notion of social control involved a particular kind of agentive individual that was homologous with connectionism. The individual was to learn to be productive within his or her assigned role as a future citizen.[3] Ross's conception of securing individual happiness in society was different from those of Dewey or Lester Frank Ward. Individual autonomy and freedom involved guardians who exercised social control over institutional conditions. Ross's avocation of cultural homogeneity was called antithetical to the spirit of America by others. Horace Kallen, a former student of Henry James, wrote about America as a melting pot and a place of cultural pluralism. Kallen argued that new immigration caused anxieties through its diversity but thought that the greatness of the republic was in the federation of nationalities that it brought together (Wald, 1995, pp. 243–244).

The securing of happiness in the sociology of Ward and the social psychology of Dewey gave focus to the manner in which social conditions influence the formation of the self. The problem of the social sciences was to artificially modify social conditions to provide for civilizing processes. Lester Frank Ward, for example, recommended moving the immigrant family of the settlement house away from the habits of the savage and the barbarian. Ward argued that education needs an "absolute universality" that was intended "to neutralize the *non-civilized* [italics in original] or it will lower all of society." The inscription of reason was to stand as a universal principle that made visible the civilized child who "can act as desired" with liberty. Methods in socialization in education were to take "the lesser of a civilization … the savage and … stagnant people" (Ward, 1883, pp. 159–160) and "to raise the *uncivilized* [italics original] classes up toward its level" (p. 595).

Dewey's "habits of the mind" entailed a rationalizing of daily life under the rubric associated with science. Science was to enable children to think and act "democratically" in a world of uncertainty. That was its hope. Fears were there as well. The fears were the debilitating effects of modern conditions.

> The existence of scientific method protects us also from a danger that attends the operation of men of unusual power; dangers of slavish imitation partisanship, and such jealous devotion to them and their work as to get in the way of further progress. (Dewey, 1916/1929a, p. 11)

Those fears were not only of the conditions of modernity. They were of the qualities of people dangerous to the future of the republic. The systematic training in "thinking" was to prevent "evil of the wrong kind of development [that] is even greater [as] … the power of thought … frees us from servile subjection to instinct, appetite, and routines" (Dewey, 1916/1929e, p. 478).

Education was to produce a mode of living that "prevents each new generation from stagnating in brutish ignorance, folly and pain. But far better education is needed to reduce the still appalling sum of error, injustice, misery and stupidity" (Thorndike, 1912/1962b, p. 72). Education, in this context, was not only to prepare children for adult life but also to adapt childhood to civilized "habits." Training "may improve in estimating others from various causes" and training might also give ideas as to how "to estimate most successfully habits of making the judgments in better ways, of making allowance for constant errors, of avoiding certain prejudices" (Thorndike & Woodworth 1901/1962, pp. 52–53).

Schooling had dual characteristics. It was to make individuals "captains of [their] own souls and their minds and 'spirit' entrusted to the future" as noble and trustful (Thorndike 1909/1962a, p. 45–46). The trust of the future engendered fears of those who did not embody such individuality. Thorndike believed that there were innate differences that education should make more efficient in order to find happiness in a differentiated society. He argued,

> degrees of emphasis on the different proximate aims that vary (1) with the nature of the individual to be educated and (2) with the nature of the educational forces besides the school which are at work. Thus (1) the emphasis in a school for the feeble-minded is not the same as in an ordinary school; the emphasis in a high school representing a selection of the more ambitious, intellectual and energetic is not the same as in a school where the selection is simply on the basis of the ability of the parents to pay tuition, (2) the emphasis in a primary school attended by the children of recent immigrants will differ from that in a school in a suburb inhabited by American professional and business families. A high school in a framing community in the Southwest should not pattern its ideals after those proper to a school in New York City. (Thorndike 1906/1962c, p. 59)

The social differentiation in Thorndike's psychology was related to a broader concern about the cosmopolitanism of the nation and who could and could not participate in the social outcome of schooling. The curriculum was, at different times, to develop labor market skills, leisure time activity of the middle class, moral character and aesthetic taste, and a healthful and creative self-expression (Freedman, 1987; Stanic, 1987).

The Alchemy of School Subjects

Although curriculum studies have approached school subjects through Herbert Spencer's question about "What knowledge is of most worth?" the question of selection and organization of school subjects had less to do with that knowledge. What became mathematics, physics, literature studies and social studies were determined through principles generated, as I argued in earlier chapters, in the converting ordinances of pedagogy. Psychology was the translation and transportation device in mapping content. Until at least 1901, school books were to organize the concepts of school subjects into the logical basis of what was considered the knowledge of the field. By 1920, teachers were to apply scientific methods of child psychology to teaching, practices that related back, for example, to earlier discussions of Thorndike's studies of arithmetic.

School subjects were ordered through the social and psychological sciences. This relation of school "content" and pedagogical knowledge can be understood as an "alchemy." The 16th- and 17th-century alchemists and occult practitioners sought the possibility of transforming base metals into pure gold, practices that are seen as contributing to the emergence of modern chemistry and commerce (McCalman, 2003; Moran, 2005; Wilford, 2006). Just as the alchemists of the Middle Ages concerned themselves with transformations from one space to another, pedagogy magically transforms sciences, social science, and humanities into "things" taught in schools (Popkewitz, 2004a).

The alchemy functions here as a "tool" to consider the limits of pedagogical models, by asking about the *cultural theses generated*. The use of the notion of alchemy is not to suggest something wrong. Academic fields of knowledge production need filtration processes and models of translation for teachers and children to work on in schooling. Children are not scientists or concert musicians. What is at issue are the particular inscription devices or intellectual tools that translate and order school subjects. When examined, the selection and organization of the curriculum have little to do with the norms of participation, truth, and recognition of academic fields associated with school subjects, whether that is mathematics, physics, or linguistics. Nor are they about the networks and relations that order the norms of participation, truth, and recognition in the academic fields associated with school subjects. School subjects are ordered by the cultural theses of cosmopolitanism and its double gestures.

Alchemy and the Science of Child Learning

The idea of school subjects was, in one sense, an invention of the 19th century. The early decades of the 19th-century school curriculum can be expressed by the names of the books read. For example, high school students were to read two books of Caesar and three of Virgil for the study of Latin. Colleges prescribed what books students should read in English for their admission and for examinations that were given for entrance up to at least 1885.

By the later decades of the 19th century, the primer books that organized teaching were replaced by textbooks designed around school subjects (see Popkewitz, 1987; also see Goodson, 1987) organized by faculty
psychology. School subjects were taught to discipline the mind by training
it in the rules of logic and reason and by shaping the powers of observation. Charles Eliot expressed this purpose in the Committee of Ten Report
discussed in earlier chapters. The curriculum emphasized the child's
membership in a world community, but that world community was realized through the technological sublime which emphasized the triumph
of science in making the nation as the apotheosis of cosmopolitan reason
(Krug, 1964, p. 356). The freedom of the child was bound to the learning
of arithmetic and reading "to acquire the feelings, sentiments, and ideas
of mankind." Government was "charged with the interests of civil society,
and thus directly concerned in the creation and distribution of wealth and
the personal well-being of the individual in the community" (U.S. Government Printing Office, 1874, p. 11). Pedagogy was for "the completion of
the individual" and involved "individual cooperation and perfecting the
development of that individuality" (Small, 1896, p. 175).

School subjects were designed to teach a universal reason that tamed
passions, desires, and sentiments. Psychology provided organizing principles. This was implicit in the Committee of Ten report about reorga-
nizing school subjects in the high school and later made explicit for the
reform of schooling. Eliot (1892–1893), the chair of the committee report,
for example, was criticized by G. Stanley Hall for not taking into consideration child study research. Eliot reflected on this omission and suggested
that psychology was essential as a principle of the curriculum. This need
entailed the consideration of the

> bodily changes in childhood and youth, and undertakes to mark off
> the years between birth and maturity into distinct, sharply defined
> periods, bearing separate names like childhood and adolescence,
> and to prescribe appropriate pedagogical treatment for each period
> in the formation of the curriculum. (Eliot, 1905, pp. 342–343)

Eliot concluded that "the idea of individual differences and a scientific
educational theory" was essential for the school curriculum.

The content of school subjects had a normative function. It signified the
moral grace bestowed on the nation and the promise of progress. Grace
was not of the pastoral garden but of the technological sublime in which
useful knowledge enabled the nation's triumph over nature. But that mastery of nature and society also embodied a continuum of values that differentiated the nation and its people as the most advanced civilization in a
natural chain of being (Lesko, 2001). The American race would civilize the

western lands once occupied by Native Americans and Americanize the immigrants coming from non-Protestant shores.

Although seeming far-fetched today, school textbooks taught that geometry and chemistry would promote this scheme of bringing progress to the lands of the west through their use in mining and smelting (Reese, 1995, p. 111). Chemistry, wrote Edward L. Youman, a founder of *Popular Science Monthly,* taught "the processes of human industry, connects its operation with our daily experience, involves the conditions of life and death, and throws light upon the sublime plan by which the Creator manages the world" (cited in Reese, 1995, p. 108). Geology taught the truths of Genesis, and zoology provided learning of classifications that placed man at the top of nature's hierarchy. "Understanding scientific laws drew people closer to God, partly by enhancing productivity," and by teaching students that life and death were shaped by a chemical process that was part of "an endless cycle of dust to dust" (Youman, cited in Reese, 1995, p. 109).

The curriculum of science and mathematics education and the newly formed school subject of social studies were to function as the instruments of progress. The teachings of science, mathematics, literature, and history were to improve "mankind" and develop a world community centered from the narratives of the nation and salvation themes of Protestant reformism (Krug, 1964, p. 342). The rise of mathematics as a school subject, for example, was considered providential. It was to contribute to the spread of Christian, republican, and civilized views about people and society. School subjects would provide what Herbert Spencer spoke about as education for complete living. The aims of the new comprehensive high school—or what some called "the cosmopolitan high school"—and curriculum theories were to order a cosmopolitan life generated by the principles of reason calculated through the sciences of the mind and communication (see, e.g., Kliebard, 1986; Franklin, 1986a; Krug, 1964, 1972).

Changes in the city and Protestant Reformism related to the Social Question provoked criticism of the school curriculum with respect to the demands of teaching "to the needs of masses of pupils" (Krug, 1964, p. 347). The criticism brought to the fore questions about learning the skills and dispositions that would enable urban children to become productive citizens. Race as well as ethnicity entered into the discussions about providing unity of all classes. Thomas Jesse Jones, associated with the settlement house movement and the 1916 report on *The Social Studies in Secondary Education,* spoke optimistically of the "Negro and Indian races" as not being able to develop properly, but would now be able to do so through education (cited in Krug, 1964, p. 343).

The fears of the backward child was expressed in the double gesture with hope. The high failure rate and pressures on children not able enough, one critic of the teaching of algebra argued, produced pressures that injured "the mind, destroyed the health, and wrecked the lives of thousands of children" (cited in Krug, 1964, p. 347). Others complained about disturbing harmony and consensus through, for example, teaching girls mathematics, which would make her "lose her soul" and contribute "nothing to their peace, happiness, and contentment in the home" (Krug, 1864, p. 347).

It is possible to think of the curriculum as the rules and standards of the conduct of the child. The content was treated solely as logical, non-temporal structures from which theories of learning and problem solving would apply. School subjects stabilized and gave consensus so that the focus on the moral qualities of the child could be attended to, calculated, and assessed (to use the language of schooling) in order to achieve the assumed desired goals. Self-realization, personal fulfillment, and individual destinies were rationally ordered in a synchronized relation from the present to the future.

The alchemy of school subjects was related to a broader shift in what Hamilton (1999) calls "the instructional turn." The development of syllabus, curriculum, and method occurred in the 16th and 17th centuries. These developments placed an emphasis on teaching rather than on learning. Prior to this, the medieval teacher was to give a faithful representation and transmission of the inherited teaching or doctrine. A new pedagogical literature directed at schoolteachers mapped the knowledge that gave rise to the curriculum (the course of modern schooling). School subjects were organized around a set of principles related to upbringing and ordered through the notion of method, and the delivery of instruction (Hamilton, 1999, p. 139). When dealing with the selection and organization of school subjects, the sciences of the curriculum focused on the logical qualities of the content to efficiently order action and reflection by intervening in the interior of the child. *The fixing of the content knowledge of school subjects overlapped with and functioned in casting principles of who the child is and should be.*

Ordering Academic Knowledge: English Literature, Mathematics, and Music Education

The school subjects of literature, mathematics, and music education are explored. At first glance, they would seem as representing different traditions of knowledge: humanities, science, and the arts. The differences, however, dissipate when the translation tools that bring these traditions in schooling are examined. They are ordered through psychological principles about modes of living.

The mapping of knowledge around psychologies of the child recognized and differentiated the children who came to the new school. The teaching of modern English literature in British mass schooling of the 19th century, for example, emerged through two different historical movements that did not evolve from prior "cultivating" aspects of writing or reading (Hunter, 1988).

First, there was the public concern for the administration of social problems. Mass schooling was opened up to the "inarticulate and illiterate" of the working classes. The child was to learn English literature to develop a cosmopolitan outlook but within the hierarchy of social structure. Second, the subject of English related to the governmental provisions for social welfare. The narrative structures and ethical messages of literary texts were to help the reader become the moral agent who embodied cosmopolitan values and its notions of "civility." The rules of moral conduct were accomplished by making the stories of literature relevant to the everyday experiences of working-class children. Relevancy was to show how the rules and standards for moral conduct could be practiced in daily life.

The high school mathematics curriculum initially was to provide for the mental discipline of the child. Character training was to occur by mentally exercising and training the mind. By the early decades of the 19th century, mathematics education was to train the individual in observation, experimentation, and reflection. Faculty psychology ordered pedagogical practices to produce "higher emotions and [the] giving [of] mental pleasure" (Stanic, 1987, p. 155). In this context, school subjects were represented as stable "entities" for children to reflect on and to order the possibilities of their worlds.

Later in the century, the principles of school subjects shifted to giving relevancy to planning everyday life. Mathematics education, for example, was seen as a practical subject that students needed for understanding everyday activities as well as necessary in "the practical needs in building homes, roads, and commerce" (Reese, 1995, p. 111). Thorndike's learning theory was influential in forming the mathematics curriculum.

My third exemplar is music education. Seemingly with different priorities about learning and knowledge than the orderly worlds of mathematics, music is perceived as expressing aesthetic, spiritual, and emotional qualities. Yet as with mathematics, music education transmogrifies the "music" found in the academy or conservatory traditions into a normalizing pedagogy about cosmopolitanism and its double gestures.

The music curriculum from 1830 to 1930 added music appreciation to that of vocal music (Gustafson, 2005). The changes were part of changing cultural theses about the child. Changes in the music curriculum marks fears of moral decay and degeneration. The inception in Boston in the

1830s of school music linked the tradition of singing in Prussian schools to the governance of the child as the future citizen. Horace Mann's 1844 "Report to the Boston School Committee" supported vocal instruction classes as a practice in which the harmony of song was the model for the child's own self-regulation in society (Gustafson, 2005). Mann discussed music education in relation to the risks that epidemic disease posed to civil society. Vocal instruction was to provide regimens to stimulate circulation that would serve to prevent poor health among the urban populations. Health was moral as well as physical. Teaching the proper songs would remove the emotionalism of tavern and revival meetings and provide a way to regulate the moral conditions of urban life with a "higher" calling related to the nation.

Music appreciation joined vocal instruction in the curriculum by the beginning of the 20th century. The curriculum was to eliminate juvenile delinquency, among other evils of society. German traditions of self-cultivation, or *Bildung*, focused on the productive use of leisure and self-cultivation in their daily lives. Its prescriptions for comportment entailed the avoidance of degenerate characteristics associated with racial and immigrant populations.

The categorizations of music establish a continuum from the civilized to that uncivilized through ethnological comparisons. Physiological psychology about the proper amount of stimulation for the brain and body was coupled with notions of musical aesthetics, religious beliefs, and civic virtue. Singing, for example, was to give expression to the home life of industriousness and patriotism that was set against racial stereotypes of Blacks and immigrants. Minstrelsy, a satiric version of Black music and spirituals, were contrasted with the complexity of music of European "civilization." A medical expert in the 1920s, employed by the Philadelphia High School for Girls, described jazz (by this time a rubric that included ragtime) as causing disease in young girls and society as a whole.

Psychology ordered the selection and organization of music. The staging of musical response in the classroom classified listening habits with age-appropriate behavior. A scale of value was constructed that compared immature or primitive human development with those of a fully endowed capacity that corresponded to race and nationality. The progression of musical knowledge outlined in teacher manuals calculated music as a form of psychometrics associated with psychoacoustics. The physical aspect of music (acoustics) was combined with the notion of a musical and interior apparatus for the perception of acoustics. The "attentive listener" was one who embodied the cosmopolitan mode of the civilized life. That child was contrasted with the distracted listener in the group. Carl Seashore, a psychology professor, claimed that a full 10% of the children tested for musical talent were unfit for musical appreciation. In teaching manuals, the child who did not learn to listen to the music in a particular way was "distracted," a determinate category bound to moral and social distinctions about the child as a drifter, a name caller, a gang joiner, a juvenile offender, a joke maker, a potential religious fanatic, having acute emotional stress, and an intense interest in sex.

Cosmopolitanism: Hopes and Fears as Recognition and Difference

Chapters 3, 4, and 5 historicized the cultural theses in pedagogy by exploring the intersections of American exceptionalism, Protestant reform movements, and the sciences of education. An amalgamation of practices focused on the distinctions and classifications through which "reason" and "reasonable people" were constructed in schooling. The universality and particularity in the cosmopolitanism in pedagogy were comparative instantiations that recognized "unhappy" populations in need of rescue and redemption. The recognition established differences that cast out and excluded those who were not of the "race" of the nation. the social and psychological sciences were technologies in which the distinctions and divisions were inscribed.

Focusing on the alchemy of school subjects in the construction of the child directed attention to the limits of the Spencerian question of "What knowledge is of most worth?" asked today in curriculum studies. The Spencierian question presupposes the systems of reason through which the cultural theses about modes of living are inscribed in school pedagogy. It assumes the models of translating disciplinary knowledge into the school. This assumption stabilizes and harmonizes disciplinary knowledge as consensual practices in the governing of the child. I will consider this stability in the next section of the book in discussions about "the knowledge base" in curriculum planning, and with reform as giving voice and empowerment as a lifelong learner.

PART 2

Twenty-First-Century Reforms, the Unfinished Cosmopolitan, and Sciences of Education

The strategy of this inquiry is a history of the present. It is to diagnose the changing cultural theses about modes of life in pedagogy, teacher education, and research. Part 1 explored cosmopolitanism as a set of historical practices that overlap in pedagogy at the beginning of the 20th century. Cosmopolitanism focused on how reason is made into a governing practice that orders and differentiates who the child is and should be. Its seductiveness, I argued, is through its inscription of sacred qualities about the individual and collective belonging: the importance of reason, rationality, and agency in the development of the self in the name of progress and the exceptionalism of the nation. The assemblies of these different inscriptions produced principles of the cosmopolitanism in pedagogical practices. Although the notions of the nature of the child and society had different foci in Dewey, Thorndike, Hall, and in sociology, for example, the different sciences of the child and education generated principles of actions and reflections tied to the social unity figured in American exceptionalism. The emancipatory project encompassed double gestures: the universality of reason and rationality was historically particular, and the hope of making the cosmopolitan child embodied fears of the dangers and dangerous people who did not fit its distinctions and classification. Cosmopolitan reason, agency, and progress embodied distinctions that differentiated and divided civilizations and "civilized" people through continuums of values.

This section of the book examines the assembly and connections of cosmopolitanism as governing principles in contemporary school and teacher education reforms and sciences of education. The arguments about the inscriptions of cosmopolitanism and its others at the beginning of the 20th century are epistemic anchors to consider shifts in the cultural theses in contemporary reforms of school standards, subjects, and teaching. Today's cosmopolitanism, I argue, is spoken about in universal terms of the lifelong learner who acts as the global citizen. I call this cosmopolitanism *unfinished* in the sense that life is continually in process and innovation through choices, with no end point in sight. The argument about the unfinished cosmopolitanism is not an updated version of the Quarrel of the Ancients and the Moderns of the Enlightenment that placed contemporary society as the most advanced civilization. My argument is different. I locate the unfinished cosmopolitanism and its Others as different than that of the cosmopolitanism of the early school reformers.

The new cosmopolitanism presents itself as a narrative of superseding and more advanced than that which preceded it. The contemporary hope of the future is also a process of abjection in which fears are given expression of those who do not embody that cosmopolitanism. That hope for the universal in cosmopolitanism links with double gestures in which fears of the dangers and dangerous populations travel along with the hope of an inclusive society.

The section examines the qualities of the lifelong learner in a continuum of values from which Others are produced as different—the child who is enclosed in the spaces of "no child left behind," to play with the phrase of the 2002 national legislation concerned with producing an inclusive society by redressing inequalities. The comparative instantiation is embodied in the phrase *all children through which a unity of the whole is posited from which to establish difference.* The subsequent and continual reiteration in policy statements about school reforms are about "all children will learn" and that programs are to "accommodate *all* students." The phrases *all children* and *the child left behind,* I argue, are mutually constituted in the theories and programs of schooling, its reforms, and research. When school reforms are spoken about to include *all* so that "no child is left behind," that space of "all children" assumes what Bourdieu (1984/1993) calls "cultural communism." It is the creation of a space of mystical participation in a common good that, in fact, differentiates and divides.

The hope of the new, unfinished cosmopolitanism and fears of those outside of its spaces in contemporary school reforms, professional education, and research are the focus of this section. The term *all children* evokes, I argue, the processes of Abjection through the inscription of cosmopolitan principles and difference. The fear is of not finding "what works," of not being successful in identifying the correct practices and strategies that will produce a progressive society. The recognition also inscribes difference and fears of those in need of remediation and rescue.

I have organized the three chapters of this section to explore various sites in which narratives and images of cosmopolitanism circulate in schooling, its reform, and sciences. These are in professional education and teaching related to performance standards, school subject teaching, and research programs.

Chapter 7 considers the cultural thesis of unfinished cosmopolitanism through the category of the lifelong learner and standards reforms in teaching and teacher education. Unfinished cosmopolitanism entails a shift of the governing apparatus in ordering cosmopolitanism. There is less talk of the social whole through which people are differentiated and divided along collective values associated with civilizations and its "civilized" people. The comparativeness operates at the micro level, related to the particular lifestyles, choices, and problem solving organized in collaborative communities. Its mode of life entails uneven and fractured sequences of time in the development of the self.

Chapter 8 focuses on the alchemy of school standards and research in school subjects. The analysis focuses on current content selection in which the translation and inscription tools of the curriculum are about modes of living that have little to do with school subjects, such as learning mathematical ways of reasoning. The alchemy of school subjects entails normalizing practices about the moral qualities of the child. Further, while the organization of school subjects and children calls for increased participation in "communities of learning," it brings a new expertise into the ordering principles of daily life and choice that narrows the range of what is open for scrutiny and, ironically, choice.

Chapter 9 focuses on the notion of design. The notion of design is assembled in different pedagogical practices of instruction and research discussed in the first section. Four sites concerned with designing the child are examined to consider the double gesture of hope and fear in the cosmopolitan mode of living. Online learning, research designs to provide scientific evidence of what works in schools, and design research to provide continuous monitoring and assessment of school reforms are examined as overlapping through principles about who the child is, should be, and abjection—the child who exists as someone who is recognized for inclusion yet different and placed in spaces designated as dangerous.

CHAPTER 7

The Unfinished Cosmopolitan: The Cultural Thesis of the Lifelong Learner

This chapter explores changes in the cultural theses of cosmopolitanism in contemporary reforms. I focus on the lifelong learner, a phrase about the new child and adult used in a vast array of European and the U.S. reforms. The lifelong learner provides a strategy to consider the "resacralization" of agency, problem solving, and communities of collaboration in present-day reforms. I call the lifelong learner *the unfinished* cosmopolitan,[1] a mode of life in which there is a never-ending process of making choices, innovation, and collaboration. The seduction of "the lifelong learner" is its enunciation of Enlightenment attitudes about a life guided by reason and compassion for others whose enclosures, internments, and double gestures are different from those at the beginning of the 20th century.

The first section examines the principles of reason and rationality in the cultural thesis of the lifelong learner. That mode of life, I argue, is problem solving in a continual process of innovation in diverse communities. The cultural thesis of the child is also that of the teacher as the reflective practitioner. The second section explores the cultural thesis of the unfinished lifelong learner in standards reform of curriculum. Standards reforms are to establish performance and outcome criteria of success for parents and the public to assess. The standards of the standards reforms and research, I argue, are not the publicly stated outcomes of teaching. The standards are about who the child is, should be, and is not that child (Popkewitz, 2004d).

The processes of abjection are embodied in the differentiation of the cultural thesis of the lifelong learner from that of the disadvantaged child or "the child left behind" as simultaneous inscriptions in the phenomenon of reform. The latter child is recognized for inclusion yet placed in different spaces that produce otherness. The final section explores the lifelong learner as producing belonging through participation and collaboration in the new systems of action and reflection. The principles of lifelong learning are inserted as the democratic obligation of the school in planning individuality and to give articulation to the new American exceptionalism. The following two chapters examine the double gestures of the lifelong learner and the child left behind as they are assembled in the alchemy of school subjects and the education sciences.

The Hope of the Future: The Unfinished Cosmopolitan as the Lifelong Learner

A Google search (which of course was not possible at the beginning of the 20th century) brought up 1,090,000 pages under "lifelong learner." The phrase crosses broad social and political arenas and geographical locations (Fejes & Nicoll, 2007; Popkewitz & Lindblad, 2004; Lawn, 2001; Simon & Masselein, 2006; Álvarez-Mendiola, 2006). European, American, and Taiwanese school and teacher education reforms, U.S. Christian religious schools, the rights of patients in medicine, among many others, evoke the term *lifelong learner* as the embodiment of who a person is and should be. The American Academy of Allergy, Asthma & Immunology Lifelong Learner (AAAAI) Bill of Rights, for example, declares the patient "a lifelong learner who has chosen to engage in continuing ... education to identify or fill gaps in knowledge, skill or performance (*Academy News,* July 2005, http://www.aaaai.org). The DePaul University School of Education (2007) teacher education mission states that it is "an urban, Catholic and Vincentian" university committed to develop "lifelong learners" whose "individual dignity, personal responsibility, and concern for values" join with the "deep respect for the poor and abandoned in our society" to foster "change in those educational and social systems and institutions which perpetuate poverty and an inequitable distribution of resources" (http://education.depaul.edu/html/about/mission_statement.asp).

Since the mid-1980s, the leading phrase of European Union social and educational policy is the cosmopolitanism of the citizen as a lifelong learner. A draft for European teacher education, for example, asserts that teachers' responsibilities for the future hinge on the development of the child who is the lifelong learner. The qualities of the child are cosmopolitan, embodying universal qualities that are to enable personal fulfillment in an equitable world. The free society, it is asserted, is one that educates *all* children in these qualities. Teachers are key players in how education systems evolve and in the implementation of the reforms which can make the European Union the highest performing knowledge-driven economy in the world by 2010. They recognize that high quality education provides learners with personal fulfillment, better social skills and more diverse employment opportunities. Their profession, which is inspired by values of inclusiveness and the need to nurture the potential of all learners, has a strong influence on society and plays a vital role in advancing human potential and shaping future generations. Therefore, to achieve its ambitious objective, the European Union needs to view the role of teachers and trainers and their lifelong learning and career development as key priorities. (European Commission, 2006)

Agency in the Continual Making of the World and Self

The lifelong learner is expressed as an age-old search for the better, more fruitful, and progressive life. Agency is enunciated by the child who problem solves and collaborates in communities—communities of learning, discourse communities, and so on—to maximize happiness through continual processes of rationally planning and organizing daily events.

In general, the appeal of the lifelong learner sounds similar to that of the early 20th century. The assemblies and connections that generate the cultural thesis about the mode of life are different. The lifelong learner manages his or her biography through self-monitoring processes that include "survival learning, adaptive learning, and generative learning, learning that enhances the capacity to create" (Simon & Masschelein, 2006, p. 1). Progress is tied to the microgoverning of life that has multiple dimensions of time—time of a regulated life, time of living in different communities where there are processes of continuous innovation, and the comprehension associated with the Internet and multitasking.

For some, the lifelong learner is the realization of the medieval alchemist's faith in finding the philosopher's stone. That stone was to unlock material and spiritual secrets by identifying the theory that unified everything. Computer learning, for many, is today's philosopher's stone. Maeroff (2003) argues, for example, that processes of online learning will unlock the unfilled promise of the new cosmopolitan citizen of the world that the Enlightenment philosophers could only have wished for. The online learning programs, "with their ability to transcend state lines and even national borders, circumvent geographic barriers," eliminate a parochialism and localism that previously were expressed by nationalism and ethnicity. Online learning is treated as revolutionary (the title of Maeroff's first chapter); that revolution is where technology makes possible the individualization of learning so that "one-on-one education may be closer at hand than ever before" (p. 1).

The new era of education brings to fruition the hope of free-market neoliberalism. The school is to produce a more equitable society and an enlightened individual by interjecting "more choice into the system, advocat[ing] reason, the richer the offerings and the greater the benefits to consumers (students and their families)" (Maeroff, 2003, p. 4).

From a different ideological perspective, Hargreaves (2003) speaks of the lifelong learner as rejecting neoliberal reforms based on choice in market competition and its materialism. The rejection of choice, however, reinserts the choices of the knowledge society that "is *really* a learning society ... [that] process[es] information and knowledge in ways that maximize learning, stimulate ingenuity and invention and develop the capacity to initiate and cope with change" (Hargreaves, 2003, p. xviii). The hope of the learning society is to prepare the child of the future with "a cosmopolitan identity which shows tolerance of race and gender differences, genuine curiosity toward and willingness to learn from other cultures, and responsibility toward excluded groups within and beyond one's society" (p. xix).

The life of the unfinished cosmopolitan is the personal responsibility and self-management of one's risks and destiny by continually maximizing the correct application of reason and rationality. The principles of this agency are assembled and connected to problem solving in multiple communities, explored in the remainder of this section. Problem solving, participation, and collaboration are shaped and fashioned by constructivist and communication theories that bring forth different connections of the self, collective belonging, and nation from earlier cosmopolitan theses in pragmatism, socialization, and behaviorist psychologies.

The Problem Solver in an Unfinished World

Problem solving is a particular salvation story that considers life to be a series of rationally ordered paths for finding solutions that is never complete and always defers the present to the future. It enunciates particular calculations about principles in making judgments, drawing conclusions, proposing rectifications, and making manageable and predictable fields of existence in school reform.

The problem solver is assembled with both continuities and dissimilarities to what I discussed earlier in pragmatism and connectionism. Problem solving then and now is to order action and plan for a world of constant changes and conditionality. Today's child problem solves through the rules of constructivist psychologies and communication theories. The psychologies talk about the production of identity in the flows and networks of ideas and "content knowledge" of school subjects. Dewey's name is given prominence but includes certain residues of Thorndike about clear goal-setting practices and curriculum standards about how teachers and children proceed to know and act.

Problem solving occurs while the child constructs knowledge. All that is solid is seen as melting, as teachers and children are viewed as actively producing, modifying, and integrating ideas in the production of meaning and the designing of biography. The constructivist notion of the child is embodied in teacher education. The Holmes Group, a group of schools of education formed in the 1980s and which serves as the forerunner to current national professional reforms, asserted that "the generic task of education" consists of "teaching students how to make knowledge and meaning—to enact culture," turning away from "a template for a single conception" of reform to "multiple models" (Holmes Group, 1990, pp. 6, 10). The teacher of online learning, as well, inscribes constructivism through the notion of choice. Online learning "gives students choices in completing tasks; lets students have some choice in the difficulty levels of assignments or tasks that they complete; and gives students some discretion about when they complete particular tasks" (Maeroff, 2003, p. 102).

The reformed child of the lifelong learner lives in a continuous course of personal responsibility and self-management of his or her risks and choices; life is now thought of in segments of time where quick actions are required to meet the challenges of new conditions and where nothing seems solid or stable. Time is flexible and heterogeneous. Not only does the child "construct" meaning and knowledge but the new pedagogical research asserts that its knowledge base makes possible different paths and flexible destinations (see chapter 9).

The salvation themes of the lifelong learner embody different relations of time and space than they did at the beginning of the 20th century. Both are strategies in which the self lives in uncertainty and certainty. The qualities of the present, however, are somewhat like Deleuze and Guattari's (1987) rhizome, an assembly of heterogeneous components and a multiplicity that functions with variation, expansion, and offshoots. The lifelong learner is a mode of living in varied communities that move at different rates of time and space. The lifelong learner is a citizen of the nation, but he or she also communicates through Internet and computer games played simultaneously around the world, and with multiple identities and disjointed narratives, just as in the television comedy of Seinfeld's that had no overarching coherence in the storyline of its four main characters.

The rhizome quality of uneven times and spaces, however, does not erase links of individuality and collective belonging. The linkages and affiliations are constituted differently.

Community and Collective Belonging

The individuality of the lifelong learner is not merely about the self in isolation of social patterns. Reason and rationality of agency are realized through patterns of communication and interactions formed in multiple social patterns. Freedom is talked about as a mode of life in which the individual is empowered by perpetually constructing his or her own practice in communities of learning. Choice in individual life is sanctioned and acts by working collaboratively. The words community and collaboration serve as the register of the social that operates as an unspoken boundary in which problem solving and choice are shaped and fashioned. Community, collaboration, and problem solving lie inside the others!

Community is not merely something added to problem solving but integral to the cultural thesis about cosmopolitan modes of living. Community overlaps and connects with the child as a problem solver and collaborator. The linking of these notions has a redemptive appeal in the virtue of the civic life of the democracy where the citizen's decision making and problem solving provide solutions in local, decentralized problem solving in schools. Community and collaboration tell of the collective obligation of the political community to promote justice and equity through the schools. The assumption of collaboration is in the procedures of interaction and association that produce paths to the common good and hospitality to others.

The "task" of community is not only for people to work out solutions to problems but a strategy that aligns and connects the scope and aspirations of public powers with the personal and subjective capacities of individuals. Community was to reestablish moral order and the pastoral faith in urban conditions and urban populations at the beginning of the 20th century. Community today circulates in a range of reforms to speak about inclusion of previously marginalized communities, as it did in the Social Question. That speech is located in a different mode of life. Individuality is bound to the site-based management of schools and home-school collaboration. School vouchers are spoken about as giving options to ethnic and racial communities. Community also functions as a noun of reform to signify commitments to democracy in classroom teaching. No longer are primary groups spoken about. Classrooms and instruction are "participatory structures" of discourse communities and communities of learners.

The narratives of community express universal values about creating the conditions for *all* individuals to achieve social or economic progress and for the revitalization of democracy. There is less talk about general social values that children are to ascribe to as in earlier Progressive education reforms; and more about children constructing knowledge and teachers as partners and collaborators. The governing of action is through communication systems and networks (discourse communities) of the reformed curriculum. Agency is spoken of in psychological notions of problem solving and the political evocation of voice and empowerment through community participation and collaboration.

The Social Question to create moral order by urbanizing the pastoral notion of community is present but unspoken. Participation and problem solving in diverse places are to enable self-realization and innovation through face-to-face interactions. In a statement that resonates across American school reforms, the National Council of Teachers of Mathematics (2000) curriculum standards joins the psychology of problem solving with the notion of community. It argues that the preparation of the lifelong learner for the future is the ever-present change, "a ubiquitous feature of contemporary life, so learning with understanding is essential to enable students to use what they learn to solve the new kinds of problems they will inevitably face in the future" (pp. 20–21). The living in a "ubiquitous" uncertain future requires "autonomous learners who are continuously involved in self-improvement" and are ready for the uncertainties of the future by working actively in "communities of learning" (see, e.g., National Council of Teachers of Mathematics, 2000; Gustafson, 2006).

Community is a universal elixir that tames the future through new territories in which personal investments overlap with registers of allegiances and responsibilities. Participation in communities is not merely the child learning to raise his or her hand before speaking in class; the participatory community is also textually related to other reforms about what rationally orders the social interactions of schooling. For example, "successful" learning in contemporary reforms are to occur in participatory structures constituted by rules that establish standards coupled with performance-based assessments, greater use of pscychology in formulating and assessing children's activities with communities and homes (Natural Commission on Teaching and America's Future, 2003; Darling-Hammond, 1998; American Federation of Teachers, 1999). Classroom community and participation link psychology of the child with norms of consensus and stability; it is where "students are well known both personally and academically and where common goals and values have been forged" (Darling-Hammond, 1998, p. 10).

Collaboration and participation are practices governed by partitioning sensibilities and principles of belonging. I will explore this further in the next two chapters, but at this point merely suggest that the rules about imaginary groups called "stakeholders" create collective representatives of the interests and values of its membership. The National Commission on Teaching and America's Future argues that its role has been in "stimulating dozens of pieces of federal and state legislation" and of "twelve states ... working collaboratively ... to develop strategies for implementing the commission's recommendations" (Darling-Hammond, 1998, p. 5). Reform agendas are to "reach across the *barriers* [italics added] that normally separate the conversations of practitioners, policymakers, and the public to seek more comprehensive, transformative change" (Darling-Hammond, 1998, pp. 5–6).

Collaboration and participation inscribe a hermeneutic objectivism in the name of the new democracy. The assumption is that each set of actors has unique experiences and points of views that are negotiated through collaborative practices; both teachers and researchers are to come to understand and respect the different perspectives they have as a method of arriving at the truth. Interactional and communication patterns provide the mechanisms in which diverse people learn from each other and respect other cultures. In an American Council on Education (1999) report about university teacher education, "local" involvement and participation follow a refrain similar to school reforms about collaboration as establishing inclusion.

The particular mantle of democracy and its registers of liberty and freedom circulate as the purposes of forming community and collaboration. Curriculum standards and professional education are talked about as involving different actors or stakeholders and through which collaboration in "shared decision making" and local site management are to replace the more bureaucratic and centralized system of school governance. The use of stakeholders gives reference to a grid of actors such as central governmental authorities, local and regional school authorities, teachers, academic research, and "community" and parent groups. Inclusion is a representative notion of interaction of "stakeholders" in the university. The report asserts that no change is possible without the participation of "all provosts, faculties, academic deans" (p. ii).

Whatever the merits of problem solving and community, they are not merely descriptive of some natural reasoning of the child that research recoups. "Democratic participation," to borrow from Cruikshank (1999), is "not clear cut or naturally occurring; it [is] something that [is] solicited, encouraged, guided, and directed" (p. 97). The language of reform evokes populist images of democracy that entails local involvement in schools and the arriving of consensus about the "goals" guiding and judging individual schools.

The salvation themes of collaboration and participation in policy and research obscure how negotiations and communication are assembled in the cultural theses of cosmopolitanism. The school and classrooms as communities of learning are sites for recalibrating the political aspirations of the individual with the new assemblies of communities as the *social*. The "barriers" breached across groups in narrations of collaboration join individual agency with the general development of society. The individuality of collaboration embodies cultural theses: the unfinished cosmopolitan who chases desire through the mode of living as making choices in a system of continuous innovation, and of an individuality that falls short or outside of the values and norms constituting collaborative and problem solving—an individuality abjected that is discussed later in this and other chapters.

The Teacher as a Reflective Practitioner: The Lifelong Learner in Communities of Collaboration

The unfinished cosmopolitan is not only the child. The teacher is also classified as a lifelong learner. The teacher is self-actualized by remaking his or her biography. The "reflective teacher" researches himself or herself through action research that brings a form of problem solving into the planning of his or her career. The teacher assesses professional growth through life histories and portfolios to document and plan for the self-management of his or her career.

Reflection is not merely about thinking. Reflection entails particular expertise in calculating and ordering thought as a problem-solving action. This ordering and mapping is through the communication systems that govern individual self-activity, desire, and personal responsibility for self-actualization. The calculation of teacher reflection has different scenarios. It entails, for example, steps to follow in which he or she deliberates, makes choices, and creates decisions about alternative courses of action. It is also a way for teachers to think and get in touch with the inner self as a form of self-analysis (for critical discussions, see, e.g. Fendler, 2003; Zeichner, 1996).

The reflection and partnership of the teacher are to investigate, map, classify, and work on the territories of individuality for lifelong learning. The teacher assesses the child through life histories or portfolios, and the child makes his or her own biography as a process of continually constructing and reconstructing meaning and knowledge.

The portfolios in teacher education provide an example of the making of biography by inscribing a rationality related to "the homeless mind."[2] The portfolio is a technology of planning and calculating life. It entails specific procedures and instruments to document the skills, knowledge, and dispositions of the student preparing to become a teacher. The procedures of documentation require objectifying and subjectifying the teacher. The portfolio

> implies that one is objectifying oneself in terms of economic value, identifying and classifying one's stock of human capital that could offer access to environments.... [It] allows one to become sensitive to the need for additional learning and to opportunities for additional

investment, easy documentation and marketization of the self as a formalization of its learning. (Simon & Masschelein, 2006, p. 19)

The teacher is a redemptive agent who embodies and imparts the norms of policy and research. The argument about teacher education reforms giving coherence to state policies is intertwined with self-regulatory capabilities of the teacher—the "teachers' knowledge, their professional values and commitments, and the social resources of practice" (Cohen, 1995, p. 16). The teachers "are the agents on whom policy must rely to solve that problem, for unless they learn much more about the subjects they teach, and devise new approaches to instruction, most students' learning will not change" (p. 13).

The teacher does not assess the truth of statements but governs the dispositions and sensitivities of the child. The cosmopolitanism of the teacher is no longer an explicator of knowledge but a coach/facilitator. Teaching is to smooth the progress of the child's internalization of the rules of interpretation and expertise of science to order conduct. Teachers become managers, developing their own learning strategies, monitoring the processes, and evaluating the results.

The "reflective teacher" of professional reforms is bound to particular sets of principles for ordering and classifying the world and the self. The teacher is responsible for "problem solving" in a world that is continually changing and unstable. The teacher has greater local responsibility in implementing curriculum decisions for children's learning—a system of capabilities and capacities homologous to the sensitivities and awarenesses inscribed in a pedagogical constructivism that organizes the lifelong learner.

Making the biography of the teacher is placed in the language of democratizing the school. The teacher engages others in communities of collaboration so that he or she may better manage daily life and be healthier and happier. The remaking of these strategies appears as constructivist pedagogies that emphasize the agency of a decentralized system that enables teacher choices. Teachers are asked to go into the community, to become part of communities to "better know" their pupils and their families, to become trusted, or to know what they should include in their classrooms from "community knowledge" (Bloch & Tabachnick, 1994; Delpit, 1995). The teacher lives out life in *communities of discourse* and *communities of learners* so that he or she can be better self-managed, healthier, and happier.

Participation, collaboration, and reflection are told as foundational stories of the democracy of the nation that (re)visions the technological sublime of the beginning of the 20th century. The mode of living appears in the universal of the learning society, a transcendental space outside of history, context, and author. Yet that transcendental space is particular, connecting the mode of life of the lifelong learner with the nation. The cultural thesis of the lifelong learner is one that fulfills the ideals of democracy instantiated in "nation-ness." The teacher, for example, is the new leadership, "energized" to "work with others," "to ensure that America and its children will have the schools they require and deserve" (American Council on Education, 1999, p. ii) and to provide "a down payment to renewal and reform" that the "American public" demands so "the nation's schools can and must serve better the citizens of our democracy" (p. 1).

Collaboration is evoked as salvation narratives about democracy. *Collaboration is assumed to constitute the democratic school.* It brings teachers and researchers together, thus "invalidating" the distinctions between those who teach children in the school and those who teach at the university (Boostrom, Jackson, & Hansen, 1993). When social exclusion is approached, collaboration and participation are spoken about as giving an "authentic voice" to those children, parents, and community members who have been excluded from the decision-making processes of schools. A common theme about inclusion in making the democratic school, collaboration provides people with a "voice" that makes the space for teachers to hear the voices of students, places their voices as part of the broader critical dialogue and encounters with social and political authority. The critical encounters are framed with the principles generated in the cultural thesis of the lifelong learner whose voice and empowerment seem all inclusive and with no outside. The production of an outside with those inside, and the processes of abjection are elided through the universalizing discourses of the unity of the whole.

Curriculum Standards: Reconnecting the Individual and the Social

School standards reforms and research are to improve the quality of teaching and to improve the equity of school programs captured in the phrase no child left behind. Curriculum standards are to serve as benchmarks of achievement outcomes to assess the quality and equality of schools for "all children," a phrase that appears increasingly to indicate the political and social commitment to equality but which I argue instantiates processes of abjection. Almost all American professional associations concerned with teaching school subjects and the states' departments of instruction have developed documents concerning standards of teaching each school subject, sometimes with great controversy (Cornbleth & Waugh, 1995). The seductiveness of standards reforms is, in part, the promise of producing a democratic society.

The curriculum standards are to make the progress of children's learning transparent and assessable, and to identify failing schools that require more resources, teacher training, and programs of remediation.

My interest in curriculum standards is not whether the claims of the reforms achieve their goal. This has been more than adequately critiqued by others (see, e.g., Valenzuela, 2005; Tough, 2006). My concern is with the system of reason that crosses the debates. The standards of these reforms are not the outcome performances of children, but in the principles generated as cultural theses about modes of living (Scott, 1998). The hope that "the national dream is not denied" and that there is no child left behind embodies processes of abjections—*fears of not fulfilling the dream of including the excluded* and *fears of populations jeopardizing that future who are rendered abject* by their modes of living.

Finding the Right Practices to Manage Democracy and Its Dangers

Professional standards reforms and research embody cultural theses about the reasoned teacher and the qualities of those children classified as *all* children. The teacher is an individual who manages time, makes the school content meaningful and joyful, and respects diversity. The teacher who manages difference is one who guides and coaches children in meaning making that is psychologically attractive and enjoyable. Teachers

> *encourage* students to consider making time for learning mathematics a priority. Above all, they do everything possible to ensure that their students learn *meaningful* and important mathematics. They are genuinely *committed* to their students, and they let their students know that they find doing and teaching mathematics *lively* and *enjoyable experiences*. They take the extra steps required to ensure that students learn, and they encourage students to advance in mathematics as far as possible. (National Board for Professional Teaching Standards, 2001, p. 7; italics added)

Wisconsin is curriculum standards follow a similar cultural thesis. The child and teacher live

> in a community of learners, collaboration and meaningful understanding [that] encourages risk-taking and empowerment ("ownership") through self-initiated learning where students take responsibility for their own learning, develops self-assessment skills, and pursues excellence from the spirit of collaboration and students perceptions of themselves as empowered learned. (Wisconsin Department of Public Instruction, 2005)

The moral and ethical imperatives of the teacher and child are framed in a cultural thesis about the civic culture of democratic systems. Teacher education reforms are to fulfill the global obligations of preserving the democracy occurring as a result of changes in America's populations, of renewing the competitiveness of the nation in a global economy, and of promoting hospitality to the other. *What Matters Most: Teaching for America's Future,* a report of the National Commission on Teaching and America's Future (1996), embodies the promise to reorganize teacher preparation programs that is not only about its organization and institutions; it is about changing people. The cultural thesis focuses on the *soul* of the teacher and the child whose enlightened qualities serve the remaking of the consensus and stability of the nation.

> We must reclaim the *soul* [italics added] of America. And to do so, we need an education system that helps people forge shared values, to understand and respect other perspectives, to learn and work at high levels of competence, to take risks and persevere against the odds, to work comfortably with people from diverse backgrounds, and to continue to learn throughout life. (p. 12)

The reclaiming of the collective soul rememorializes the optimism of American exceptionalism to correct the past by providing for progress. "Reclaiming the soul of America" is a narrative of loss and the hope of redemption. That hope is expressed as a commitment to fulfill the dream of a democratic society. That dream is to forge consensus and harmony. Teacher education is to generate collective values in learning communities whose mode of living "respects others," "takes risks," and works with "diverse people" by making an individual who makes choices in which there is no choice not "to continue to learn throughout life."

To Touch the Future: Transforming the Way Teachers Are Taught, the report of a professional organization representing presidents of the leading research universities, places changes in teacher education as a moral imperative of the nation: "With each passing decade, education has become more critical to economic and social survival" (American Council on Education, 1999). America, the report continues, entered into a new era in which its unity needs to be recreated to achieve the American dream and aspirations:

> This nation will begin a new century with an economy that depends far more than ever before on knowledge—its acquisition, analysis, synthesis, communication, and application and the school becomes important ... [and] for the creation of wealth and well being.... The

quality of teaching in our schools must match *our dreams and aspi-ration as a nation* [italics added]. (p. 1)

The language, at first glance, seems to privilege the economy. That language, however, quickly morphs into images and narratives of the collective national belonging that are given expression through the language of "our dreams and aspiration." On one layer, one can argue that schooling is utilitarian, concerned with well-being as the creation of wealth. Yet reduction to economic criteria would elide the cultural and social registers about modes of living in the phrase about the collective "aspiration" of the nation.

The standards reforms connect agency and participation in what might seem as an oxymoron of political theory—centralized and decentralized patterns of government. Standards are outcomes to standardize the dream of the nation to ensure equal outcomes across diverse classrooms. The dreams are expressed in the No Child Left Behind reforms, the National Commission on Excellence in Education report, entitled *A Nation at Risk* (1984), and the contemporary efforts to improve teacher education cited above. They express American exceptionalism and its narrative of the nation as a unique experience in democracy. Standards are to promote participation of parents and communities who actively assess and work with schools in achieving their communal democratic purposes. Ravitch (1996), a historian of education and former deputy in the U.S. Department of Education, advocates national curriculum standards accompanied by testing as "setting a new course in a democracy" (p. xvi). National standards, Ravitch argues, are collaboratively developed to respect traditions of local control with the participation of professional organizations and the national government. The inscription of standards in teacher education follows the script of the democratic ideal of groups collaborating on standardized outcomes.

Where there are critiques of the standard reforms, the critiques revolve around whether the reforms will actually provide greater inclusion, such as with the children of the poor, racial minorities, and certain ethnic groups. The counterarguments bring forth the cosmopolitanism thesis. The achievement standards, it is argued, do not concern the "whole" child and do not allow the flexibility needed to educate the child in humanistic values (Ohanian, 1999). Other critiques suggest that standards are biased against groups that have not been served successfully by the school (see, e.g., Boaler, 2000). The counterposition to the standards leans back to the standards argument about a greater democracy through teacher, parent, and community participation in making the choices about what is best for children. The concern for the whole child standardizes unspoken principles of the new unity without questioning the rules and standards through which the objects of schooling are constructed.

The Unity of "All" Children and Its Casting Out

The democracy of the standards is not merely bringing the practices of schooling into a relation with normative ideals. The *all* in the standards reforms and research—*all* children learn, *all* children have high achievement, and so on—expresses the broad political commitment that schools are a positive social institution that should serve all segments of society equally. The reforms equally serving all children is not about the unity of the whole. The distinctions and categories enunciate cultural theses about the unfinished cosmopolitanism and its Others, generating double gestures that function to qualify and disqualify individuals for participation. The hope that "*all* children learn" recognizes and divides.

The hope of community and lifelong learning is to reclaim the lost dream of American exceptionalism. The dream engenders fears of not providing the correct strategies to rescue the fallen groups, and fears of the dangerous populations that threaten the republic's future. The title of the second report of the National Commission on Teaching and America's Future (2003), *No Dream Denied: A Pledge to America's Children,* memorialized the nation as providing the unity of the whole. The unity is signified as what is natural to all children as their "educational birthright" scaled with the constitutional rights of the citizen.

The birthright is, on one layer, bound to *being* a lifelong learner in "a culture of continuous learning." The natural birthright of the child, however, requires school performance standards that provide "students opportunities to learn and to evaluate whether all students have access to these opportunities" (Darling-Hammond, 2004, p. 1945). The securing the birthright of the child required accountability to "resolute(ly) and relentless(ly)" ensure clear goals (Hunt, 2003, p. 3).

The securing of the child's "birthright" ties to the consensus assumed in the statements of "clear goals," and ironically entails the double gestures of cosmopolitanism. There is the gesture to the universal qualities of human reason and rationality that emancipates and liberates. The school where "*all* children learn" is a comparative injunctive about fears that not engaging in the reforms that include will prevent the realization of the dream of the nation. The National Commission on Teaching, for example, asserts that schools need to develop a comprehensive policy that "confronts the laissez-faire Darwinism that currently reserves most high quality teaching to affluent schools, substantially segregated 'upper tracks' and a few alternative schools that exist on the margins of the system" (Darling-Hammond, 1998, p. 6).

The principles ordering the standards are given as universal cosmopolition qualities about freedom and agency. While no longer evoking the earlier Social Question, the moral disorders of the city still occupy reforms in narratives of the dangers and dangerous populations. The Social Question is transmogrified into the optimism of the new American exceptionalism that rescues and rectifies failures by turning to reforms about the child as the unfinished cosmopolitan and the rescue and redemption of targeted populations. The signifying of *all* children, however, is an iteration of cultural communism (Bourdieu, 1984/1993). Its fears are doubles: not providing the correct strategies to include, and the fears of the dangers and dangerous qualities of those different.

The Democratic Community as Double Gestures

As in the beginning of the 20th century, reforms direct attention to the soul of the teacher and child in the name of the democratic ideal. The soul of the unfinished cosmopolitan is made as an empowered, problem-solving individual capable of responding flexibly to problems that have no clear set of boundaries or singular answers.

The unfinished cosmopolitan stands in a diverse grid of practices reformulating relationships that evoke populist sentiments of participation, collaboration, and agency in shared decision making and individual autonomy. The location of responsibility, however, has internments and enclosures different from those described in the first section of the book. Responsibility is no longer traversed through the range of social practices directed toward a single public sphere—the social. Responsibility is located today in diverse, autonomous, and plural communities perpetually constituted by one's own practice in communities of learning that seem to have no boundaries or internments. This does not mean that the social is not being reconstituted. It is, as I indicated, through the discussion of the revisioned American exceptionalism.

The different versions of collaboration in making the democratic school embody the same rules and standards of the reason in constructing the subject. The reforms and their critiques *assume that equity and inclusion are separate entities from exclusion.* The division between inclusion and exclusion works with the assumption that solving the exclusion through the right mixture of policies and research will eliminate (at least theoretically) exclusion and inequities. School improvement and teacher education standards proclaim that "all children should learn"; if the prescriptions are followed, all children *will* learn (see, e.g., Ravitch, 1995). The cosmopolitanism ordered through principles of reason, agency, the planning of biography, and the rationalization that accompanies "the homeless mind" are left unquestioned, as well as the processes of abjection.

The changes in cosmopolitanism are morphologically related to other changes in the cultural theses about modes of living. A characteristic of life science for example, is that life appears to be open to shaping and reshaping at the molecular level—by precisely calculated interventions that prevent something from happening, alter the way something happens, or make something new happen in the cellular processes themselves. There is an individualizing of human worth that naturalizes variations in human capacities, reduces social phenomena to the aggregates of individual actions, regards human beings as merely technical resources to be managed in light of the considerations of efficiency or worth, from the point of view of the requirements of the race, nation, or state, and seeks to constrain or exclude those found biologically abnormal or defective (Rose, 2001, p. 26). Today, the state does not resolve society's needs for health. The state is enabling, facilitating, and animating—as is the reflective teacher.

The hopes of the future travel simultaneously with double fears that I focus on in the next chapters. There is the fear that the school will not adequately recognize and identify the correct strategies that work for inclusion, and there are fears of difference, of those children who pose dangers to the future imagined in the qualities of the lifelong learner. The child who has not succeeded is recognized and made different so that he or she may be worked on and rescued for inclusion. Yet these practices of rescue and remediation also differentiate and divide the child from the normalized qualities of reflection and action.

CHAPTER **8**

The Alchemy of School Subjects
Designing the Future and Its Unlivable Zones

This chapter continues to examine unfinished cosmopolitanism as double gestures by moving to the standards reform and research in teaching school subjects. In chapter 6, I discussed the alchemy with respect to schooling as performing a magical transmutation. As academic knowledge moves into the spaces of schooling, an odd thing happens: the different school subjects have a certain homogeneity in stated outcomes (see Popkewitz & Gustafson, 2002; Popkewitz, 2004a). The national music curriculum standards and the mathematics curriculum would seem at first glance to be knowledge that is either divergent and humanist or rational and scientific. However, they are not divergent but relate to a mode of living of unfinished cosmopolitanism: participation, decision making, problem solving, communication ("defending an argument" and "working effectively in a group"), work habits ("acquiring and using information"), and interactional proficiency that enables community collaboration and participation. The unspoken and unexpressed optimism of the standards reform is that the school will produce a more enlightened and cosmopolitan mode of living. Paired with this assumption are engendered threats to the unity of the whole. The joining of the hope and fears is visible in the phrase "all children," which produces recognition of the difference of the child who is left behind.

The first section of this chapter examines the standards of teacher education that underlie the school subject reforms. I argue that the teacher education reforms have less to do with overt statements of performance outcomes standards and more to do with the cultural theses about modes

133

of living and processes of abjection. The second section examines policy reforms and research of school subject standards in mathematics education to consider what counts as the teacher's knowledge of school subject matter and pedagogical content knowledge, phrases of significance in contemporary professional education. Mathematics is the exemplar; it was chosen because mathematics is presented as a universal, objective knowledge that has no cultural theses other than what are in the numbers itself. The relation of school subject standards to the cosmopolitan hope and processes of abjection are explored.

The selection and organization of school content are ordered by psychological inscriptions that focus on the interior dispositions or the *soul* of the child. Returning to the 19th-century Spencerian question of "What knowledge is most important?" the selection and organization of school subject standards are ordered to meet the demands of theories about children's growth, development, and moral character. The normalizing procedures of pedagogical reform are placed in constructivist psychologies that reassemble and reconnect the pragmatism of John Dewey (there is no mention of Thorndike, although learning theories still look for clear goals) and Lev Vygotsky, who emerged from Russian psychology to design modes of living as the unfinished cosmopolitanism (Popkewitz, 1998a). Pedagogical practices order and divide conduct, personality, relationships, and dispositions (emotions and attitudes) as modes of living and to locate the dangers and dangerous populations.

The Desire for Future and Abjection in Teacher Education

The National Commission on Teaching (1996, 2003) discussed in chapter 7 captures much of the concern with standards in contemporary teacher education reform. The performance standards of teacher education, it is asserted, are to provide "clear and consistent visions of teaching and learning," to further the integration between university instruction and clinical practices, and to guarantee adequate knowledge for the teacher of school subjects. These commitments embody the cultural thesis of the professional teacher as the lifelong learner whose autonomy, self-responsibility, and problem solving is enacted collaboratively with other teachers, parents, communities, and stakeholders. Unfinished cosmopolitanism's hospitality to others is expressed as teacher sensitivity to cultural diversity and the different communities. The commitment to diversity and sensitivity that seems all inclusive is a process of abjection. Particular populations are recognized for inclusion, yet as different from unspoken norms of the family and community where "all the children who learn" reside.

Standards reforms envision an American exceptionalism as the epic of the nation that embodies the unfinished cosmopolitanism. The title of the National Commission on Teaching's 2003 report, *No Dream Denied: A Pledge to America's Children,* and other reform reports express the hope of the inclusive schooling for "poor and minority communities" (see, e.g. Darling-Hammond, 2004 p. 1961; also American Council on Education, 1999). The rhetorical use of the "dream" and "pledge" in the commission's report reawakens 19th-century promises of the nation claiming an evangelical future. That future is again written as the hope of future freedom and liberty that now is given as the natural and universal "birthright" of all children to "competent, caring, qualified" teachers and that will provide the technologies that bring the teacher success (National Commission on Teaching and America's Future, 1996, p. 10).

The "sense of urgency" and the "high stakes" of professional reforms are to produce the unity of the participatory society where all individuals "need skills once thought only for the few," since most assembly-line manufacturing jobs disappeared by the early 1990s (National Commission on Teaching and America's Future, 1996, p. 10).

> In this knowledge-based society, the United States urgently needs to reaffirm a consensus about the role and purposes of public education in a democracy ... the challenge extends far beyond preparing students for the world of work. It includes building an American future that is just and humane as well as productive, that is as socially vibrant and civil in its pluralism as it is competitive. (National Commission on Teaching and America's Future, 1996, p. 11)

The promise of the better future engenders hopes and fears that circulate in each other. The vitality and pluralism of the future of American society is threatened, the report continues, by economic disparities produced by the fast disappearance of high-wage jobs and the divisions of race and class that makes "the backbone of our national life, the great American middle class ... left wondering about the future" (National Commission on Teaching and America's Future, 1996, p. 11). The new teacher and school are to protect against the dangers that threaten the future cosmopolitanism. The future is viewed initially as the natural preparation for participating in the democracy ordered by reason and rationality: "If every citizen is to be prepared for a democratic society whose major product is knowledge, every teacher must know how to teach students in ways that help them reach high levels of intellectual and social competence" (National Commission on Teaching and America's Future, 1996, p. 3).

The optimism of the future thoughtful, reflective, and active child or teacher engenders fears that have at least two layers. One is the fear that if the reforms are not carried out, the manifest destiny and the collective good of the republic will not be fulfilled. Drawing on the rhetorical style of the Puritan sermon in the American Jeremiad, the 1984 federal report *A Nation At Risk* and current mathematics and science achievement scores (National Commission on Teaching and America's Future, 1996, p. 4) stand as testimonials that the problem of the future is not race or the split between wealth and poverty. The future is bound to the unified whole where there is no difference as all children learn.

> There has been no previous time in history when the success, indeed the survival, of nations and people has been so tightly tied to their ability to learn. Today's society has little room for those who cannot read, write, and compute proficiently; find and use resources; frame and solve problems; and continually learn new technologies, skills and occupations. (National Commission on Teaching and America's Future, 1996, p. 3)

On a different layer are fears about the dangerous moral and social qualities that menace the fulfillment of the future destiny. The dangers are attached to categories related to the poor and minorities, categories that have particular social distinctions and divisions that are not merely statistical summaries of achievement scores. If the distinctions were merely statistical divisions, then the poor and racial groups would far outnumber the "real" minorities, such as the group whose ancestors were the Puritans—but everyone "knows" who is in the enclosed spaces of "minority," and that space is not of the small number of ancestors of the Puritans.

Further, the dangers to national survival are at first glance about economic distinctions, but those distinctions quickly morph into moral, social, and cultural distinctions about the qualities and characteristics of the excluded. The task is for all Americans, it is asserted in one national report, to have a critical interest in building an education system to counteract such statistics as:

> Low levels of literacy are highly correlated with welfare dependency and incarceration—and their high costs.

> More than half the adult prison population has levels of literacy below those required by the labor market.

> By the year 2010 there will be only three workers for every Social Security recipient, as compared with 16 in 1950. If all these future workers are not capable and productive, the older generation's retirement security and our social compact will be in *grave danger* [italics added].

> We cannot afford the continued expansion of prison populations, public assistance programs, and unemployment. (National Commission on Teaching and America's Future, 1996, p. 12)

The hope and different characteristics of the dangers travel with each other through complex interactions of recognition and difference. Social and cultural distinctions are erased in the insertion of unity, stability, and consensus of the whole that teacher education standards are defined as articulating. The unity is given as the expertise that is now available to shepherd reforms and the reforming of teachers. "We have achieved a national consensus that what teachers know and can do is the most important influence on what teachers learn" (National Commission on the Teaching and America's Future, 2003, p. 6).

That consensus and stability is placed in the democracy of schooling produced through the participatory structures of reform. "Democratic" participation is creating "communities that work toward shared standards, developing common curriculum goals and working in teams" (National Commission on Teaching and America's Future, 1996, p. 9). The communities are not just places where people interact. The interactions and communications practices are tied to developing particular principles of ordering the possibilities of teaching. These principles relate to "high standards, coherent, high-quality curriculum across the grades, designed to support teachers' collective work and learning on behalf of their students; and structured to allow for ongoing parent engagement" (National Commission on Teaching and America's Future, 1996, p. 3).

The democracy in which participation occurs has particular instrumental qualities. Participation is for more efficient planning. The location and direction of that planning is in the psychology of the child.[2] The failure of schools is in "inconsistent expectations" and "a haphazard hodgepodge of polities" (National Commission on Teaching and America's Future, 1996, p. 9). Diversity is demonstrated when teachers consider the issue of the most effective practices for different groups of students. These effective practices re-inscribe homogeneity in which to see difference.

The insertion of diversity is of a unity through the reduction of cultural difference into psychological aspects of self-expression, differences in solving problems and happiness. Diversity in the curriculum is the various routes in which the mind solves the problem at hand or in the recognition of the characteristics of the child or family that need reordering (see, e.g., Grossman, Schoenfeld, & Lee, 2005). Joyfulness and happiness are a criterion of diversity in the Wisconsin standards for music education. Pursuit of happiness brings back Thorndike's aim of schools in relation to others, who are the "unhappy" in contemporary school reforms. Diversity is singing with "improvisation" as an important means of self-expression in all cultures and as an integral part of students' musical heritage (Wisconsin Department of Public Instruction, 2005, p. 6). Diversity is "sing[ing] music representing diverse genres and cultures, with expression appropriate for the work being performed" (p. 3). The words of "meaningful," "enjoyable," and "lively experiences" express the optimism of teaching about making democracy through the making of the child.

> The curriculum standards of pedagogical content knowledge provide the assertion of diversity as ensuring the unity of difference. Culturally responsive pedagogy recognizes that diverse sense-making practices, carries with it a more egalitarian values, and ensures that linguistic minority students acquire the mainstream literacies they need to succeed in school and beyond. (Grossman et al., 2005, p. 225)

At this point, one might say that there are variations, fluidity, and flexibility to the standards and that something is needed to provide greater accountability to schools. For example, states have adopted their own approaches to accountability and standards. Wisconsin mandates that teacher education program establish its own priorities. The standards for the individual program standards are clearly stated as performance outcomes. The institutional and organization approach, however, does not take into account the unifying system of rationalizing through decentralizing and the double gestures that are included in the standards and its systems of recognition and difference.

The Standards of School Subjects: Mathematics and the Cultural Theses of Pedagogical Knowledge

The organizing concepts of professional reforms consist of teachers learning "school subject knowledge" and "pedagogical content." The terms enunciate a common sense that teachers should know the subjects that they teach and should have adequate skills to effectively teach that school subject. That common sense, however, is ordered and classified within a grid that brings disciplinary systems into principles about the lifelong learner.[3]

In the sections that follow, I explore an assemblage of practices in mathematics education as principles are generated about agency, planning of the self, and science in ordering action and reflection: (a) the translation tools that bring mathematics into the imagination of pedagogical psychology; (b) problem solving as an ordering device to classify and govern the child; (c) research on classroom "communities" and communication processes that relate individual self-realization with public or collective capacities.

Mathematics in Service of the Pedagogical Child

The reforms that call for pedagogical content knowledge characterize instruction as bringing classroom interactional patterns into closer proximity with those found in the academic discipline of mathematics. Teacher education reforms begin with an assertion that teachers "should possess deep knowledge of the subjects they teach" (Grossman et al., 2005, p. 201). That deep knowledge of school subjects is to capture the cultural norms of the discipline of mathematics in classroom instruction. Speaking of standards reform, "Classrooms are mathematical communities *writ small* and key reform documents envision the classroom as a mathematical culture governed by roughly the same norms of argument and evidence as govern discourse within communities of scholars in the disciplines themselves" (Nelson, Warfield, & Wood, 2001, pp. 6–7).

When mathematics education is examined more closely, mathematics education is not pedagogy about mathematics. It is pedagogy about changing children by differentiating them. The community of mathematics as a "humanistic field" in which collective knowledge continually grows and is revised (see Nelson et al., 2001, p. 6) is translated and transported in the curriculum as the psychological qualities of the child. The psychological conceptualization of school subjects is assumed, drawing from Dewey's phrase in *The Child and the Curriculum* (1902) about the need to "psychologize the subject matter" (cited in Grossman et al., 2005, p. 207).

Of course, this is not the intent of reformers but inscribed in the system of reason that orders what is seen, talked about, and acted. The research about mathematics education is to govern the moral conduct of the child through standards of communication, participation, and social relationships in the classroom. Lampert (1990), for example, calls for "moral courage" in learning mathematics. That moral courage seems, at first glance, as a process without content. Mathematics education should "strive for the use of intuition and the practices of 'conscious guessing,' 'the taking of risk,' and a problem solving that 'zig-zags' in refutations and proofs en route to identifying (pp. 30–31). If we pose this as a cultural thesis about the mode of life of "all children," it is the child who expresses tentativeness and attentiveness to the nonlinear qualities of mathematics.

The curriculum quickly transmogrifies into sociopsychological conceptions of child development that are to produce a life of continuous learning where the making of the self is never complete. The mathematics standards of the National Council of Teachers of Mathematics (NCTM, 1989) are about the psychological ordering of a mode of living, assessing "what students know and need to learn" (p. 11), and constructive psychology about students who are "actively building new knowledge from their experience and prior knowledge" (p. 18) and using "knowledge flexibly, applying what is learned to one's setting appropriately in another" (p. 20).

The constructing of knowledge is not only personal but linked with collective belonging that is ascribed as the foundational condition for humanity. Mathematics education provides the principles for the realization of a shared culture through which citizens act. Sutherland and Balacheff (1999) state this boldly. The problem solving of mathematics is the

> modern social answer to the need to enable children to become citizens—that is, members of a society who have access to both a shared culture and who are empowered with intellectual and emotional tools to face problems within the workplace and everyday life. (p. 2)

The pedagogical content knowledge is not about a shared culture of the community of mathematics. It is the psychological calculating and ordering of the interior of the mind to give direction to the uncertain future. The fixing of what is to be known that children "construct" is captured in the seemingly innocent distinction between conceptions and misconceptions. The teacher is to assess, for example,

> the ability to anticipate and respond to typical student patterns of understanding and misunderstanding within a content area, and the ability to create multiple examples and representations of challenging topics that make the content accessible to a wide range of learners. (Grossman et al., 2005, p. 201)

Educational research is to find efficient technologies that replace children's "intuitive" reasoning in which misconceptions are contained with new sets of rules for acting and seeing. Truth is in the structure of mathematics knowledge. The flexibility and fluidity of knowledge is treated in response to a given transcendent structure or base knowledge from which misconceptions are found. The notion of misconception inserts the assumption of an essential, universal core of rules and standards from which the child's growth, development, and future actions as a cosmopolitan citizen can be assessed.

Teacher education is built on a cultural thesis that complements that of the child's undoing misconceptions so as to have stable rules for accessing the phenomena of the world.

> Making the right choices as a teacher depends on knowing what kinds of errors or mistakes students are likely to make, being able to identify such mistakes when they occur, and being prepared to address the sources of the students' errors in ways that will result in student learning. (Grossman et al., 2005, p. 205)

The salvation of the teacher and the school is, as it is for the more general school subject standards reform as well, for research to identify the universal good works that exemplify high standards and the collective practices that enable "the replication" of universal good.[1] Research formulates, classifies, and provides the ordering principles to administer what functions as the classifications of the child's ability to reason. The task of instruction is to move students from their own intuitive understandings into what is labeled as conventional mathematics (see, e.g. Ball, 2001).

The narratives of constructing knowledge, experience, and flexibility embody the individualizing of the unfinished cosmopolitan in American exceptionalism. Ball (2001), for example, uses a narrative about her own teaching as a research "site of practice." The teaching is narrated as an exemplar of children using their everyday lives and interests in learning to problem solve. As if in service to the democratic ideal and its earlier 20th century populist ring directed to the soul, learning mathematics is

> to create a practice that is responsive to students' ideas, interests, and lives. I strive to hear my students, to work with them as they investigate and interpret their worlds. I want to respect who they are as well as who they can become. (p. 13)

To instruct properly is a gesture to include what is now characterized as the child's mathematical promise, which distances the self and the teacher from the immediate by theorizing about the daily practices of teaching. The theorizing, however, is talked about as merely a reporting of the observations of experience. The teacher is to

> hear below the surface features of children's talk and representations … so teachers will not miss the mark by considering a student wrong who has in fact an interesting idea or is carrying out a nonstandard procedure, but one with mathematical promise. Suspending one's *desire* [italics added] for students to get answers right and thinking mathematically about what a child might mean are among the most difficult problems of teaching. (Ball, 2001, p. 19)

Research is to order the new democracy of the classroom as constructing knowledge through participation and collaboration.[4] We find a "classroom in which differences are valued, in which students learn to care about and respect one another, and in which commitments to a just and democratic society are embodied and learned" (Ball, 2001, p. 13). In a similar vein, Nelson et al. (2001) argue that teaching entails the "vision of mathematics instruction that takes seriously the fact that children construct their mathematical knowledge" (pp. 6–7).

The narrations of mathematics education embody cosmopolitanism principles of the individual acting through the use of reason and rationality, with mathematics as the privileged knowledge of the learning society. That learning of mathematics is the ostensible impartial management of children's thought and the mere application of an administrative task of learning to problem solve. Children's involvement and agency in this calculation of reason is spoken of as finding relevancy and individual interests. The suspension of the teacher's "desire" for the child's right answer quoted above has a double quality. It involves being responsive and relevant to "students' ideas, interests, and lives" (Ball, 2001, p. 13), but it is also a pastoral strategy that opens the child's inner thought for scrutiny, comparison, and management.

Like the water that the fish swims in, the psychological principles traveling in pedagogy are so much part of the reason of education that one does not question the medium of pedagogical translation but only discusses which terms are more effective or how to unify them.[5] The pedagogical "eye" is so naturalized that psychological inscriptions are assumed in the translation and transportation of academic fields into school subjects. The lenses for "seeing" and "thinking" mathematics in schooling are treated as if they are, in fact, what mathematics is and is not; and not about in moral principles of agency or the planning of the self.

Governing the Soul: Problem Solving as Ordering the Interior of the Mind

I argued in chapter 7 that problem solving is central to the assembly of cosmopolitanism of the child. I will turn to this quality of cosmopolitanism by focusing on two functions of problem solving that are served in research.

One is to develop more efficient procedures of teaching through calculating the interior mind of the child. Returning to the discussion in the first chapter, problem solving fabricates who the child is and should be through the categories and distinctions for mapping and administering thoughts, feelings, and actions. The research about mathematics education links psychological distinctions (constructing meaning), social interactions (community), and replacing misconceptions with the proper conceptions of subject content. The assembly and connections of these different practices form as the cultural thesis of the child as the lifelong learner.

Second, problem solving governs the principles of conduct as moral principles that relate to unfinished cosmopolitanism rather than about mathematical reasoning per se. Problem solving is not merely solving problems! Effective instruction is to have children "want to" as well as "be able to" (Brousseau, 1997, p. 12). The teacher is to *monitor students' capacity* [italics added] and inclination to analyze situations, frame and solve problems, and make sense" (p. 19). Pedagogical content knowledge is to provide an order for shaping children's capacities and inclinations: "Effective teachers recognize that the decisions teachers make shape students' mathematical *dispositions* and can create a rich setting for learning" (National Council of Teachers of Mathematics, 2000, p. 18, italics added).

Problem solving is posited as learning to deal with the uncertainty of the future—"the ubiquitous feature of contemporary life" discussed earlier—and learning how to meet the obligations of the individual in a democracy. The uncertainty with which the problem solver faces the future is not that uncertain. It embodies a cultural thesis about a child's ethical obligation to work for self-improvement and self-motivation: "A major goal of school mathematics programs is to create autonomous learners" (NCTM et al., 2000, p. 21). The mode of living as an autonomous and continuous self-improving problem solver forms characteristics of the unfinished cosmopolitan.

Consensus and harmony that remove conflict are at the level of thought and cognition. One mathematics educational research project, for example, posits its purpose is to identify how "connections are formed between new information and existing knowledge structures or when new information leads to cognitive conflict and, therefore, to the reorganization of existing structures in order to resolve that conflict" (Warfield, 2001, p. 137). The words *connections* and *reorganization* in this sentence have little direct relation to mathematics, although the content serves as the backdrop. They are ways of thinking about and organizing children's dispositions, sensitivities, and awarenesses through the teaching of mathematics.

The cultural thesis of the child is of the global citizen whose homeless mind enables the application of universal principles of reason given an association with mathematics. The autonomy is a mode of living that entails continuous self-improvement in which choices are bound by the deferral of the present to the future. The standards and rules of reason through which one's freedom and empowerment are enacted join the rationalities of problem solving with the stability of the propositions provided by mathematics. The cultural thesis of this unfinished cosmopolitanism is regulated and calculated through the procedures that order the inner qualities or soul of the child.

Community and Classroom Communications in the Struggle for the Soul

To pursue further the assembly of the unfinished cosmopolitan with respect to problem solving is to return to the intersections with collaboration in communities. "Community" is an intellectual tool in which the problem solver learns thinking skills by participating in the classroom community—"a discourse community" (NCTM, 1989, p. 7) and in "a *community of knowers* who share in the construction of beliefs or knowledge" and whose knowledge "is created through discursive processes and negotiation of meaning carried out in accord with the norms of the group" (Nelson et al., 2001, p. 6).

Earlier 20th-century notions of the classroom spoke about a place of socialization in which the child was to internalize preestablished universal, collective norms of identity. Today's reforms return to community to promote solidarity, consensus, and collective belonging. Community is connected with problem solving as a salvation theme about the empowerment assumed by all citizens who take on its responsibilities. The *classroom community* is a social space of moral relations in which individuals form obligations and allegiances in multiple communities.

Community assumes the consensus of meaning through which individual self-improvement, autonomy, and the responsible life are conducted. The *community of learners, discourse community,* and *community of knowers* direct attention to the development of "shared norms" based on an "equilibrium" and "consensus" about knowledge (Cobb, Yackel, & Wood, 1992; Cobb, 1994). Teaching mathematics is "the development and justification of use of mathematical generalizations" (Russell, 1999). The statement presupposes that a fixed and stable logical structure of knowledge is the object through which children learn. Students "put themselves in relation to the establishment of valid arguments in the discipline" as their answers are located as "mathematically legitimate" (Lampert, 1990, p. 54).

The taken-as-shared interpretations of mathematics stabilize the world that the child is to act on and make possible the revisioning of the Puritan converting ordinances about salvation and redemption. The technological tools of instruction are the "learning psychologies" that focus on identity mediated through the communication systems of the classroom community (see, e.g., Steffe & Kieren, 1994, 1995; Cobb et al., 1991; Cobb et al., 1992; Cobb, 1994). The classroom community is thought of as a "participation structure" through which agency of the child and teacher is effected. Classroom participation is organized as the tasks of learning. Lampert (1990) speaks of the classroom as a "discourse community" where truth is reached by children "figuring out what is true, once the members of the discourse community agree on their definitions and assumptions" (p. 42).

Community is a narrative of social psychology. The intersubjective life is one of consensus in meanings and understandings. "Collaborative learning" in mathematics education is to "arrive at a taken-as-shared interpretation of the problem" (Simon, 1995, p. 120).

The overlapping of problem solving with "participatory structures" revisions the homeless mind. Mathematics is to order life and enable the child to be both an object and subject of knowledge. The learning of valid arguments is what provides a universal knowledge that transcends the local. Its mastery provides boundaries for autonomy and freedom. Instruction is directed to the soul of the child by constituting the principles of action and reflection. The distinctions and differentiations about the qualities constitute the criteria about success "for all" and paradoxically those who cannot put themselves into the mathematical community that stands as writ large for the total community.

Pedagogical Inscriptions, School Subjects, and the Iconic Images of the Expert

Ironically, the populist and democratic impulses in children's construction of knowledge are not about constructing knowledge but about constructing paths to identifying the already known structures of a given content. Children's construction of knowledge is to find multiple ways of making apparent the presupposed logical and analytical foundations of mathematical properties. The stability of the knowledge of schooling connects with the selection of conventional ideas as the core of mathematical education. The notion of "conventional" is used to identify the foundational rules of the "nature" and logical "structure" of knowledge taught to children (see, e.g., Simon, 1995, p. 120; Cobb et al., 1991).

Principles and Standards of School Mathematics (NCTM, 2000), for example, assumes that mathematics consists of logical and analytic structures. School subjects are classified as "bodies of knowledge"—systems of concepts, proofs, generalizations, and procedures—that children learn. The linguistic quality of curricular words—"bodies," "content," "content coverage," "conceptual knowledge"—treats disciplines as inert, unchanging, and unambiguous "things" (concepts or proofs) whose structures organize the base of children's learning. In accordance with the standards, students are expected to

> identify the characteristics of various quadrilaterals in grades 3–5. In grades 6–8 they may examine and make generalizations about properties of particular quadrilaterals. In grade 9–12, they may develop logical arguments to justify conjectures about particular polygons. (p. 16)

Identifying conventional knowledge of physics or mathematics "makes sense" if pedagogy is understood as cultural theses about modes of living. To fix and stabilize the content knowledge of disciplinary knowledge in the school curriculum enables the focus on psychological principles assigned to the child's developement. However, the notions of community, negotiated meanings, and problem solving of mathematics education are shaped by the governing practices of pedagogy rather than by the disciplinary practices of mathematicians.

The alchemy in which the selection of conventional mathematical ideas (its language and symbols) occurs provides a consensus and harmony in the *a priori* structures that enable the focus on the soul of the child. The normalizing is put into a populist democratic language about "enhancing learning," negotiation, and the autonomy that comes with making one's own meaning. Research on mathematics education, for example, is to produce teachers' "discussion and negotiation of meaning with students to add to the tools they are able to use to enhance their thinking" (Lampert, 1990, p. 47). In classroom dialogue, students are to internalize and make their own the logical standards of conventional mathematical ideas: "The ideas that governed classroom interaction came to parallel the tradition of argument in the mathematical community more closely, as truth came to be determined by logical argument among scholars" (p. 35).

The classroom focus on students learning the rules of argument is not only a process of modeling truth. It is also a process of normalizing the inner characteristics of the students by modeling the social through the rules of participation for "constructing knowledge" in what might seem to be a mutation of the "ontogeny recapitulates phyologency" of G. Stanley Hall and Herbartians of the early 20th century. In a widely cited text, it is asserted that instruction is "*regulating* [italics added] the interaction among children rather than just regulating the individual action" (Cazden, 1986, p. 450).[6]

Conceptions of "participatory structures" and a "community of learners" in the curriculum standards research are part of the normalizing practices. They emphasize children's involvement and constructing knowledge that has already been confirmed in the *a priori* world of schooling and mathematics education research. Participation and problem solving are to test and confirm the givens of the empirical world. The National Council of Teachers of Mathematics' (2000) principles and standards, for example, assert that curriculum should "offer experiences that allow students to see that mathematics has powerful uses in modeling and predicting real-world phenomena" (pp. 15–16).

The focus is on the structures of knowledge that inscribe stability and consensus to the curriculum. French theory of didactical situations, a variant of constructivist pedagogy, illustrates the relation of a certain, stable world with that of the universal of reason that "finds" its structures and relations; mathematics education becomes a metonym for *a priori* of the nature of society. Mathematics functions in the curriculum as a highly formalized body of knowledge whose ontological status serves as a model for testing reality that is separate from questions of epistemology (see, e.g., Brousseau, 1997). The reason and rationality of the child are modes of living for "testing" the revelation of the given world's order through the practices of modeling and predicting. Problem solving is for accessing and confirming the external world and to arbitrate truth and falsehood in one's personal life.

The attention to the structure and nature of mathematics is ironic. Current reforms speak about the social construction of knowledge. The uncertain and ubiquitous future that the mathematical standards refer to is in fact not so uncertain or ubiquitous after all. The ubiquitous future is fixed and ordered by the truth-telling practices embodied in the nature and structure of conventional mathematics. Problem solving gives flexibility in finding the given solutions to the problems set in the curriculum designed through psychology and not academic disciplines. The notions of nature and structure of subject content knowledge stabilize and regularize the procedures for interpretation of that uncertain future. At the same time, the inscriptions of the problem solver redefine the parameters of human agency, and what is open for scrutiny is circumscribed by the expertise that stabilizes and harmonizes the world of participation.

The Eliding of Mathematics as a Field of Cultural Practices

The attention given to the logical structures and the nature of conventional ideas elides the disciplinary fields of school subjects as *fields of cultural practices*. Mathematics, like other school subjects, involves an amalgamation of institutions, authority relations, analogies, memories, and images that come together at different times and places to order and classify the objects of reflection and action. To borrow from Bakhtin's (1981) discussion of literature, the dynamics and possibilities of the knowledge of mathematics are "permeated with concrete judgments, they knit together specific objects and with belief systems of certain genres of expression and points of view particular to particular professions" (p. 289).

Mathematics can be considered as a field of competing intellectual traditions whose relations form that academic field. A particular system of generalizations and procedures of inquiry is crystallized in the curriculum. The conditions of participation, norms of inquiry, and rules and standards of recognition and truth that form the field of professional mathematics are omitted. The National Council of Teachers of Mathematics' principles and standards, for example, refer to "mathematical sciences" in determining what is to be treated as core knowledge.[7] This designation may refer to the distinction between applied mathematics as opposed to mathematics "for its own sake," although it is not clear in the NCTM's 1989 and 2000 documents. But this designation of "scientific mathematics" as the field of mathematics obscures the variety of traditions and networks of associations through which knowledge is produced in the field of mathematics.

At this time, one might ask: What is lost when conventional ideas from a subfield of an academic discipline are inscribed as the organizing principles of pedagogy, such as those derived from "scientific mathematics"? Hacking's (2002) discussion of science and mathematics offers some partial answers to this question. Hacking argues that mathematics embodies different ways of thinking about and creating new objects. "Each style of reasoning in mathematics," Hacking continues, "opens up different objects for scrutiny and provides classificatory schemes by which lives are experienced, truths authenticated, and futures chosen." Hacking compares algorithmic and combinatorial styles of reasoning with spatial styles of reasoning in mathematics (p. 2). The different reasoning styles are "self-authenticating." That is, each style "introduces its own criteria of proof and demonstration, and ... it determines the truth conditions appropriate to the domains to which it can be applied" (p. 4). Thinking of mathematics in this way directs attention to its practices as more than "a group of techniques for bringing new kinds of facts to our awareness" (p. 4).

The field of cultural practices in the disciplines can be thought of as ways of producing truths that work in an immense world of institutions, authority relations, "connotations, stories, analogies, memories, and fantasies" (Hacking, 2002, p. 9). The various styles of reasoning introduce different registers of debates about the ontological status of the objects seen as true. Truth has historically both stable and unstable qualities.

Approaching science and mathematics as fields of cultural practices that construct their objects and truth statements is a way out of the controversies that divide education into realist and antirealist camps, the unproductive separation of epistemology and ontology, and the division between subjectivist and objectivist worldviews.[8]

Hacking's approach to thinking about mathematics as the open space in which different systems of reason meet goes against the grain of the pedagogical alchemy that solidifies conventional knowledge. The pedagogical translations produce iconic images of an expertise that constitutes what is known about the world and the rules to find that truth. To stay with the exemplar of mathematics, its formulas are consecrated as models of truth for decision making in daily life. The agency of the child is directed through particular stable qualities to the world contained by the propositions of mathematics. The processes of choice are interned and enclosed by particular rules and standards assigned as mathematical "reasoning."

The alchemic selection of "bodies of knowledge" from the subfield of "scientific mathematics" crystallizes and fixes what is to be known. The cultural theses about ways of acting are to make the future citizen. Reason is shaped and bounded to testing and predicting what is proved as the real of the world. The uses of "real" and "nature" establish a certainty that existed in prior times with God. The mathematics of the school is the arbitrator of the real through the rules that order the meaning of propositions. There is no room left for doubt except in the learning procedures to access the natural and real world. The turn to the conventional ideas from a particular subfield of mathematics provides flexibility as the paths taken arrive at given conclusions. In contrast to the translation models of pedagogy, one can think of "doing" mathematics as making the familiar strange, examining the mysterious and unfamiliar, and questioning precisely that which is taken for granted and conventional. This rethinking of curriculum translation does not do away with the need for alchemic practices because schools do not practice the disciplinary production of knowledge. It does suggest, however, an alternative to the limits of current tools.

Standards of Social Inclusion as Exclusions

Although the aims of problem solving and belonging to a community are described as student "empowerment," the alchemy inserts the expertise of science as a secure model for telling the truth of a given reality while obscuring the social mooring of the academic field. In this section, I return to the production of standards of social inclusion and exclusion in the alchemy of school subjects.

Reforms and standards are thought of as redressing the lack of academic success among particular groups or populations in society. The commitment to equity is expressed through the phrase "all children"—"All students, regardless of their personal characteristics, background, or physical challenges, must have opportunities to study—and support to learn—mathematics" (NCTM, 2000, p. 12). The phrase "all children," as I argued in previous chapters, compares and distinguishes two human kinds—the cosmopolitan child who has all the capacities to learn, problem solve, collaborate, and achieve in schooling and the child recognized for inclusion and yet different—the child left behind.

A digest of personal facts fashions territories of members and nonmembers in the category of *all* children and overlaps the reforms identified in the federal No Child Left Behind Web sites that list programs about "What Works," standards reform and research, and teacher education research. The recognitions of division and the differentiation of the child not up to the achievement standards are quickly filled in. The child who is not problem solving or living with autonomy is cast into unlivable spaces that overlap with social and psychological qualities that circulate as the principles of "the child left behind." The psychological categories are of the child who lacks self-esteem, has "low expectations" (NCTM, 2000), or lacks motivation, with the latter as the cause of not learning from online classes discussed in the next chapter.

Assembled with the psychological traits and attitudes are social characteristics. The low expectations connect with children

who live in poverty, students who are not native speakers of English, students with disabilities, females, and many nonwhite students who have traditionally been far more likely than their

> counterparts in other demographic groups to be the victims of low expectations. (National Council of Teachers of Mathematics, 2000, p. 13)

This category is further given coordinates as

> students who are not native speakers of English, for instance, and may need special attention to allow them to participate fully in classroom discussions ... as students with disability may need increased time to complete assignments, or they may benefit from the use of oral rather than written assessment. (p. 13)

The social and psychological distinctions of the category of the child left behind overlap to signify qualities dangerous to the cosmopolitan future of society, such as the child placed in the spaces of *urban* or *rural* settings (NCTM, 2000, p. 373). That child is one of a population of "poor and minority students" (p. 368) who have "unique mathematics needs" and thus are in need of rescue through additional help so as not to be at a disadvantage when starting school. These categories and distinctions of difference are practices of inclusion continually placed against the background of something simultaneously excluded (see Popkewitz, 1998b).

Ironies of Autonomy and Participation: The Alchemy and the Narrowing of Possibilities

The very translation models of disciplinary knowledge into school subject content may increase participation and problem solving, but that participation is increasingly defined by the iconic expertise of the givenness of the nature of the world that problem solving illuminates. Although not the intent of reforms, the child is a tourist and a consumer in the world of the propositions and generalizations of school subjects. The child is more active in the sense of the modeling of a particular argument and questioning in school subjects, but the child is less active in defining the terms and extending the possibilities and boundaries of that engagement. The uncertainty is the flexible problem solving that allows diversity in the paths to the truth of the "real" opened by the knowledge of mathematics. Participation, problem solving, and collaboration give children flexibility in learning how to appreciate the majesty of that already given reality. On the other hand and equally important, the pedagogy fixes the cultural relations (community) in which the images and narratives of school subjects are sought.

The alchemy of mathematics in the curriculum produces the agency, participation, and community within particular internments and enclosures. Mathematics is a strategy of reason to distance oneself from the immediate through an abstract and seemingly universal knowledge of humanity that constitutes the homeless mind. That distancing loops back into the accounting of the principles to guide everyday life.

Equally important, the alchemy of school subjects embodies double gestures. It produces comparative differences that congeal as human-kinds that the school acts upon—the problem solver, the disadvantaged, the urban child, and the child left behind. A continuum of values is established to recognize, differentiate, and divide. In this process of normalization, exclusion is not an act of deliberate avoidance but a paradoxical result of the distinctions and differentiation that map the inclusion of the child.

If we relate the increased emphasis on children's involvement and collaboration to the alchemy, the naturalizing of the world in school subjects may actually narrow the spaces open for participation and action. Curriculum today has been rewritten to produce greater student involvement and participation, personal relevance, and emotional accessibility. But as McEneaney (2003) reported on the international changes of science teaching, the attention given to student participation is a double-sided practice. The increased participation entails increased and wider scientific authority over claims about the management of the natural world. Children's participation and problem solving are organized to learn the majesty of the procedures, styles of argument, and symbolic system that assert the truthfulness of the expertise of science.

The curriculum disowns the fragility or conditionality of the world by assembling a particular programmed agency for the child in its stead. This produces limits on "thought" and reason, reducing the problems of the curriculum to protocols of "participation." The conclusions of academic expertise are located outside the bounds of children's questioning and problem solving. The latter serves as procedures through which to ascertain the givenness of reality, what I earlier referred to as the conventional knowledge of a discipline. Pedagogy fixes the cultural relations (community) in which the Platonic images of mathematics are sought. Where uncertainty leads the personal explorations, there is the certainty of outcome that has flexibility in the routes that the child takes.

CHAPTER **9**

Designing People in Instruction and Research: Processes of Abjection

Agency and the Fears of Those Left Behind
in Instruction and Research

The notion of design at the beginning of the 20th century (discussed in chapters 4 and 5) is reassembled in instructional designs, research designs, and design research. Design was to order the "nature" of people and things, bringing God's design into human affairs (see, e.g., Becker, 1932). The notion of design in reforms and social sciences were political strategies to act upon others by getting them to act in their own interest. It entailed a specialized knowledge to estimate, calculate, measure, evaluate, discipline, and judge ourselves. Today, teachers and children design their own learning or research in order to fulfill cosmopolitan narratives of democracy, empowerment, and human agency in globalization presumed in the unity given to the "learning society."

The first section of this chapter continues the earlier discussion of reforms as democratizing and producing agency and the expertise of designing the cosmopolitan principles of reason and rationality. The following sections explore three sites of designing schools and designing people: (1) instructional design in online learning, and two research approaches to produce successful reforms that seem ideologically different, (2) the federally sanctioned research to produce rigorous research designs that provide "evidence-based research," and (3) design research as a pragmatic strategy for the continual assessment and modification of school practices. The different research embodies constructivist and behaviorist psychologies that overlap with theories about social systems. The final section examines how sameness and difference are inscribed in the projects of design. The imaginary unity of "all children" is the product of the processes of abjection.

The discussion further considers the distinctions and differentiations of the cosmopolitanism of the past chapters. Design embodies qualities of the conditionality of life spoken of earlier as the ubiquitous future, where one participates in self-generating systems that are premised on the school as a system that does not allow chance to be in charge. The search for "useful knowledge" in different projects of design stabilizes and tames change to give focus to the making people. The provisions for enlightened participation, I argue, exude distrust of those participating and processes of abjection.

Design as the Philosopher's Stone

Design enunciates values and desires that include the hope of democracy and its cosmopolitan future. Projects of design are to provide greater involvement and participation. As with the alchemists and then later in the quarrel of the Ancients and Moderns (who believed that the 18th-century philosophers and their modes of living were superior to their closest ancestors'), contemporary policy and research utilizes the problem of design as the faith that research has found enlightened paths that show "what works" as school reform. The instruments of design are today's philosopher's stone that unlocks the secrets of what unites everything to ensure choice and continuous innovation.

Today's philosopher's stone is in the reassembling of the earlier 20th century's term of social engineering. The tasks of planning is concerned, at one level, with the unfinished cosmopolitan. The life of choice and innovation is, ironically, spoken about as engineering through replication; that is, identifying successful programs (and the people who operate in them) as universally transportable models to the universe of schools. Replication is an interesting word choice, carrying an image of isomorphic compliance across contexts and people. The replication is embedded in the quest for designing methodological rigor for "stable explanations" (National Research Council, 2002, p. 3). Education sciences function with unspoken norms about what is possible" and desirable (p. 49).

Teacher education as well as school reforms assume the same qualities of research. The continual assertion in contemporary research and policy is an already at-hand knowledge necessary for the complete success of the new professionalization projects. This is possible because of "the replication of successful programs" through studies of expert teachers: What teachers do as expert teachers is known[1] and replicable, as "studies show that teacher expertise is the most important factor in student's achievement (National Commission on Teaching and America's Future, 1996, p. 6). That expertise now "has discovered" what is necessary for producing successful teachers, and this research has declared that the "new standards-based curriculum [is] working" (Grossman et al., 2005, p. 221).

The certainty of the knowledge now at hand circulates across professional associations as the principle to direct reflection and practice. The American Council on Education asserts that "persuasive new research, when combined with past findings" (American Council on Education, 1999, p. 1) will make the school successful. The teachers' union, the American Federation of Teachers (1999), argues that "Scientific research has achieved the knowledge necessary to teach children to 'read well' for all but a handful of severely disabled children" (p. 5). Only the foolhardy would not recognize that the scientific knowledge available will open the door to the progressive future! Teacher educators must be conversant with the new research findings for, "given what we know about how teachers learn and develop", it is possible to create "teacher education programs that are effective in enabling teachers to acquire the knowledge, skills, and dispositions that will allow them to succeed?" (Hammerness, Darling-Hammon, with others, 2005, pp. 390–391). The enlightened teacher is designed and internalized through particular forms of expertise formulated through standards.

Designing Instruction, Designing Research, and Designing People

The expertise of science is expressed as in the service of democratic ideal in pursuit of the unfinished cosmopolitanism. The sentiment of design is collaboration, participation, flexibility, and multiple solutions given as evidence of democracy; the idea of just powers is derived from the consent of the governed, or at least the adult governed.[2] It is argued, for example, that school decisions are best made at the site where problems arise. Efforts among local authorities, parents, and teachers are viewed as yielding better policies, increased teacher expertise, and innovation because teachers are in charge of their own practices.

The participatory practices of design are strategies of ordering and governing who people are and should be. That governing is embodied in the concern with "useful" knowledge about what works.

Instructional Design as a Foundational Story of Future Cosmopolitanism

The *design of instruction* is a commonly used phrase to talk about the management of curriculum and teaching. Instructional design is a term that goes back to at least the scientific management of curriculum movement in the 1920s. Today, that field is heavily influenced by overlapping of cognitive and behaviorist psychologies and more recently by "information-processing" approaches.

Instructional design is given in the name of democratic schooling. That classroom democracy has a practical quality with reference to the teacher. It assumes a consensus and stability for dealing with, ironically, ambiguity and uncertainty. Agency is linked to a consensus about social and human goals and purposes in working on the child and teacher. Wiggins and McTighe (2005), for example, focus on instruction as "backward design." Backward design is analogous to an architect's planning. Design starts with the desired but unspoken goals of instruction or reform, and then works backward to the search for materials and methods to enable the choices for teaching to achieve the "desired" results (p. 13). The nature of the desired results is not specified other than the results are to serve democratic principles. Backward design is to identify the specific learning sought by the teaching, identifying the evidence of success, and then set the travel plans to get to the destination in a developmental sequence. Instructional designs are to identify the "timeless, essential and overarching knowledge" (p. vii).

I use here the previous discussion of online learning to discuss instructional design as a technology of making people (Maeroff, 2003). Online instruction revisions (and visions) the foundational stories of the early 20th-century American exceptionalism in today's use of the computer. Online instruction embodies the prophecy of the new national beginning and the perfection of cosmopolitanism. Online learning "will be an enabling one, as printing presses have been to the production of books" (p. 3). The electronic cosmopolitanism is a borderless humanity that sheds the provincialism of the nation and of the harmful effects of past traditions through its universality to reach across borders. "These programs, with their ability to transcend state lines and even national borders, circumvent geographic barriers." The new educational practices are to produce a world citizen through the virtual spaces of online learning, with the erasure of provincialism that is enclosed in the educational systems that "were often used in the past to protect campus-based education from competition" (p. 4).

The 17th-century Puritan sermons of Jeremiad's describe the fall of man and then the finding of grace. Today they are given in a new pulpit. The rhetorical style of the American Jeremiad in online learning locates the causes of school degeneration through student failures and then predicts progress for all children. The idea of degeneration or fall is in the "system that has often been inflexible and reluctant to change" (Maeroff, 2003, p. 18) and in the teacher who does not embrace the prophecy of technology and does not find the fulfillment of the future cosmopolitan world. "Instructors who in coming years ignore the potential of web-based embellishments will be as remiss as their peers in past years who did not expect students to enrich their learning by consulting sources beyond their books" (p. 3). To prevent the fall is to have the vision of the new delivery system. "Such a shift will require a vision of educators who recognize that education can be education regardless of its form of delivery" (p. 3).

Design is to bring the unfinished cosmopolitan into existence. The child is to live a life of continual choices, personal responsibility, and self-management of one's risks and destiny. Instructional design makes possible the continuous self-actualizing of an unfinished life. Online learning "gives students choices in completing tasks; lets students have some choice in the difficulty levels of assignments or tasks that they complete; and give students some discretion about when they complete particular tasks" (Maeroff, 2003, p. 102).

The making of choices is placed in psychological registers. Agency is produced through one's desire, motivation, satisfaction, and self-responsibility. Individualized instruction is the technology to make possible those desires. Online instruction is to enable all children who "desire to make education more convenient" (Maeroff, 2003, p. 76), "have greater achievement and satisfaction" (p. 83), and assume "self-responsibility and motivation" (p. 95). The design of instruction erased differences through the psychological unity of "all children."

Democracy, as a practice of instructional design, is stabilizing the system of participation. That stabilization is to work psychologically on the child who is motivated, satisfied, and self-responsible for pursuing life as the unfinished cosmopolitan.

*Design as Research: The Expertise of Empowerment
in Continuous Innovation*

Closely aligned with the field of instructional design is design research. The object of design research is to provide a finer-tuned relation between the conditions of schooling and the self-government of people. The word *reengineer* is used to talk about the mode of living in which the teacher and child continually "innovate" through principles homologous with unfinished cosmopolitanism.

As with online learning, democracy is the purpose of design. "Design and engineering are generative and transformative" (Kelly, 2003, p. 4). Research is anchored to the everyday life of schooling to enable individual participation and agency. Design research is the continual and fluid process of inventing tools that bring reform and the ongoing development of the system in an intimate relationship with the participants. Using mathematics teaching as an exemplar that enunciates sentiments of popular participation and the significance of the relevancies of personal life, "learning should be contextualized, and of ideas that mathematics learning should be more closely tied to students' experience" (Design-Based Research Collective, 2003, p. 5).

The alchemist and the philosopher's stone return, with design as the substance to bring enlightenment and to conclude with the great work of the pursuit of happiness and progress. Individual happiness is placed in the landscape of professional knowledge. Design research is formulated as a technology of direct and continuous intervention in which there is harmony and consensus between individual actions and the function of the systems of instruction.

Certainty is uncertainty in instructional design and research is enunciated through the apparatus of "system" that orders reform as its central assumption of coordination. The notion of a system was used in social and political theories of the 1970s to argue the need to treat social events as systems of interrelating parts and networks through which consensus and stability are achieved in public policy (see, e.g., Easton, 1965).

The particular use of system in the design of instruction has a relation to the prior discussions about school reform and research. The literature takes on the characteristics of the school and reform as a problem of social "systems."[3] The more general reform discourses suggest that past reforms have been too piecemeal in their approaches. Change is viewed as requiring a more scientific and coherent approach that coordinates the implementation of practices demonstrated as working. Conceptualizations are about systems of interrelated structures and overlapping functions through standards reforms and research can produce effective reforms in which there is "no child left behind."

The assumption of systems is important as it assumes an equilibrium and consensus that circulate in the different sites of teaching and teacher education, the design research programs, and plans about partnerships and local flexibility (see, e.g., Porter & Smithson, 2001). The National Commission on Teaching and America's Future (1996, 2003), for example, focuses on system variables to coordinate different layers of recruitment, retention, and performance standards. The goal is "clear and consistent visions of teaching and learning," the integration between university instruction and clinical practices, and performance standards that "guarantee" adequate professional and subject matter knowledge.

Design research designs agency within the boundaries of an open system. The open system is one that continually changes and yet is anchored in the continual monitoring and conceptualizing to order the process to provide direction to change itself. "The educational system may be described as open, complex, nonlinear, organic, historical, and social" (Kelly, 2003, p. 3).

The openness of the system is in fact to provide tidiness and consensus through constant monitoring in the delivery of instruction. The stability and universality are inscribed through the notion of "sustainable intervention." "Sustainable intervention requires understanding how and why an innovation works within a setting over time and across setting" (Design-Based Research Collective, 2003, p. 6). The evolution and improvement of the complex systems entails negotiation processes to provide harmony between the "interests" of the intervention system and the specific classroom situation (p. 3). Design is the procedures of researchers listening to people affected in the contexts and responding to them as active agents. "Thus, emergent behaviors of students in response to activities [drive] development of the intervention and development of theory" (Design-Based Research Collective, 2003, p. 6).

The openness and "listening" is bounded through the research ordering and framing the spaces of action in schooling. Action is the designing of the continual flow of events and communication. Research conceptualizes, organizes interventions, and mediates between the "interests" of reform and a complex set of individual actions and dispositions. Participation and collaboration are to make "the system's actions relevant to its own evolution and improvement" (Kelly, 2003, p. 3). Research is in a close relation in the "interactions between intervention and setting" that ironically is labeled "open" (Design-Based Research Collective, 2003, p. 5).

A more subtle notion of design in this genre is the design experiment as an instructional theory. The design experiment is "both to develop sequences of instructional activities and associated tools, and to conduct analyses of the process of the students' learning and the means by which that learning is supported and organized" (Cobb, 2001, p. 456). Learning is viewed as an ecology of a complex, interaction system. Research is to "engineer" particular forms of learning and systematically study the activities of teaching that supports that learning (see, e.g., Cobb, Confrey, diSessa, Lehrer, & Schauble, 2003; also see Halverson, 2004).

Cognitive theory and instructional practices overlap as a process of monitoring teachers and children to bring external system goals into the internal norms and values of school practices. The intervention of learning combines social and individual qualities of the interior of the mind to increase efficiency in learning. Design research is the continual processes of testing and modifying "conjectures as informed by ongoing analyses of both students' reasoning and the classroom learning environment" (Cobb, 2001, p. 458). The children's learning is brought into a functional relation with teachers and school administrators to order action through the practical knowledge or "wisdom" of the ongoing processes of schooling.

The idea of system is a particular theoretical intervention about the unity of the whole. The open system directs attention to uncertainty of the future yet is designing that uncertainty in stable systems from which rules and principles are generated to order the change, agency, and participation and collaboration. The system places actions in a functional structure (system) given equilibrium by coordinating ongoing implementation processes grounded in the everyday life of the school. The function of research is to provide a complete knowledge that will "close the credibility gap between unscientific research and detachment of researchers" (Design-Based Research Collective, 2003, p. 5).

Democratization is formatted with the epistemological boundaries of the system. It is, for example, taking into account those who participate on the ground—teachers, students, and parents; but within the rules of "reason" through which action is organized conceptually within what constitutes the operational system. That ground "listened" to is not merely teachers' experience. Experience is organized and classified through "anchored instruction" and as the technology for bringing research closer to reforming conditions and people.

The research anchors classroom communications and interactions in a seamless process of theorizing and intervening that brings order out of what might otherwise be chaos. The anchoring is a "micro-analysis," whose intervention produces close monitoring as a continual feedback loop for designing the will to act. "Micro-analysis of student interactions with activities based on that principle enabled redesign and refinement of activities, and ultimately refinement of the underlying interest-drive learning framework" (Design-Based Research Collective, 2003, p. 6).

The processes of calculating, ordering, and changing through design are portrayed as neutral to the system's goals. Design Research asserts an impartiality of assisting in interventions to change and innovate in schooling. Science brings

> the values and problems of the society that supports it and sets its goals.... Educational researchers [use their professional language] to generate distinctions and descriptions for the system. The distinctions and descriptions themselves and interventions designed from them make the system's actions relevant to its own evolution and improvement. (Kelly, 2003, p. 3)

The neutrality is to allow the impersonal system of the school to achieve its purposes by utilizing a language of "the scientific processes of discovery, exploration, confirmation, and dissemination" (Kelly, 2003, p. 3).

The impersonality is not neutral. Design research is political in the sense that I have been using that term. It erases differences in a democratic gesture of participation that simultaneously scripts the rules that order conduct. The design procedures order and classify the everyday activities of classrooms as a system in a harmonious and consensual set of relations. The flexibility and continual assessment tame chance through giving order and tidiness to the "things" and the people to be changed.

The system of instruction is to produce more efficient interactions between the social "context" and its individuals. That efficiency, as in early progressive movements, entails a particular populism. Yet that populism has certain internments and enclosures.

One's life is made into an event of planning with a coterie of experts to assist in that planning (Berger et al., 1974). The psychological classifications and distinctions inscribe principles of cosmopolitanism, the child who lives a life of continual choice and change that matches the system in which action is anchored. The working of the open system is bounded by the ordering and classifications of psychological theories of learning, motivation, communication, and individualization that are to change "the metacognition of the child and the teacher" (Kelly, 2003, pp. 3, 5). The science of complexity is ironically the desire towards certainty—to "lose the credibility gap" and the incompleteness of knowledge. The openness of the design process is a closed-loop system that is driven by its own internal logic.

Research Designs and "Evidence-Based" Reforms: Replications as Change

The philosopher's stone does not disappear in the National Research Council's (2002) commissioned report for the implementation of U.S. congressional legislation, No Child Left Behind (2002). The National Research Council's report is to identify the precise criteria of science that will provide warranted data about school reforms. The report uses the language of "rigorous" design procedures and replication in the focus on design technologies of research.[4]

The warrant of this report, as is design research, is a democratic, inclusive society. The use of rigorous design procedures is bound to "the nation's commitment to improve the education of all children requires continuing efforts to improve its research capacity" (National Research Council, 2002, p. 21). In these guarantees, the normative assertions about democracy and an inclusive society are taken for granted. They are treated as a previously agreed-upon consensus and in no need for any discussion. The problem is only instrumental in identifying "What Works," the title of the federal clearinghouse on research to set apart proven success reforms tied to the No Child Left Behind legislation.

There are certain overlaps and distinctions between the two designs in research. The purpose of design in "evidence-based research" as well is the engineering of people. Both research approaches are to find useful knowledge about what works through the design of the most efficient methods of intervention. The criterion of usefulness of knowledge is not the same. One is through continual interventions and monitoring in the engineering of people; the other is in the control of variables that generates "verifiable" knowledge in "re-engineering" that follows the "gold standards" of randomized trails of medical and drug testing.[5] These gold standards are the "real" science, as design experiments do not control variables and verifiable knowledge that enable testing to judge competing hypotheses and replication (Shavelson, Philips, Towne, & Feuer, 2003). The methodological problem of design is ultimately to provide stable, harmonious systems of practice about what works for the purpose of engineering.

Rigorously designing the methods of research offers a different version of the disinterested (neutral) science than design research for the rational assessments of reforms.[6] The report asserts, for example, that the only interest of the education sciences is to support a dialogue that contributes to "a comprehensive perspective in which 'scientifically-based' education research" contributes to "improving education policy and practice" (Alberts, 2002, p. viii). More powerful than the doxologies of previous religious cosmologies, the proper design is to enable the prescriptions of what works as successful reforms and thus contributes to broader goals of society without bias to political parties or ideology. "The scientist discovers the basis for what is possible" (National Research Council, 2002, p. 49).

The design of science is the shepherd that steers others in the name of democracy. The name for democracy is the collaboration among "various stakeholders." These various stakeholders are researchers, policymakers, and practitioners who work in partnership in deciding what is best for schools. To encourage the close proximity of research knowledge to classrooms, the National Research Council calls for "partnerships between researchers and practitioners" to bring the expertise of research directly into schools and classrooms (National Research Council, 2002, pp. 94–95). In contrast to Design Research, collaboration is to identify the rigorous designing of methods and generating the appropriate data in order to find out what works and thus which reforms should be replicated to attain more effective schools. The sciences of education provide politicians, citizens, and school systems with "hard evidence," "impartiality," and "reasonable, rigorous, and scientific deliberation" (pp. 12–13).

One might argue that the National Research Council's claims of what constitutes methods have weak evidence in the history, sociology, or philosophy of science (Popkewitz, 2005), or that the word *stakeholders* is to define a representational and instrumental notion of collaboration and participation that has a weak relation with modern political theories of the substantive qualities of democracy. One could also suggest the report lacks any historical grasp of the particular and unique patterns of government and social science in the development of American exceptionalism, as discussed in chapter 3.

My interest in the National Research Council's report, however, is not with its own failures to use evidence to establish the claims of science that the report asserts as standards (Popkewitz, 2004b). The National Research Council's report is of interest because of the unspoken cultural theses of the lifelong learner and others that overlap with instructional design and design research. Science has the dual qualities discussed earlier as classifications, distinctions, and calculations to order and plan (design) changing the world that operates to change people. The useful knowledge of science is the inscription of the particular calculated democracy to "make people."

The Erasures of the System: All Children Are the Same and Different

The engineering of the designs of instruction and research is a cultural thesis of the whole that erases difference. The imaginary whole and unity were captured in previous chapters through the juxtaposition of the phrase that "all children will learn," with the child left behind whose qualities are recognized for inclusion and cast out of the boundaries of the "civilized"—the mode of life of the lifelong learner who has esteem, self-responsibility in making choices, problem solves, works collaboratively, and continually innovates. The "all" unites all parts of the social whole into a particular sameness from which individual children are classified, measured, and divided.

The Hope of Inclusion and the Difference of Dangerous Populations

The complexity of abjections is in the distinctions embracing the qualities of the "all" in the inclusionary project. The Principles and Standards for School Mathematics, for example, states that "All students, regardless of their personal characteristics, background, or physical challenges, must have opportunities to study—and support to learn—mathematics" (NCTM, 2000, p. 12). The unspoken qualities of "all students" refer to the qualities of the lifelong learner whose mode of life differentiated from the distinctions and differentiations of the child not living as the unfinished cosmopolitan.

Differences are placed into statistical and probability theories of populations that homogenize and differentiate the unity. The distinctions of Others circulate through overlapping psychological, social, pedagogical, and political distinctions.

The child who does not succeed is characterized by what the child psychologically lacks. To return to online learning, motivation is what "all" children must have to live as the unfinished cosmopolitan. The children who are motivated design their own life to give them "choices in completing tasks; lets students have some choice in the difficulty levels of assignments or tasks that they complete; and gives students some discretion about when they complete particular tasks" (Maeroff, 2003, p. 102).

The lack of progress of struggling students, it is asserted, stems from their feeling that they lack any power over their own learning. This struggle and lack of power are given as the psychological quality of the lack of motivation. The proposed future is threatened by child who is not motivated. The child of difference is the nontraditional child, a term that assumes the juxtaposing qualities of tradition with what is outside of that space. This latter child lacks the motivation to control his or her life and exercise the agency of the new revolutionary life. Online courses, it is argued, offers a breakthrough, a way to put them in control for the first time (Maeroff, 2003, p. 218).

The category of "nontraditional students" quickly morphs into social distinctions that do not allow inclusion. The nontraditional student becomes a determinant category about moral/immoral life that revisions the beginning of the 20th-century Social Question about the moral disorder of the urban child and family. The fears of the "nontraditional" students are registered as not profiting and failing to learn from online learning because of their lack of motivation, preventing them from obtaining the proper education.

The fear of reform seems as though it is not being inclusive. That fear is expressed as not reaching the nontraditional student and thus preventing the cosmopolitan mode of life as an expression of the equitable society. The fear of not including erases difference. The child who fails is one lacking equal opportunities because his or her life is surrounded by the crime and violence of the inner city:

> [S]tudents who live in inner-city neighborhoods are so besieged by crime that travel between school and home is a threatening ordeal. The chance to stay at home and attend virtual classes might provide some relief. As it is, crime, violence, and drug dealing have forced school systems in some urban locales to consider holding classes in community rooms at housing projects so that children would not have to venture onto unsafe streets. (Maeroff, 2003, p. 216)

The deployment of the category of motivation simultaneously erases difference through its insertion of difference. The erasure is found in the solution that is to make everyone the same. "While poor children drill on the computer, higher-achieving students have more chances to work with data bases, spreadsheets, and graphics, for example" (Maeroff, 2003, p. 221).

The erasure is also a psychologicalization of the cause of failure. Motivation is inserted as something natural to the child and missing in some children. Motivation is inscribed in the instructional design of online learning as strategies of individualized instruction. That is, individualized instruction is a technology to produce children who "desire to make education more convenient" (Maeroff, 2003, p. 76), have greater achievement and satisfaction (p. 83), and have self-responsibility and motivation (p. 95).

Designing the interior of the child's desire, to which motivation is linked, has particular historical configurations in psychology and pedagogy (Danziger, 1997). Early psychology did not provide explanations of everyday conduct. It was not until the emergence of mass schooling that an interest emerged about removing children's "fatigue" in learning through calculating and influencing the children's will, motives, interests, needs, and desires. This treatment of inner thought, daily life, and experience was the object of administration. Motivation became a key player in this administration; it is neither a disinterested and impartial grouping nor a neutral category. Its historical configuration is important in considering how psychology mutates to the present to inscribe principles about who the child is.

If I return to the child who constructs knowledge and meaning, the erasure of difference is inscribed in the pedagogical constructivist psychologies. Standards reforms of school subjects are cast as a responsive pedagogy to the diverse sense-making practices of children. The diversity is a glance to the egalitarian values of pedagogy and a strategy to ensure the success of "linguistic minorities students [who] acquire the mainstream literacies they need to succeed in school and beyond" (Grossman et al., 2005, p. 225). The cosmopolitan hospitality to others is responding to the diversity of the classroom in which teachers "consider the issue of the most effective practices for different groups of students. One set of practices might include culturally responsive pedagogy, and what this might look like in different subject matters" (p. 225).

The call for diversity is met with engineering to the conditions of schooling that changes children. "Moreover, to address the challenges of, for example, low-performing schoolings, the 'achievement gap,' and language diversity, educators today require new knowledge to reengineer schools in effective ways" (National Research Council, 2002, p. 12). That reengineering of schools entails reengineering and abjecting people. As one travels to the U.S Department of Education's Web site to document programs supported by rigorous evidence (U.S. Department of Education, December 2003; http://www.ed.gov/nclb), the "proven interventions" are narratives of the dangers of dangerous populations.

The hopes and fears of difference are scaled in the What Works Clearinghouse. The listing of programs continually recognizes the rescue of populations for inclusion that establishes difference.[7] There is fear of the federal government, the states, school districts, schools, and teachers who do not implement the reforms properly through the dictates of approaches based on scientific evidence. There are hopes and its fears of students, parents, and communities expressed in the language of participation and collaboration and of those who do not have the proper upbringing habits in the home. There is the fear of the achievement gap between rich and poor, between the Anglo and minority, with the latter categories as universalized as if everyone knows who fits and does not fit the distinctions. The category of "disadvantaged students" provides another category of the dangers to the unity of the whole and an inclusive society. The fears are articulated in discussions about teacher quality and limited-English-proficient students, sexuality ("Just say no to premarital sex"), and the need for faith-based education to overcome moral disorder. The dangers are also of others outside of the United States, such as those classified by national security issues that are given expression in teaching the "uncommonly taught languages" such as Arabic, Chinese, and Farsi.

If I use one program identified at the Web site for What Works, there are fears of children "at risk for developmental delays and school failure" (Carolina Abecedarian Project, http://www.promisingpractices.net). The hope of the reform is "to create an educational, stimulating, and structured environment to promote growth and learning and to enhance school readiness." The hope is also the fear circulating in the populational statistics that racializes the processes to create inclusion. Specialized categories of the child are produced, for example, by creating populational groups of children who attend day-care centers 6 to 8 hours a day, or dysfunctional families as counted by the number of visits that resource teachers make to homes of populations targeted for intervention. The rigorous scientific evidence of these calculations generates divisions in assessment indexes that compare normalcy by defining high-risk children as those who match "13 socio-demographic factors associated with poor intellectual and scholastic progress" with specific racial groups (98% participating are African American).

The Child Not in the Space of "All": The Urban Child Left Behind

The cultural territory of the child left behind is a space of fears; fears that the search for useful knowledge and the right procedures of reform will not provide for redemption and total inclusion; and a territory that threatens the civilization and its "civilized" people through the modes of living of the populations of the child and family who are disadvantaged, at risk, and urban. The child and family embodied in the interventions targeted for rescue are determinate classifications about the "unhappy" populations who do not or cannot pursue happiness. The qualities that constitute the unhappy populations function as a determinate category produced by the succinct chronological, cultural, physiological, and psychological characteristics that I discussed above.

Who is placed in the unlivable spaces of the unhappy populations that are outside and different from the constituted distinctions of *all children?* Using an ethnographic study of an alternative teacher education program for urban and rural schools (Popkewitz, 1998b), the child left behind is the cultural thesis about the urban child. At the start of the 20th century, the urban child was racialized as different; immigrant groups from southern and eastern Europe, Irish, or African American. 'Urban' also included people who did and did not live in the city, Asians and Native Americans. Then and today, the urban child has multiple qualities to differentiate through cultural theses about who he or she is and should be. The urban child in contemporary schooling is functionally related to the succinct categories generated about the child left behind and comparatively part of yet different from the lifelong learner.

To consider the construction of difference and division is to recognize that the geographical designation of urban is not about a physical place but a cultural space. This is evident when the word is examined. American cities, for example, are spaces with great wealth and a cosmopolitan urbaneness that coexist with the spaces of poverty and racial segregation. Urban can be urbane, the cosmopolitan value about the civilized and culturally sophisticated. Children who live in the high-rise apartments and brownstones of American cities appear as urbane and not urban. The urbane coexists with the urban, who are the child and family of poverty, racialized groups, and those signified as "immigrants." These determinate categories of kinds of people function as cultural theses of modes of living cast as outside and as the "unhappy" populations.

That cultural thesis of those cast outside is evident is the classifications associated with urban education, a political designation of populations targeted for social inventions. Urban education and the urban child live in suburbia and rural areas as well as in the "inner city." The categories and classifications of the child in a teacher education program in urban and rural schools around the U.S., for example, were identical (Popkewitz, 1998b). The troubled/troubling child was discursively assembled through the same sets of distinctions in pedagogy. The child had "low expectations," low self-esteem, family dysfunctions, and different learning styles. The child was recognized as disadvantaged, in need of rescue, and the mode of life feared as culturally dangerous.

In linguistic and practical terms, then, urban and rural children are ordered through the same universalizing sets of distinctions. They both are urban in the sense of the characteristics and qualities that make up who they are. The categories and characteristics of those classified as children left behind are like those of all "urban" children. The urban child occupies unlivable spaces, threats to the cosmopolitan ordering of individuality and belonging.[8]

The child left behind is also the family left behind. The federal Web site concerned with reforms that respond to the "achievement gap" between children left behind and "all children" emphasizes the mode of living in the family that will provide success for the child (http://www.ed.gov/nclb/methods/whatworks/). The reforms are given as evidence of democratization of schooling enhanced by parental participation in changing the modes of living in the family. Parents are to participate in reforms of site-based management, home-school collaboration, parent "choice" vouchers, and the new charter schools.

The errant family is both inside and outside of normalcy. The distinctions and divisions of the urban child organize school-family connections in the recalibrations of the cultural theses of cosmopolitanism and its others. Research on the family and children's school failure, for example, classifies the child as living in a "fragile" and "vulnerable" family (Hildago, Siu, Bright, Swap, & Epstein, 1995, p. 500). The parents are differentiated as having a lower level of education and socioeconomic status, as immigrants (the length of time living in country), and through categories of ethnicity (living or not living in ethnic enclaves), among others (p. 501). The social and economic classifications of the child and family linked social structural relations and communications patterns to gender, such as whether the mother is a single or teen parent (p. 501; David and Lucille Packard Foundation, 2002). The aggregate of the "fragile" and "vulnerable" family acquires the abstraction of the sciences for the seemingly impersonal management of the reason that defines personal capabilities and the capacities of people.

The distinctions and division of the urban child and child left behind are shaped and fashioned with the very construction of the lifelong learner discussed in chapter 7. The child left behind exists in an in-between place of requiring rescue and excluded as different. That difference is the partitioning of the sensible and "reasonable" in which the lifelong learner and the urban, left behind child form a continuum of values. Each is dependent on its Others as they are part of the same phenomenon in the construction of the child.

Democracy as Designing People

The designing of classrooms and people is a governing practice that is never merely descriptive of some natural reasoning of the child, idiosyncratic to a particular classroom, or a description that captures good teaching practices and "what works." The different traditions of design in pedagogy and research embody the "promise of social renewal," which is one of the important objects of social and educational sciences (Wagner, 2001b). That idea is that intellectuals had to move closer to action, and the theories of social science needed to become much more pertinent and applicable, by developing a useful knowledge with which they could direct change. This notion included European and North American policy sciences that crossed ideological barriers. For example, action research (*conricerca*) of the Italian Quaderni Rossi group, a leftist Italian political group, criticized traditional workers' organizations and sought to engage in research that would produce the autonomy of workers dissociated from established union organizations and that would reject the capitalist state, society, and its way of life. The design research projects discussed are also moves for action research through the planning to calculate the knowledge that is to be used (useful) for democracies to arise.

The expertise of design as "in service of the democratic ideal," an expression of progressive reform movements, is connected and reformulated in contemporary registers of social administration, freedom, and difference. The reengineering of the child and teacher today is told as a salvation theme of empowerment by applying the proper technologies of change.

The educational site of online learning, the design procedures of science, and design research are to move closer into the domains of what constitutes experience, designing "what works" in planning conditions and people. Reforms offer a self-governance that echoes the older Puritan notions of instruction as converting ordinances. Whereas the Puritan converting ordinances related to evangelizing works to bring one's salvation, the principles generated through contemporary designs are secular acts about the future and the happiness of the cosmopolitan is a double gesture of abjection.

Whatever the merits of the different approaches to designing classrooms and designing research, the salvation themes of empowerment and democracy appear without history. Views of the child as an empowered actor and the community as the enactment of democracy are made possible by a range of historical discourses that related concepts of society and the individual as elements of modern government.

CHAPTER 10

The Reason of School Pedagogy, Research, and the Limits of Cosmopolitanism

This final chapter brings together some issues of the politics of schooling that emerged in the prior study of cosmopolitanism. My intent is not a summary or conclusion in a more traditional sense but to use the analysis to think further about the problematic enterprise of schooling and its research. The chapter begins with considering the internments and enclosures of unfinished cosmopolitanism as a fatalism that inscribes comparative instantiations. The next section examines the fears of democracy that circulate in reform and the question of "useful" knowledge. Ironically, the search for useful knowledge and what works is pessimistic about the cosmopolitan attitude toward freedom and democracy. I then consider the limits of the study of cosmopolitanism as it is bound by its general attitude about reason and rationality. The final two sections explore the principles about equity in educational studies and its limitations for the study of schooling.

The historian Carl Becker in *The Heavenly City of the Eighteenth-Century Philosophers* (1932) wrote about the 18th-century shift in philosophical thought. He argued that 18th-century thinkers moved from knowledge given by God to knowledge residing in nature. The city of man [*sic*] would find progress in the secular world. The shift in location of the subject matter from God to nature, however, did not entail a change in the system of reason about the pregiven rules to order "things."

Becker's argument has analogies to cosmopolitanism, pedagogy, and the age of reform. From the 18th century to the present, I have argued that cosmopolitanism functions as a set of sacred universalized values about reason and science in the emancipatory project of progress. The age of reform directs attention to this continuity of inscribing cultural theses of cosmopolitanism in the making of people. The universality was never universal, but particular. Cosmopolitanism in different times and spaces instantiated particular historical systems of reason. Those systems of reason divide the "civilized" child from those outside its unity. Further, cosmopolitanism was not one thing, but complex relations of inclusion and exclusion that function as processes of abjection. Today, the abject are given the categories of the disadvantaged, urban, at risk, and left behind child; recognized for inclusion and paradoxically radically cast out as different.

The age of reform is a historical trajectory of things of difference in the cultural theses about modes of living. The inclusive dream in planning lifelong learning, the learning society, or the information society in the contemporary landscape of school reform is not produced through the same assemblies, connections, and disconnections that ordered American progressive education and its sciences of the child. Nor are those past and present reform programs merely to find effective paths to a utopian future. What is taken as natural and sacred in the commonsense of reform are particular internments and enclosures. Theories of learning, development, community, and problem solving articulate double gestures as comparative principles about the honored feats of the noble with the fears of the threats and dangers to the civilized future.

In making this argument I realize that I have suggested a different approach to change and the politics of schooling from the conventional wisdom of education science. The wisdom articulated as knowledge has to be useful for progressive change. The idea of use and practicality moves across different ideological positions, expressed as bridging the gap between research and practices. I have argued historically in this book about the politics of the idea of useful through exploring the idea of planning people. This way of "telling truth" is not naturally "there." The planning to be "useful" is an effect of power rather than merely the desire of being "useful."

While I have explored the politics of the planning for useful knowledge in the social and education sciences, I want to turn here to its particular rhetorical politics in public policy and research. That rhetorical style is of the American Jeremiad (Bercovitch, 1978). The formulation about change is drawn from the Puritan's sermons. It is to first decry the evils that produce the downing of the walls of the temple and then prescribes the optimism of resurrections. The rhetoric form of the Jeremiad today would read as, "Critique is not enough. What is needed are actions to confront the challenges of modern societies and schooling." Pessimism is out and optimism is in. But the optimism is joined with the promise of useful knowledge. What is needed is something useful to guide and direct how to get to the utopian future.

The historicizing of cosmopolitanism is in fact optimism within the imperative of planning people. That optimism is in the Enlightenment's faith in reason as a method of scrutinizing the present in the hope that other alternatives are possible to present arrangements. The strategy is to make conditional what has seemed natural, disrupting the givenness of the present. Once we agree that inequities exist, express outrage to the sufferings encountered, utter the words that the world is socially constructed and thus changeable, and continue with the topoi that every child should learn, these agreements defer to the givenness of difference that marks out divisions as sites of intervention. The politics of schooling is in the givennesses and its partitioning of sensibilities.

The denaturalizing of cosmopolitanism does not eliminate its commitments to a humane and just world. It is a strategy to continually test the limits to the manner in which the objects of reflection and acts are produced to honor those commitments. The inclusive dream in planning lifelong learning, the learning society, or the information society is not merely to find effective paths to the utopian future. The strategy of study, to play with the analysis, is concerned with agency and change by making visible the limitations of the normative prescriptions that circulate about the "useful" knowledge of research and identifying what works.

The Unfinished Cosmopolitanism, Cultural Theses, and Processes of Abjection

Two questions were raised in the first chapter. They were about (1) the changes in cultural theses of cosmopolitanism in pedagogy, teacher education, and the sciences of education; and (2) the processes of abjection. These questions are examined here in order to consider the limits of school reform and its principles in the governing conduct.

I begin with the efforts for an equal and equitable school expressed in the phrase "No Child Left Behind" and standards reforms for school subjects and teacher education, and the different uses of design in research and instruction embodied in the principles of pedagogy. My interest in the intersection of the different sites of school reform is to make visible the system of reason that orders the reforms and the particular solutions and plans for action offered. Underlying prior chapters is the question, "How is it possible that such reforms are seen, felt, talked about, and acted as plausible even in their critiques?" Cosmopolitanism is a strategy to consider that grid of intelligibility. On one layer, the different reforms to produce an equitable institution take the givenness of difference as the framework in which to search for inclusion. That hope of finding useful knowledge through cosmopolitanism, if I may play with the terms, embodies its opposites. The hope of cosmopolitanism is the unity of the whole expressed in the assertion that "all" children learn. The deferrals that inscribed difference as "the child left behind."

Further, a paradox. The cultural thesis of the cosmopolitan in school reform and research entails a fatalism. The fatalism is in the given-ness of globalization and the Learning Society through which individuality is structured. The social structures of life appear as inevitable. Self-actualization, innovation, and collaboration are seen as fulfilled within that preordained destiny.

The fatalism is, ironically, given as the optimism to develop useful knowledge. The fatalism in the notion of useful knowledge, as discussed in past chapters, as stability and harmony are inscribed as a response to the seeming omnipresence of globalization, the regularizing of the temporal order in which the self is placed, the alchemy in pedagogy, and the processes of abjection.

The fatalism is embodied in what seems at first glance to be the lack of a center or whole in which collective values and goals are articulated. Today's unfinished cosmopolitanism is bound to multiple communities that seem to have no center. One lives in discourse communities, classroom communities, communities of learners. The catchwords of today are diversity, flexibility, and the uncertainty of the future.

The only certainty seems to be globalization, the ubiquitous presence that is there to shape daily life but has no author or history. Globalization is often treated as a given that schools and people adapt to in order to find happiness and routes to salvation. Here lies one trajectory of the fatalism of the world as given. "Social" unity seems to move to the sideline as teachers, children, parents, workers, and whoever else is around work hard and innovate continuously to make life better in the face of globalization. During meetings of European and American university presidents and in interviews with teachers and administrators in multiple European countries, people spoke of globalization as something that is there, and the problem of schools is to produce modes of living so children can live a happy and rewarding life. The ubiquitous globalization brings forth calls for more planning, more standards, greater harmony, and unity of the whole from which difference can be defined.

The ubiquitous globalism and the fragmentation of the nation without a center are not without social belonging and "home." It is just that the social is located differently than it was at the beginning of the 20th century. The nation has not disappeared in the narratives of globalization, as earlier chapters illustrated with respect to the mobilizations occurring in reform reports and research. The nation as a site of belonging is given expression through the plurality of communities that generate the allegiances of cosmopolitanism in the epic contemporary struggle for happiness. We may not talk about the primary group any longer as a problem of communities or use words to talk about socialization, but the child, family, and schooling are still a primary site through which the social as collective belonging is performed.

The citizen, the child, and the nation are placed in a particular scaling of relations of "global" capitalism, interstate institutions (the European Union, OPEC, or NAFTA, for example), with the nations placed in continuous flows and networks through which individuals respond to the seeming inevitability of globalization. The information and learning societies, for example, are narratives of things given a naturalness as a product of globalization and requiring particular pedagogical responses through, for example, online learning to design life.

The scaling in which belonging and home are inscribed seems, in one scenario, less of a fatalism when the relations of time and space are examined. The unfinished cosmopolitan is located in variegated and nonevolutionary time expressed in theories of communication, community, and interaction. The openness of identity and the multiplicity and inconsistency of values have overlapping boundaries and territories of belonging. The corridors of action are expressed through talk about individuals in temporary dimensions of flows, networks, and nodules, concepts that move across psychological and sociological theories in a manner that disrupts any ideas of continuities or a single dimension of time. The language of learning, social organization, and world systems embodies metaphors about "discourse communities" in which agency, reflection, collaboration, and participation are located. Life is a process and a flow of information in which flexible modes of living are judged and acted. The family is reclassified as the site of learning and communication in which child rearing is brought closer to pedagogical models of interactions and cognitive development.

Fatalism seems out of place in a time that is varied and compressed. The different temporalities in the theses of unfinished cosmopolitanism and fatalism go against conventional logic, or so it seems. Whereas early 20th-century pedagogical psychologies focused on behaviors and development in evolutionary processes, constructivist psychologies and designing the child today talk about the conditionality of the self in flows and networks, such as how meaning is made or solutions found to school problems. The learning society and the lifelong learner mix regulated time and varied time. There seems no fixed sequence to how children learn and the rates of learning except there needs to be choices along the way. One is always becoming and having multiple careers in one's life. The discontinuous quality and interdependence of time provides epistemological/ontological structures of a fleeting time and indeterminate zones in which one lives that appear as if outside the constraints and necessity.

This might seem as just the opposite of fatalism. Yet to look closer, freedom and flexibility require stabilizing and the assumption of consensus to tame the uncertainties of the future. The constructivist psychologies of pedagogy provide this stabilizing. Research is mapping the practices and processes of reason that enable autonomy, self-responsibility, and freedom. The mapping generates principles that order the conduct of conduct.

There is a counterintuitive logic present if we return to the discussion of the alchemy. Classrooms have increased participation, collaboration, and problem solving—yet these strategies entail the increased mapping of the world as given through particular expertise of science and mathematics. This narrowing occurs through the alchemic selection of "conventional ideas" that offer formulaic notions of the knowledge of physics, mathematics, and history in the curriculum. Pedagogy is to provide flexibility in the designed routes of learning the majesty of that formulaic knowledge, administering problem solving in the micromanaging of classroom communication and interaction.

The fatalism is embodied in the alchemy through the relation of school subjects and the psychology of the child. The pedagogical reforms and sciences make it less possible to relate the individual to the social and to critically inquire into the historical constructions that order the present and its possibilities. The design and engineering of the child is directed to a life shaped and reshaped at the molecular level. There are finer and finer distinctions in ordering life as calculated interventions that prevent, alter, and make new things happens in cellular processes aimed at the enhancement of capacities.[1] This is not only in the studies of children learning mathematics as described in chapter 8 but also evident in the statistics about the conditions of education. Whereas the 1960s statistics of education were defined around social mobility and social class, in one current report there were 50 categories in which to order psychological, social, economic, and pedagogical distinctions about the characteristics of the failing child in schools. The psychological categories of deviance (self-esteem, efficicacy), for example, overlapped with categories of race and ethnicity, social categories (single-parent families), and economic categories (poverty).

Fatalism travels in the erasures of difference that reinscribe differences and exclusions. The processes of abjection are not in the categorical imperatives of reason that Kant spoke about as directing one's responsibilities and obligations. The processes of abjection are embodied in the very systems of reason through which intention and purpose circulate through the rules and standards that order action and reflection. The problem is not whether people have good intentions or not, or are reasoning properly. I assume that people have good intentions but different paths to bring happiness and to correct for those classified as the unhappy, if I may use the phrase of past chapters. My argument about abjection is to think of the complexity of what is both inside and outside, both rescued and cast out as threats to cosmopolitanism, and thus as the unlivable spaces of moral disorder and deviance.

The comparative distinctions that differentiate and divide people and their qualities of life along a continuum to recognize the excluded for inclusion and produce those qualities as different. The contemporary reform to include "all children" creates a sense of the unity of the whole that recognizes the child left behind for inclusion *and* constructs spaces of difference as outside the reason of normalcy. The comparative, dividing qualities in processes of abjection are no longer expressed in words such as civilized (usually!) but in the qualities of the children recognized for inclusion yet different. The inclusion as difference makes it not possible for the latter child as ever "being of the average." This double space of outside and inside is not adequately considered as a binary, and the doubles that I speak of are intersecting doubles in the same phenomenon of schooling and its reforms.

The fatalism that I mentioned above is not one of the universal church of medieval times or that of the salvation narratives of the Reformation and Counter-Reformation. It is located in the regulation of freedom that embodies systems of reason that naturalize the present, its systems of abjection as inclusion, and reason and science as learning the majesties of the given world. This fatalism evokes the shepherd's plan by providing "useful knowledge" to order and guide the promises of the coming democracy.

Fears of Democracy: Enclosures and Internments in the Ordering of the Present

The fatalism and processes of abjection overlap with a particular inscription of democracy as the planning of people, a paradox of schooling and cosmopolitanism. As I think about the past discussion, it seems that wherever one turns, agency, participation, and collaboration are seen as the contemporary elixir of a democracy that will bring progress, happiness, and the elimination of exclusions. Vouchers will enable the poor to participate and act with the same interests as the wealthy through school choice! Critical pedagogy calls for democratic education through collaboration and judges reforms through what stands in the way to authentic participation. This entails that the teachers' and children's empowerment recognize diversity and promote communities that foster equity and social justice.[2]

The seductiveness of narratives of democracy and its redemptive theses of cosmopolitanism instantiate particular assemblies of practices that shape and fashion what constitutes the emancipatory potential of humanity. Participation in communities is democratic because it is assumed to enable one's personal and collective voice to be heard and one's experiences given public significance in decision making. The rise of qualitative studies in the United States since the 1970s can be understood in this symbolic structuring. The phenomenological versions of qualitative research operate with the assumption that the natural utterances and experiences of people in schools are truer and real—and thus the need for a "grounded theory" to capture the naturalness of context. The practices of collaboration and participation as well as those about individual autonomy and voice are naturally there to be found by the researcher but historically given intelligibility through a grid of institutions, ideas, and technologies. A different version of this democratization is "hearing" particular relevancies of teachers, communities, and the child as the base or starting point of reform.

My point here is simple. Democracy is not an ideal reached through the right mixture of policies and research. Democracy is an ongoing practice constituted through historical assemblies and connections to "securing social cooperation necessary to keep state intervention at a minimum and also enlarge the sphere of individual liberty" (Cruikshank, 1999, p. 8). The linking of the social whole with the citizen has its paradox. It embodies its Others.

The naturalizing of experience becomes the metaphysics of democracy, the origin of explanation, and the grounds of what is known. Naturalizing experience ignores how experiences are not merely the autobiographical "I" speaking, but historically produced through the relationships of distinctions, oppositions, and differentiations through which the world is catalogued prior to our participation. It is experience itself that needs to be explained rather than deferred to the givenness of divisions that mark out its difference. Scott (1991) speaks to this issue.

> There is a need to attend to the historical processes that, through discourse, that is, agency is made as ahistorical, ignoring the ways in which practice and agency are shaped by relations of production that are discursively established. Position subjects and produce their experiences. It is not individuals who have experience, but subjects who are constituted through experience. (p. 26)

The naturalizing of experience and grounded theories are not the consumation of democracy. The democratization entails fears of the people from which democracy needs to be protected. Rancière (2006) argues that the new discourses of the Enlightenment and the positivist sciences ordered differences as the necessity of the state rather than as an arbitrary order. Difference was to be rehabilitated to bring the universal of progress in which

> the prior Aristotelian ideal of community governed by the Good overlapped with theories of interpretation that traces a circle that excluded by disclosing the differences in ethos in which the people who constitute difference are "incapable" of ever acquiring a taste for the philosophers goods—and even of understanding the language in which their enjoyment is expounded. (p. 204)

The construction of unequal situations through which sensitivity to difference is installed inserts the shepherd, who guides actions and directs that casting out of what does not belong to the whole. The consensus and stability of the unity of the whole become a representative democracy of populations and roles that are mediated through an expertise of knowledge. This was explored in design research as systems that gave consensus and stability to the ongoing events of classrooms and school reforms. The assumption is to establish the idea of consensus through which each is to be allotted comparable shares, and in that allotment is the casting out of those not represented and thus surplus.

> Consensus is more that the reasonable idea and practice of settling political conflicts by forms of negotiation and agreement, and by allotting to each party the best share compatible with the interests of other parties. It is a means to get rid of politics by ousting the surplus subjects and replacing them with real partners, social groups, identity groups, and so on. Correspondingly, conflicts are turned into problems that have to be sorted out by learned expertise and a negotiated adjustment of interests. (Rancière, 2006, p. 306)

The practice of consensus, Rancière continues, closes the spaces of democracy but rids it of politics as the tasks are producing consensus that patch over the possible gaps. The talk of stakeholders and of different populations of actors participating in school and university reforms are examples of the practices of consensus guided by shepherds who speak about pedagogical knowledge and professional standards as having a consensus about "desired" outcomes in teaching, learning, and so on.

The fear of democracy requires planning to mediate participation parallels the discussion of abjection. Each entails the radical differentiation that casts out others that paradoxically is to include an undifferentiated part of the whole. The "ousting the surplus subjects" that Rancière speaks about creates an undifferentiated unity from which others are placed in unequal situations and that installs difference.

Equity Research: The Radical Differentiation, Repulsion, and Paradoxical Inclusion

Earlier discussions of research designs and design research (see chapter 9) can be used to consider the limits of the sciences of schooling and its claims about planning and finding useful knowledge for emancipating the future. I turn to the question of "useful knowledge" and its corollary of "what works" that is presupposed in the different research traditions by focusing on the particular way of thinking and organizing research that my colleague Sverker Lindblad (Popkewitz & Lindblad, 2000) called "the equity problematic." As part of a European Union research project on educational governance and social exclusion in nine countries, we did an extensive review of Anglo-American educational research to consider the principles that order the problems and methods (Popkewitz & Lindblad, 2000). We considered the problematic to interpret the principles generated in research about what can be known, what must be done, and what may be hoped (Foucault, 1984, p. 38). The discussion about the equity problematic brings together and provides a further reframing of the limits of cosmopolitanism explored through chapters 7, 8, and 9.

Schematically, the equity problematic entails the project of science in planning for agency and freedom through the organization of research. Schemes of social intervention are to change social conditions and to change people. Research identifies the necessary knowledge to understand the factors that increase or hinder representation and access of individuals and social groups handicapped in existing school programs. The assumption of research is that once the factors and their mechanisms of inequity are made apparent, more efficient policies and programs are possible to bring forth progress. These assumptions circulate in policy and research through four overlapping principles.

First is *the politics of representation.* The politics of schooling lies in identifying those excluded and then seeking practices that redress that exclusion. Statistical reporting in cross-national reports of education compares different characteristics of populations to school performance indicators: comparing ethnic or racial groups and gender populations to norms about school attendance, achievement levels, and graduation rates, among others. Qualitative research provides narratives of the interactions, communications, and cultures of classrooms to understand how bias is mobilized to prevent inclusive principles.

Second, change is finding *the right mixture of policies to produce an inclusionary institution* and thus eliminate (at least theoretically) exclusion and inequities. The juxtaposition of "all children will learn" with the strategies to remediate and rescue the child left behind is to find the right procedures to close the achievement gap between the affluent and poor students within a specified time. The closing of "the gap" overlaps with other distinctions and norms assumed in the phrase that reform serves "desired goals" or purposes. Further, the design in instruction, design research, and research designs of methods discussed in chapter 9 overlap as strategies for dealing with contingencies of schooling by regulating the systems of practices for producing "desired results." The differences in the particular paths to inclusion aside, the problem of research is to tame change and to provide stability and consensus by producing the right mixture of policies and practices for administering school conditions and people.

The third principle is that *knowledge is to serve human purposes and intention*, to be "useful" in making possible efficient planning. The policymaker, researcher, and teacher look at knowledge as a tool in service of universal human goals. The teacher asks, "What does this research tell us for improving classroom teaching?" The university researcher is heard to say, "How can this research be made relevant to what teachers do in the classroom?" Others ask, "What reforms work?" The political activist implores that research serve as an agent of change and social reconstruction. The unspoken principle is that knowledge is the servant of humanity. That servant is to change people to enable their effecting of agency in the pursuit of happiness.

Fourth, inclusion and exclusion are *separate categories in planning*. The unhappy populations are to be rescued so that they may pursue happiness. It is seen as a zero-sum game; inclusion is to eliminate exclusion. The increase in one decreases the other. The unity of the whole of "all children" erases differences through the application of proper procedures and planning. As I argued in earlier chapters, curriculum and teacher education standards reforms proceed as if the combination of teacher's cultural sensitivity, clear statements of learning standards, better content preparation, and pedagogical knowledge will produce inclusive schooling.

There are difficulties in these assumptions. They beg, paradoxically, empirical evidence to the contrary. There are no ultimate causes of the present, and the search for "what works" and "useful" knowledge is a chimera that has material consequences. I say this for different analytical and historical reasons. The "finding" of what works is concurrently a process of abjection. The "causes" of the present are assembled and connected from different historical practices that have no single origin. The outcomes of interventions are not processes of replication because there is no total knowledge of the present to control and regulate what is and what should be. And while the faith in science as providing mastery of the social world persists and is seductive when feeling uncertainty arises about the future, it is dangerous to almost any notion of democracy except that which requires shepherds. In spite of claims to the contrary, my reading of the history of the social and education sciences leads me to conclude that the enduring literatures that enable transgressions are more provoking of the doubts to the present than they are in its planning directives offered by the social services as the shepherds of democracy.

Diagnosing the limits of the foundational tools, to draw on Gilroy's (2001) discussion of a theory of antiracism, might seem as "a betrayal of those groups whose oppositional, legal, and even democratic claims have come to rest on identities and solidities forged at great cost from the categories given to them by their oppressors" (p. 52). It is not! While the politics of the representation for marginalized groups is important, the strategy for change leaves intact and unquestioned the very systems of reason and their processes of abjection. To recognize those for inclusion does not exorcize exclusion.

It is the processes of abjection that need to be made visible to consider the internments, enclosures, and casting out produced in the forged identities. The seductiveness of the sacred words of education in mobilizing people should not be confused with the necessary historical and analytic work to consider the assemblies and connections that govern what is constituted as our very humanness. The very questions of differentiations and divisions require, to borrow from Franz Fanon, the psychiatrist and anticolonial activist from Martinique, that "people must give up their too-simple conception of their overlords" in the constructions of given identities (cited in Gilroy, 2006, p. 57).

Cosmopolitanism and the Study of Schooling: Limits to Its Cultural Thesis

It is plausible to ask: If cosmopolitanism embodies processes of abjection in its inclusive impulses, does the study of its limits reinscribe the paradoxes and the violence committed in its name? My response is possibly too simple. The very deployment of critiques about ourselves as historically determined reassembles an attitude of the Enlightenment. Are we condemned as Sisyphus to continue inscribing what we set out to change? Are the only possibilities the dogma of the shepherd and the hatred of democracy that plans to change the conditions of a society that changes people, and the gestures of inclusion in processes of abjection?

This conundrum is bound to what Foucault (1984) called the blackmail of the Enlightenment. To open spaces beyond what exists as the common sense is not to shed the attitudes of cosmopolitanism and its concerns about agency, reason, and rationality. If I use Foucault's essay on the enlightenment and the study of the limits of present, he argues that

> Enlightenment is a set of events and complex historical processes-located in the development of European society that includes elements of social transformation, types of political institutions, forms of knowledge, projects of rationalization of knowledge and practices, technological mutations that are difficult to sum up in a word even if many of the phenomena remain important today. (Foucault, 1984, p. 43)

This quote brings to the surface principles of the Enlightenment and cosmopolitanism that help explore the limits and possibilities of the present. Foucault's use of a historical register is different from that of Hegelian dialectics and analytic-empirical traditions of research. The phrase "a set of events and complex historical processes" employs a variable, *discontinuous time that has no single origin,* a view that underlies this study.

The strategy of this study is a history of present. It diagnosed cosmopolitanism as not a history of continuities but of discontinuities that produces objects of reflection and actions. The present is not, as the pragmatists of the early 20th century argued, to overcome the traditions of the past to create something new. Cosmopolitanism is cultural theses whose changing configurations and overlapping principles intern and enclose about what is seen, talked about, acted on, and felt as natural and unquestionable.

Notions of agency and change, other cosmopolitan aspects, are embedded in Foucault's text. They are given expression when he talks about the history of the present as the "grasping for freedom and liberty" historically by the "practical test of the limits that we may go beyond, and thus work carried out by ourselves upon ourselves as free beings" (Foucault, 1984, p. 47).

Cosmopolitanism and its agency are located differently than in the insertion of the people to be changed embodied in the equity problematic and the fears of democracy that I referred to earlier. Agency is in the possibilities of testing of the limits of the present; freeing ourselves from the particular dogma of the present. Resistance is to make conditional what seems inevitable and necessary by "modifying the rules of the game, up to a certain point" (Foucault, 1984, p. 48). The hesitation—"up to a certain point"—is in the conditionality that makes it not possible to find complete and definitive knowledge of what constitutes the past and present.

The testing of the limits of the Enlightenment and cosmopolitanism is paradoxical. It does not give up notions of freedom and agency. What is given up is the notion of planning people is the social sciences that stabilizes and fixes the boundaries of freedom. There is no absolute knowledge of freedom. Resistance is continually pushing against the boundaries by historicizing what we are and what we have become. Critical thought is directed to "what is accepted as authority through a critique of the conditions of what is known, what must be done, what may be hoped" (Foucault, 1984, p. 38). Agency is embodied in specific inquiries that denaturalize present common sense by exploring the limits of what constitutes the necessary and what is "no longer indispensable for the constitution of ourselves as autonomous subjects" (p. 43).

The attitude of critique in this study through historicizing the present is not to reject the *attitudes* of cosmopolitanism or notions of agency, progress, and rationality. It is to make visible its rules and standards as part of the problem of the present. Freeing oneself from the present while being immersed in it is a funny juggling act—to engage in an interrogation of the limits of the present while not giving up on the attitude of cosmopolitanism about reason and commitments to freedom, justice, and hospitality to others. The tracking of shifts in the cultural theses of schooling is a tactic in that juggling act by which we may challenge the habitual ways of working and thinking in school reform, teacher education, and the sciences of education.

Methodology and Epistemological Obstacles

To think about the limits of the present and its enclosures in the equity problematic entails pushing the "epistemological obstacles," to borrow from Gaston Bachelard (1984), to focus on the divisions and oppositions of the common sense of schooling. I approach the obstacles here through the oppositional/binary logics of contemporary policy, research, and practices of pedagogy and teacher education.

One obstacle is the division between freedom, individuality and the social. There is no individuality without the social. Historically, as I argued in the first chapters, both are dependent on the other. The cosmopolitan universals about freedom, agency in the projects of pedagogy, are never "merely" of the person alone. The individuality that portrays child development or lifelong learning are mutually produced with notions of "community" and its social patterns of communication and interaction. The individual and social are constitutive of each other. Take away the nice-sounding words of schools as *places of learning, finding children's potential,* and *self-actualization,* and there stands pedagogy as registers of social planning that require the simultaneous inscription of the child in the classroom and schooling.

Another obstacle is the distinctions between ideas, texts, and knowledge, as oppositions to the "real," lived experiences of the teachers in contexts. These oppositions function in contemporary social and educational theories as Kantian categorical imperatives that have little value for interpreting the politics of modern life. The distinctions generally place "ideas" as an epiphenomenon to the materiality of school, that which is "real." Knowledge, as I have argued, is not an epiphenomenon to the materiality of life but works in that materiality and is part of that phenomenon! The notion of fabrication was deployed to recognize this relation. The lifelong learner is not merely a fiction but simultaneously real as things are manufactured or made through the books written, theories developed, and programs and assessments created to ensure a life of continual learning, growth, and development, as well as principles produced to order teachers and parents administering the deviations that arise.

A different set of distinctions that requires rethinking in the theories of schooling is that of certainty and uncertainty. This often inscribes certainty. It is the social in those things that constrain and restrain uncertainty in the daily vicissitudes of schooling and teacher education. Certification programs require school and society classes for students to understand structures and cultures that shape boundaries (give certainty) to teaching. The other end of the spectrum is the concern about the whole child, the subjective, and the giving of agency, empowerment, and voice to a world that is uncertain.

However, uncertainty and certainty travel together and are not opposites in practice. The individuality lives in a world where external verities and certainties no longer seem safe. The spaces of change are stabilized and tamed through the calculations of principles of reflection and action. The joining of uncertainty and certainty confront each other not as opposites but in the same phenomenon and as limits of governing. Modern governing, I argued, is the "taming" of social contingencies through inscriptions that orders the future by disciplining the conduct of conduct.

The questioning of the limits of the system of reason through this study might be misread as a regression into relativism where all claims in the political cultures are formally equivalent. That would be a philosophical misrecognition of the concept of relativism as well as a misreading of the very categories and method of study undertaken. The foci of the doubles gestures of cosmopolitanism in schooling are to take seriously our current predicaments and commitments to questions of democracy, diversity, and inequity that do not treat them as categories of the ideal.

The issue at hand could be read as a form of Occidental rationalism and Eurocentric thought about identity in the universal history that projects a series of binaries on the rest of the world (Mehta, 2000, p. 631). While it is ideologically pleasing to talk about "outside of the West", the critiques are continually made with the tools of reason even in seeking to subvert them (see, e.g., Mehta, 1997; Chakrabarty, 2000). Gilroy (2006) argues that Black antiracism thinkers have confounded the conventional distinctions between nationalism and cosmopolitanism through visions from pan-Africanism passed on to the anticolonial movement. These movements do not necessarily descend from "the template landscape of liberal pieties" (p. 92), but the works of Fanon and DuBois that Gilroy analyzes center on the subjectivity that brings back the European hope of remaking cosmopolitanism by challenging the suffering, estrangement, and disenchantment of the present.

The rethinking of cosmopolitanism as different relations of time, space, and biography is taken up sometimes outside the problematic of the design of people. Rajchman (1997), for example, poses a way to think about constructions free from the problematic of regulated faculties in which all meaning is kept within the bounds of logical constructions and the salvationist problematic of judgment. He proposes that it can be connected to an unfinished, indeterminate, complex time of the possible "compositions" of our lives in which the life constructed is less perfect, and the characters in the resulting drama more flexible. Society is an "experiment and a labyrinthine construction that we must enter and exist in many ways and by many ways since 'the way' does not exist" (Rajchman, 1997, p. 5). The disunities and tacit or indeterminate rules are also filled "with voids and interstices, always leaking and changing shapes according to its lines of leakage" (p. 7). Life becomes a question of what a work is and not a question of what works. The problem of research is to look for provisional points of contact and alliance in a new idiom no longer belonging to the recognized language of either (p. 9).

The search to engage the politics of schooling takes on qualities that are somewhat like Deleuze and Guattari's (1987) rhizome, an assembly of heterogeneous components and a multiplicity that functions as variation, expansion, and offshoots. The lifelong learner is a mode of living that seems to fit the Internet and computer games played simultaneously around the world as well as the fragmented narratives that travel in media in which daily life is one of ongoing changes with no overall storyline. The expression of the multiplicity of functions in time in the pedagogical projects discussed, however, is emptied of history. Difference is denied in the insertions of diversity.

The search for alternatives remains. Yet that search is a search that bears the conditions of the present and is not outside of it. And that present is still within the Enlightenment attitudes toward reason, rationality, and freedom, although not necessarily the insertion of progress as the Shephard's movement and evolution of regulated time. This is the charge of Gilroy's (2006) bringing together cosmopolitanism, antiracist theory, and multiculturalism. Gilroy uses notions of conviviality and suffering to orient a cosmopolitanism that has a universalistic agenda that is historicized through antiracial theory. Such a theory, he argues, is to reconstruct and reconsider the tensions between the cosmo and polis, the global and local, the worldly and the parochial by historically examining the racializing, embodied in what he calls "raciology," the inscriptions of identities as essential oppositions of binaries of White/Black, settler/native, and colonizer/colonized. Frantz Fanon, the Enlightenment's Montesquieu, W. E. B. DuBois, Malcom X, Sigmund Freud, Lévi-Strauss, and the Italian political philosopher Giorgio Agamben are drawn into a conversation to visualize and conceptualize a politics of knowledge and the cultural thesis that works off different assumptions of cosmopolitanism than the mastery assumed in the equity problematic. Related explorations to rethink the epistemological limitations and the politics of knowledge are present in a range of philosophical, literacy, social science, arts, and pedagogical literatures.[3]

I mentioned these briefly because, although they are not the focus of this book, the different studies seek the limits of the present yet are not outside of its sensibilities about reason and rationality for organizing the self and agency. To say this, however, does not free one from the obligation of poking holes in the causality of the present and the limits produced. It is to recognize the dangers that go along with commitments but not to give up those commitments even as they are historicized. The optimism thus returns. Making visible the arbitrary as conditional and the possibility of alternatives other than those framed by its contemporaneity are a form of resistance and a theory of change.

Notes

Chapter 1

1. See, for example, Hofstadter, 1955; Rodgers, 1998; Popkewitz, 1991.
2. I could also talk about ages of reform, as I am thinking about the emergence of reform as a project of joining individuality and society that forms in the Enlightenment and mutates to the present.
3. This internationalization is evident in reading through the programs of the European Research Association and the American Educational Research Association.
4. For a critical discussion of globalization, see, for example, Steiner-Khamsi, 2004; Steiner-Khamsi & Stolpe, 2006; Lindblad & Popkewitz, 2004.
5. Chapter 9 discusses these research programs; here, my purpose is only to create a place for them in the age of reform.
6. While drug testing is in the biomedical field it is still about the effectiveness of drugs and may not be the same as the study of people and their condition.
7. I use the notion of "play with" as I draw on Foucault in relation to the range of other historical and cultural theories about knowledge, the production of subjectivity, and social inclusion and exclusion. My argument is at once modern and postmodern in its theoretical assembly to tackle the problematic of contemporary schooling and its limits. Hopefully, the formulation of this amalgamation will be more apparent through the manner in which the argument is pursued in the book.
8. Among discussions to historicize its uses are, for example, Pagden, 2000; Brennan, 1997; Breckenridge, Pollock, Bhabha, & Chakrabarty, 2002; Cheah & Robbins, 1998.
9. This term emerged in work that I did with Jamie Kowalczyk (see, e.g., Kowalczyk & Popkewitz, 2005) and related to Kristeva (1982; also see Butler, 1993). Feminist theory draws on psychoanalytic concepts. My interest is to explore systems of reason. For other uses or related concerns, see Shimakawa's (2002) study of Americanness and the Asian body as "abjection" and Shapiro's (1999) concern with the doubles of inside and outside as fluidities and contingencies in which individual and collective subjects are constituted.

10. Political theory in the works of Michael Shapiro (see, e.g., 1992, 1999) and William Connolly (e.g., 1987), as well as the philosophical works of Agamben (1998, 2005), Foucault (2003, 2005), Rabinow (1984), and Rancière (1983/2004b) are counter examples to this statement.

11. If my informants are correct, Diogenes is more correctly translated as talking about the universe and not "the world," as the latter would provide a different set of meanings.

12. I will discuss this quality of cosmopolitanism in chapter 2. Here, I should say that I am not following the institutional theory of Berger, Berger, and Kellner (1974) but using it to explore the social epistemological breaks in cosmopolitanism.

13. Once said, there will be someone who finds the counter example. But as I read through Cassirer (1932/1951) and other readings of social, philosophical, and educational theories from the 19th century to the present, including Marx, this judgment persists.

14. The relation of the social and agency permeates different social interests of knowledge, to borrow from Habermas (1971) in projects of social planning. Heilbron, Magnussion, and Wittrock (1998) list four notions of agency (p. 25). There is a *rationalistic-composition* conception of agency in which society is viewed as formed through the collective actions of individuals. A *statistical-inductive* conception of agency is formed through a populational reasoning that focuses on society as a *systemic aggregate. A structural-constraining* conception of agency corresponds with thinking about society as an *organic totality*. And finally there is a *linguistic-interpretative* conception of agency in which society emerges as a totality formed by communicative patterns.

15. It is not that the poor, for example, do not act, but these actions are often deemed as deviant, antisocial, or counterproductive to a normative notion of action and participation.

16. I do not mean to suggest that the particular applications of theories of the child and teaching are the same in the iconic figures of American education; I do, however, suggest that there is a family of resemblance, to borrow from Wittgenstein (1996), that can be discerned historically.

Chapter 2

1. This notion of time underlies the historicizing use of cosmopolitanism as assemblies, connections, and disconnections. See, for example, Deleuze and Guattari's (1987) notion of rhizome and Shapiro (2001).

2. I borrow this phrase from Hacking's (1990) study of statistics. In it, he talked about chance and processes of normalizing populations. I use taming to talk about the administration of change in relation to different but overlapping historical registers.

3. See, for example, Beck (1992); Baker and Simon (2002).

4. Horace Mann was one of the founders of the modern school in the United States and Secretary of Education of the Massachusetts schools in the 19th century. This problem of the social administration of the soul is posed by Durkheim (1938/1977) when discussing the moral formations of society

through the Reformation and Counter-Reformation, although the soul of modernity has different historical configurations and relations of knowledge and power that I want to explore.

5. See, for example, Butler (1993), Kristeva (1982), Shimakawa's (2002) study of Americanness and the Asian body as "abjection," and Shapiro's (1999) with the doubles of inside and outside. My discussion leans to the cultural and historical rather than the feminist's incorporation of psychoanalytic theories.

6. These "others" were in particular the poor, Native Americans, and different Europeans in the 19th century. At certain times in American history, the British are the "other" in relation to the German and the French; and other times, the relations move to another axis, such as that of the post–Civil War, World War I, and World War II.

7. There is a vast literature on time as a cultural and historical concept. The historical school of the Annales, for example, differentiates three different notions of time in the study of the past; Grosz (2004) explores different dimensions of time to think about the "untimely," that is, how to break from the traditions of the past and present in creating possibilities of the future; Kosselleck (1985) provides a semantic history of time and Norbert Elias (1992) a cultural historical analysis.

Chapter 3

1. The terms *America* and *American* are used interchangeably in the text with that of the United States, as the terms were used interchangeably by the historical figures I discuss. My usages are therefore historical and not ideological.

2. Oliver Cromwell was a Puritan military leader and leader of the English Commonwealth in the 17th century.

3. I am using "America" here and elsewhere as it appears in the literature about the nation and not to claim its appropriateness as a generic term for the nation.

4. At certain times in American history, the British are the "other" in relation to the German and the French; and other times, the relations move to other axes, such as during the post–Civil War, World War I, and World War II eras.

5. The report was prepared for a meeting of state superintendents in order to send representation to a conference in Vienna to talk about conditions of education in the United States. The statement was signed by Superintendents Doty of Detroit and William Torrey Harris of St. Louis, the latter an influential member of the American Herbartian Society and later head of the federal Bureau of Education.

6. John D. Rockefeller's founding of this new university was to maintain his Baptist religious affiliation. It is important to note that eastern elite universities such as Yale, Columbia, Harvard, Dartmouth, and Princeton were initially schools to train clergy.

Chapter 5

1. Images of Protestant moral and ethical life were overlaid with the categories of science to humanize and personalize individual disciplines (see, e.g., Greek, 1992).

2. Kvale (2003) notes that the discipline of psychology is generally most prominent in Protestant countries and many of the founders of modern scientific
psychology were sons of ministers; also see Tröhler (2000).

Chapter 6

1. The U.S. Declaration of Independence's list of such rights comprises "life,
liberty, and the pursuit of happiness."
2. I use the notion of a welfare state as a way to signify the manner in which the
state assumes responsibilities for the care and welfare of its citizens rather
than as a normative concept of contemporary discussions with the Nordic
state as its ideal. In this more "commonsense" notion, all modern states are
welfare states that provide, for example, unemployment insurance, some
forms of health care, old age insurance, laws concerning the workplace, and
so on. A welfare state appears in the U.S. as government-organized interstate
commerce, pensions for widows from the American Civil War, a war department, agricultural policies, and initial laws for equality among the freed
slaves, among other practices to guide economic and social development.
3. I used agentive because the child was to bring purpose and intention into his
or her planning of biography; this notion of agency is more prescribed than
Dewey's or Lester Frank Ward's.

Chapter 7

1. The phrase *unfinished cosmopolitan* emerged in a conversation with Ruth
Gustafson. I appreciate her thinking through with me some of the intellectual and historical questions raised in this chapter.
2. This was discussed in the first two chapters and relates to a particular modern consciousness that makes possible the self as an object and subject of
reflection. It is intricately tied to cosmopolitanism.

Chapter 8

1. To speak of alchemy and salvation is not necessarily mixing metaphors. The
alchemists worked with magical powers in the hope of affecting longevity, if
not an immortality, that embodied God's way. But I do not want to push the
analogy too far, as analogies are always limited.
2. The use of psychology in the curriculum was not a forgone conclusion. William James spoke against it; G. Stanley Hall defended it as a central discipline in forming the soul.
3. For critical discussions of this, see, for example, Valero (2003) and Bishop,
Clements, Keitel, Kilpatrick, & Laborde (1996).
4. Although it is possible to talk about norms of community and notions of
participation, democracy, and individualization in science or mathematics,
these notions and their nuances do not necessarily collapse into or directly
overlap with the political rationalities and political regime of a nation. Thus
they need to be investigated rather than assumed in pedagogy. One can

compare the meanings of collaboration in the French and U.S. scientific communities, for example, to understand how norms of partnership and cooperation differ in relation to the different cultural and political regimes in which science is produced (Rabinow, 1999).

5. French didactics gives explicit recognition to the need for translations into pedagogy, but without questioning the alchemy itself. See, for example, Brousseau (1997).

6. Mathematics educators make distinctions between different strands of pedagogical research. See, for example, Cobb and Bowers's (1999) distinction between cognitive and situated learning perspectives of constructivism, and Hershkowitz and Schwarz (1999). See also Sutherland and Balacheff (1999), who clarify the distinctions between constructivist psychologies and a theory of didactical situations. In relation to the argument in this article, the different strands and nuances of research are internal discussions to the rules and standards of the same alchemic strategy in constituting the curriculum. I discuss some of the similarities in Popkewitz (1991). I do not consider other mathematics education traditions, such as ethnomathematics or the tradition of the Freuthenthal Institute, Utrecht, Netherlands.

7. I appreciate Sal Restivo for making this distinction as I thought about this issue.

8. This provides a way to undo the binaries that underlie debates about science and mathematics that are concerned with uncertainty and certainty, idealism and realism. These can be thought of as a double inscription. Platonic notions of certainty in mathematics exist even when we consider the cultural qualities that produce its systems of knowledge (Restivo, 1993). The Platonic certainty of mathematics is continually worked on through a field of cultural practices as mathematicians produce its foundations. For example, mathematics can be thought of as embodying a logic that is about the truth of the world; as a collection of synthetic propositions and the *a priori* of Kant; or as the relations of classes determined by its context (such as the properties of summing and discounting, and measurement problems). Even if a Platonic notion of certainty is accepted, the seemingly self-evident classes of the categories of numbers embody norms of ranking and divisions that relate to the cultural resources available for the classifying. One can think of the classification systems of social surveys or the types of mathematical problems related to development of computer sciences or by the Defense Advanced Research Projects Agency (DARPA) to consider the issues of epistemic drift in the field of mathematics through resources both internal and external to the field.

Chapter 9

1. It is interesting that what is "known" about teachers is nothing like that which is known about an engineer who makes a bridge, but is instead a form of romantic, progressive beliefs that overlap with research to provide hope and faith. What is known is that schooling needs a strong learning community, teachers need to know content knowledge, and schools that "provide every child with competent, caring, qualified teachers" (National

Commission on Teaching and America's Future, 2003, p. 9). When examined, the design problem of this science is not only to obtain evidence to describe what works, but it is also to *rigorously* order the phenomena of schools so as, to use the word of the report, *reengineer* not only the contexts of the school (p. 12) but also to *reengineer* the child.

2. See, for example, Weiss (1993) for a historical discussion of the emergence of this notion.

3. Smith and O'Day (1990) discuss reform as systemic; but while the conceptualization has been maintained in the broader reforms, it is rarely given reference or is the epistemological idea of "social" system addressed. It is also obvious that the word *system* has multiple theoretical qualities that are not linked to finding consensus and equilibrium. My use of "systems of reason," for example, in this text is concerned, for example, with the changing principles generated about reflection and action, what I called a social epistemology.

4. For a critical discussion of the assumptions of this report, see the special issue of *Qualitative Inquiry* (2004, October).

5. The call of this notion of science as science and everything else as something different raises all sorts of questions about its politics in closing the boundaries of what is sanctified as possible to ask and study. There is also the problem of the complexity and limitations of what is called "the gold standard" of research in medicine (see, e.g., Welch, Woloshin, & Schwartz, 2007).

6. For a historical discussion of this "neutrality," see Popkewitz (1984).

7. This summary is related to the review of the Web sites of the federal government related to What Works by Cecile Eren Argit from Turkey, who was an Honorary Fellow with me during the 2006–07 year.

8. The processes of abjection do not disappear in critical research. Although describing inequities in the distribution of resources in urban education, there is a near romanticized view of the oppressed inscribed in the youth of the poor and working class (see, e.g., Fine, Burns, Payne, & Torre, 2004).

Chapter 10

1. This condition of the relation of the normal and pathological is not only in education. It is related to biogenetics, for example, in the micromanagement of disease and changes possible in cosmetic surgeries (Pollock, 2006; Belkin, 2005).

2. Carlson (2005) focuses on democratic renewal projects and the forces in and out of schooling whose power relations prevent participation and collaboration. While accepting the good of collaboration as a path to progress, he also warns of the expertise of the university as talking for marginalized groups that makes the "voices" of those groups as natural and outside of historical practices.

3. See, for example, Bernadette Baker (2001), Gunilla Dahlberg and Marianne Bloch (2006), Patti Lather (2007), and Hillevi Taguchi (2006).

References

Agamben, G. (1998). *Homo sacer: Sovereign power and bare life* (D. Heller-Roazen, Trans.). Stanford, CA: Stanford University Press.

Agamben, G. (2005). *State of exception* (K. Attell, Trans.). Chicago: University of Chicago Press.

Alberts, B. (2002). Foreword. In R. J. Shavelson & L. Towne (Eds.), *Scientific research in education* (pp. vii–viii). Washington, DC: National Research Council.

Álvarez-Mendiola, G. (2006) Lifelong learning policies in Mexico: Context, challenges and comparisons. *Compare, 36*(3), 379–399.

American Academy of Allergy, Asthma, and Immunology. (2005, July). *Academy News.* Retrieved July 25, 2006 from http://www.aaaai.org

American Council on Education. (1999). *To touch the future: Transforming the way teachers are taught: An action ag.enda for college and university presidents.* Washington, DC: American Council on Education.

American Federation of Teachers. (1999, November). *Educational issues policy brief.* Washington, DC: American Federation of Teachers.

Anderson, B. (1991). *Imagined communities: Reflections on the origin and spread of nationalism* (Rev. ed.). London: Verso.

Appiah, K. (1996) Cosmopolitan patriots. In M. Nussbaum & J. Cohen (Eds.), *For the love of country: Debating the limits of patriotism* (pp. 21–29). Boston: Beacon Press.

Appiah, K. (2006). *Cosmopolitanism: Ethics in a world of strangers.* New York: W. W. Norton.

Apple, R. (2006). *Perfect motherhood: Science and childrearing in America.* New Brunswick, NJ: Rutgers University Press.

Ariès, P. (1962). *Centuries of childhood: A social history of family life* (R. Baldick, Trans.). New York: Vintage Books.

Bachelard, G. (1991). Epistemological obstacles. In M. M. Jones (Ed.), *Gaston Bachelard, subversive humanist: Texts and readings* (pp. 81–84). Madison: University of Wisconsin Press.

Baker, B. (2001). *In perpetual motion: Theories of power, educational history, and the child.* New York: Peter Lang.

Baker, K. (1994). Enlightenment and the institution of society: Notes of a conceptual history. In W. Melching & V. Wyger (Eds.), *Main trends in cultural history* (pp. 95–120). Amsterdam: Rodopi.

Baker, T. & Simon, J. (Eds.). (2002). *Embracing risk: The changing culture of insurance and responsibility.* Chicago: University of Chicago Press.

Bakhtin, M. (1981). *The dialogic imagination: Four essays* (C. Emerson & M. Holquist, Trans.). Austin: University of Texas Press.

Balibar, E. & Wallerstein, I. (1991). *Race, nation, class: Ambiguous identities.* New York: Verso.

Ball, D. (2001). Teaching with respect to mathematics and students. In T. Wood, B. S. Nelson, & J. Warfield (Eds.), *Beyond classical pedagogy: Teaching elementary school mathematics* (pp. 11–21). Mahwah, NJ: Lawrence Erlbaum.

Beck, U. (1992). *Risk society: Towards a new modernity* (M. Ritter, Trans.). Beverley Hills, CA: Sage.

Beck, U. (2000). The cosmopolitan perspective: Sociology of the second age of modernity. *British Journal of Sociology, 51*(1), 79–105.

Becker, C. (1932). *The heavenly city of the eighteenth-century philosophers.* New Haven, CT: Yale University Press.

Belkin, L. (2005, November 6). A doctor for the future. *New York Times.* Retrieved from http://www.nytimes.com

Bell, D. A. (2001). *The cult of the nation in France: Inventing nationalism, 1680–1800.* Cambridge, MA: Harvard University Press.

Bellah, R. (1975). *The broken covenant: American civil religion in time of trial.* Chicago: University of Chicago Press.

Bercovitch, S. (1978). *The American Jeremiad.* Madison: University of Wisconsin Press.

Berger, P., Berger, B., & Kellner, H. (1974). *The homeless mind: Modernization and consciousness.* New York: Vintage.

Bhabha, H. K. (1990). *Nation and narration.* New York: Routledge.

Bishop, A., Clements, K., Keitel, C., Kilpatrick, J., & Laborde, C. (Eds.). (1996). *International handbook of mathematics education.* Dordrecht, The Netherlands: Kluwer.

Bledstein, B. (1976). *The culture of professionalism, the middle class, and the development of higher education in America.* New York: W. W. Norton.

Bloch, M. (1987). Becoming scientific and professional: An historical perspective on the aims and effects of early education. In T. Popkewitz (Ed.), *The formation of school subjects: The struggle for creating an American institution* (pp. 25–62). New York: Falmer.

Bloch, M., & Tabachnick, B. R. (1994). Improving parent involvement as school reform: Rhetoric or reality? In K. M. Borman & N. P. Greenman (Eds.), *Changing American education: Recapturing the past or inventing the future* (pp. 261–296). New York: State University of New York Press.

Boaler, J. (Ed.). (2000). *Multiple perspectives on mathematics teaching and learning.* Westport, CT: Abex.

Boon, J. (1985). Anthropology and degeneration: Birds, words, and orangutans. In J. Chamberlin & S. Gilman (Eds.), *Degeneration: The dark side of progress* (pp. 24–48). New York: Columbia University Press.

Boostrom, R., Jackson, P., & Hansen, D. (1993). Coming together and staying apart: How a group of teachers and researchers sought to bridge the "research/practice gap." *Teachers College Record, 95*(1), 35–44.

Bourdieu, P. (1993). *Sociology in question* (R. Nice, Trans.). London: Sage (Original work published 1984).

Boyer, P. (1978). *Urban masses and moral order in America, 1820–1920.* Cambridge, MA: Harvard University Press.

Braudel, F. (1980). *On history.* Chicago: University of Chicago Press.

Breckenridge, C., Pollock, S., Bhabha, H., & Chakrabarty, D. (Eds.). (2002). *Cosmopolitanism.* Durham, NC: Duke University Press.

Brennan, T. (1997). *At home in the world: Cosmopolitanism now.* Cambridge, MA: Harvard University Press.

Brickman, W. (1949). John Dewey's foreign reputation as an educator. *School and Society, 70*(1818), 257–264.

Brousseau, G. (1997). *Theory of didactical situations in mathematics: Didactique des mathematiques, 1970–1990* (N. Balacheff, M. Cooper, R. Sutherland, & V. Warfield, Trans.). Dordrecht, The Netherlands: Kluwer.

Butler, J. (1993). *Bodies that matter: On the discourse limits of "sex."* New York: Routledge.

Carlson, D. (2005). Hope without illusion: Telling the story of democratic educational renewal. *International Journal of Qualitative Studies in Education, 18*(1), 21–45.

Carolina Abecedarian Project. *Promising Practices Network.* Retrieved from http://www.promisingpractices.net

Cassirer, E. (1951). *The philosophy of the enlightenment* (F. Koelln & J. Pettegrove, Trans.). Princeton, NJ: Princeton University Press (Original work published 1932).

Cazden, C. (1986). Classroom discourse. In M. Wittrock (Ed.), *Handbook of research on teaching* (3rd ed., pp. 432–463). New York: Macmillan.

Chakrabarty, D. (2000). *Provincializing Europe: Postcolonial thought and historical difference.* Princeton, NJ: Princeton University Press.

Chamberlin, J. & Gilman, S. (1985). Degeneration: An introduction. In J. E. Chamberlin & S. Gilman (Eds.), *Degeneration: The dark side of progress* (pp. ix–xiii). New York: Columbia University Press.

Cheah, P. & Robbins, B. (Eds.). (1998). *Cosmopolitics.* Minneapolis: University of Minnesota Press.

Childs, J. L. (1956). *American pragmatism and education: An interpretation and criticism.* New York: Henry Holt.

Cobb, P. (1994). Where is the mind? Constructivist and sociocultural perspectives on mathematical development. *Educational Researcher, 23*(7), 13–20.

Cobb, P. (2001). Supporting the improvement of learning and teaching in social and institutional context. In S. Carver & D. Klahr (Eds.), *Cognition and instruction: Twenty-five years of progress* (pp. 455-478). Mahway, NJ: Lawrence Erlbaum.

Cobb, P. & Bowers, J. (1999). Cognitive and situated learning perspectives in theory and practice. *Educational Researcher, 28*(2), 4–15.

Cobb, P., Confrey, J., diSessa, A., Lehrer, R., & Schauble, L. (2003). Design experiments in educational research. *Educational Researcher, 32*(1), 9–13.

Cobb, P., Wood, P., Yackel, E., Nicholls, J., Weatley, G., Trigatti, G., et al. (1991). Assessment of a problem-centered second-grade mathematics project. *Journal for Research in Mathematics Education, 11*(1), 3–29.

Cobb, P., Yackel, E., & Wood, T. (1992). A constructivist alternative to the representational view of mind in mathematics education. *Journal for Research in Mathematics Education, 23*(1), 2–33.

Cohen, D. (1995). What is the system in systemic reform? *Educational Researcher, 24*(9), 11–22.

Commager, H. S. (1950). *The American mind: An interpretation of American thought and character since the 1880s.* New Haven, CT: Yale University Press.

Comte, A. (1975). *Auguste Comte and positivism: The essential writings.* New York: Harper & Row (Original work published 1827).

Connolly, W. E. (1987). *Politics and ambiguity.* Madison: University of Wisconsin Press.

Cooley, C. H. (1909). *Social organization: A study of the larger mind.* New York: Charles Scribner's Sons.

Cornbleth, C. & Waugh, D. (1995). *The great speckled bird: Multicultural politics and education policymaking.* New York: St. Martin's Press.

Counts, G. S. (1980). Dare the school build a new social order? In L. Dennis & W. Eaton (Eds.), *William George S. Counts: Educator for a new age* (pp. 98–107). Carbondale: Southern Illinois University Press (Original work published 1932).

Crary, J. (1999). *Suspensions of perception: Attention, spectacle, and modern culture.* Cambridge, MA: MIT Press.

Cremin, L. (1962). *The transformation of the school: Progressivism in American education, 1976–1957.* New York: Alfred A. Knopf.

Cronon, W. (1996). The trouble with wildernesses or getting back to the wrong nature. In W. Cronon (Ed.), *Uncommon ground: Rethinking the human place in nature* (pp. 69–90). New York: W. W. Norton.

Cruikshank, B. (1999). *The will to empower: Democratic citizens and the other subjects.* Ithaca, NY: Cornell University Press.

Dahlberg, G. & Bloch, M. (2006). Is the power to see and visualize always the power to control? In T. Popkewitz, K. Petersson, U. Olsson, & J. Kowalczyk (Eds.), *"The future is not what it appears to be": Pedagogy, genealogy and political epistemology* (pp. 105–123). Stockholm, Sweden: Stockholm Institute of Education Press.

Danziger, K. (1997). *Naming the mind: How psychology found its language.* London: Sage.

Darling-Hammond, L. (1998). Teachers and teaching: Testing policy hypotheses from a National Commission Report. *Educational Researcher, 27*(1), 4–10.

Darling-Hammond, L. (2004). Inequality and the right to learn: Access to qualified teachers in California's public schools. *Teachers College Record, 106*(10), 1936–1966.

David and Lucille Packard Foundation. (2002). Welfare reforms and children. *The Future of Children 12*(1).

Dean, M. (1994). *Critical and effective histories: Foucault's methods and historical sociology.* New York: Routledge.

Deleuze, G. & Guattari, F. (1987). *A thousand plateaus: Capitalism and schizophrenia.* (B. Massumi, Trans.). Minneapolis: University of Minnesota Press.

Deleuze, G. & Guattari, F. (1994). Conceptual personae. Introduction: The question then… (H. Tomlinson & G. Burchell, Trans.). In G. Deleuze (Ed.), *What is philosophy?* (pp. 61–84). New York: Columbia University Press.

Delpit, L. (1995). *Other people's children.* New York: New Press.

Depaepe, M. (1987). Social and personal factors in the inception of experimental research in education (1890–1914). *History of Education 16*(4), 275–298.

Depaepe, M. (1997). Differences and similarities in the development of educational psychology in Germany and the United States before 1945. *Paedagogica Historica, 33*(1), 69–97.

Depaepe, M. et al. (2000). Order in progress: Everyday education practice in primary schools—Belgium: 1880–1970. *Studia Paedagogica, 29.*

DePaul University School of Education. Retrieved 8-02-05 from http://www.depaulteachered.asp.htm

Derrida, J. (2001). *Cosmopolitanism and forgiveness* (M. Dooley & M. Hughes, Trans.). New York: Routledge.

Design-Based Research Collective. (2003). Designed-based research: An emerging paradigm for educational inquiry. *Educational Researcher, 32*(2), 5–8.

Desmond, A., & Moore, J. (1991). *Darwin: The life of a tormented evolutionist.* New York: W. W. Norton.

Dewey, J. (1929a). American education and culture. In J. Ratner (Ed.), *Character and events: Popular essays in social and political philosophy* (Vol. II, pp. 498–503). New York: Henry Holt and Co. (Original work published 1916).

Dewey, J. (1929b). Individuality, equality, and superiority. In J. Ratner (Ed.), *Character and events: Popular essays in social and political philosophy* (Vol. II, pp. 486–492). New York: Henry Holt and Co. (Original work published 1922).

Dewey, J. (1929c). Our educational ideal. In J. Ratner (Ed.), *Character and events: Popular essays in social and political philosophy* (Vol. II, pp. 493–498). New York: Henry Holt and Co. (Original work published 1916).

Dewey, J. (1929d). Philosophy and the social order. In J. Ratner (Ed.), *Character and events: Popular essays in social and political philosophy* (Vol. II, pp. 435–442). New York: Henry Holt (Original work published 1927).

Dewey, J. (1929e) The schools and social preparedness. In J. Ratner, (Ed.), *Character and events popular essays in social and poltiical philosophy* (Vol II, pp. 474–478). New York: Henry Holt (Original work published 1916).

Dewey, J. (1929f). *The sources of a science of education.* New York: Horace Liveright.

Dewey, J. (1998). *How we think: A restatement of the relation of reflective thinking to the educative process.* Boston: Houghton-Mifflin (Original work published 1933).

Diggins, J. P. (1994). *The promise of pragmatism: Modernism and the crisis of knowledge and authority.* Chicago: University of Chicago Press.

do Ó, J. R. (2003) The disciplinary terrains of soul and self-government in the first map of the educational sciences (1879–1911). In P. Smeyers & M. Depaepe (Eds.), *Beyond empiricism: On criteria for educational research.* Studia Paedoagogica 34 (pp. 105–116). Leuven, Belgium: Leuven University Press.

Drost, W. H. (1967). *David Snedden and education for social efficiency.* Madison: University of Wisconsin Press.

Durkheim, E. (1977). *The evolution of educational thought: Lectures on the formation and development of secondary education in France* (P. Collins., Trans.). London: Routledge & Kegan Paul (Original work published 1938).

Dussel, I. (2006). Changing the patterns of social regulation in schools: A look at cohabitation rules in post-crisis Argentina. In T. S. Popkewitz, U. Olsson, & K. Petersson (Eds.), *"The future is not what it appears to be": Pedagogy, geneaology and political epistemology, in honor and in memory of Kenneth Hultqvist* (pp. 124–136). Stockholm, Sweden: Stockholm Institute of Education Press.

Easton, D. (1965). *A systems analysis of political life.* New York: Wiley.

Eisenstadt, S. N. (2000). Multiple modernities. *Daedalus, 129*(1), 1–29.

Eksteins, M. (1985). History and degeneration: Of birds and cages. In J. E. Chamberlin & S. Gilman (Eds.), *Degeneration: The dark side of progress* (pp. 1–23). New York: Columbia University Press.

Elias, N. (1978). *The history of manners: The civilizing process* (E. Jehcott, Trans., Vol. 1). New York: Pantheon (Original work published 1939).

Elias, N. (1992). *Time: An essay.* Cambridge, MA: Oxford University Press.

Eliot, C. (1892–1893). Wherein popular education has failed. *Forum, 14,* 411–428.

Eliot, C. (1905). The fundamental assumptions in the report of the Committee of Ten (1893). *Educational Review,* 325–343.

European Commission. (2006). *Draft common European principles for teacher and trainer competences and qualifications.* Brussels, Belgium: European Commission, Directorate-General for Education and Culture.

Faragher, J. M. (1994). Introduction: "A nation thrown back upon itself": Frederick Jackson Turner and the frontier. In J. M. Faragher (Ed.), *Rereading Frederick Jackson Turner* (pp. 1–11). New Haven, CT: Yale University Press.

Fejes, A. & Nicoll, K. (2007/2008). *Foucault and lifelong learning: Governing the subject.* London: Routledge.

Fendler, L. (2003). Teacher reflection in a hall of mirrors: Historical influences and political reverberations. *Educational Researcher, 32*(3), 3–15.

Ferguson, R. A. (1997). *The American enlightenment, 1750–1820.* Cambridge, MA: Harvard University Press.

Fine, M., Burns, A., Payne, Y. A., & Torre, M. E. (2004). Civics lessons: The color and class of betrayal. *Teachers College Record, 106*(11), 2193–2223.

Foucault, M. (1984). What is the enlightenment? Was ist Aufklärung? In P. Rabinow (Ed.), *The Foucault Reader* (pp. 32–51). New York: Pantheon Books.

Foucault, M. (1991). Governmentality. In G. Burchell, C. Gordon, & P. Miller (Eds.), *The Focault Effect: Studies in Governmentality* (pp. 87–104). Chicago: University of Chicago Press.

Foucault, M. (2003). *Society must be defended. Lectures at the Collège de France, 1975–1976* (M. Bertaini & A. Fontana, Eds.; D. Macey, Trans.). New York: Picador.

Foucault, M. (2005). 24 March, 1982, First hour. In F. Gros (Ed.), *The hermeneutics of the subject: Lectures at the College de France 1981–1982* (G. Burchell, Trans.) (pp. 451–475). New York: Palgrave MacMillan.

Franklin, B. (1986a). *Building the American community: The school curriculum and the search for social control.* New York: Falmer.

Franklin, B. (1986b). The first crusade for learning disabilities: The movement for the education of backward children. In T. Popkewitz (Ed.), *The formation of school subjects: The struggle for creating an American institution* (pp. 190–209). New York: Falmer Press.

Fredrickson, G. (2002). *Racism: A short history.* Princeton, NJ: Princeton University Press.

Freedman, K. (1987). Art education as social production: Culture, society and politics in the formation of the curriculum. In T. Popkewitz (Ed.), *The formation of school subjects: The struggle for creating an American institution* (pp. 63–84). New York: Falmer Press.

Friese, H. & Wagner, P. (2000). Modernity and contingency: Not all that is solid melts into air. In M. Featherstone & S. Lash (Eds.), *Spaces of culture: City, nation, world* (pp. 101-115). London: Sage.

Furstenberg, F. (2006, July 4). Spinning the revolution. *New York Times,* A17.

Ganonkar, D. P. (Ed.). (2001). *Alternative modernities.* Durham, NC: Duke University Press.

Gee, J. (2003). *What video games have to teach us about learning and literacy.* New York: Palgrave Macmillan.

Giddens, A. (1987). *Social theory and modern sociology.* Stanford, CA: Stanford University Press.

Gilroy, P. (2001). *Against race: Imaging political culture beyond the color line.* Cambridge, MA: Harvard University Press.

Gilroy, P. (2006). *After empire: Melancholia or convivial culture.* New York: Routledge.

Glaude, E., Jr. (2000). *Exodus! Religion, race, and nation in early nineteenth-century Black America.* Chicago: University of Chicago Press.

Goodson, I. (1987). *International perspectives in curriculum history.* London: Croom Helm.

Gorski, P. (1999). Calvinism and state-formation in early modern Europe. In G. Steinmetz (Ed.), *State/Culture: State formation after the cultural turn* (pp. 147–181). Ithaca, NY: Cornell University Press.

Greek, C. (1992). *The religious roots of American sociology.* New York: Garland.

Grose, H. (1906). *Alien or Americans? Forward mission study courses, edited under the auspices of the Young People's Missionary Movement.* New York: Easton & Mains.

Grossman, P., Schoenfeld, A., & Lee, C. (2005). Teaching subject matter. In L. Darling-Hammond, J. Bransford, P. LePage, K. Hammerness, & H. Duffy (Eds.), *Preparing teachers for a changing world: What teachers should learn and be able to do* (pp. 201–231). San Francisco: Jossey-Bass.

Grosz, E. (2004). *The nick of time: Politics, evolution, and the untimely.* Durham, NC: Duke University Press.

Gustafson, R. (2005). *Merry throngs and street gangs: The fabrication of whiteness and the worthy citizen in early vocal instruction and music appreciation, 1830–1930.* Unpublished doctoral dissertation, University of Wisconsin-Madison, Madison.

Gustafson, R. (2006). Circulation of the blood and the American public school music curriculum: A means and a metaphor to insure the future. In T. Popkewitz, K. Petersson, U. Olsson, & J. Kowalczyk (Eds.), *"The future is not what it appears to be": Pedagogy, geneaology and political epistemology, in honor and in memory of Kenneth Hultqvist* (pp. 136–158). Stockholm, Sweden: Stockholm Institute of Education Press.

Habermas, J. (1971). *Knowledge and human interest* (J. Shapiro, Trans.). Boston: Beacon Press.

Hacking, I. (1986). Making up people. In T. C. Heller, M. Sosna, & D. E. Wellbery (Eds.), *Reconstructing individualism: Autonomy, individuality, and the self in Western thought* (pp. 222–236, 347–348). Stanford, CA: Stanford University Press.

Hacking, I. (1990). *The taming of chance.* Cambridge, MA: Cambridge University Press.

Hacking, I. (2002). Inaugural lecture: Chair of philosophy and history of scientific concepts at the Collège de France, 16 January 2001. *Economy and Society, 21*(1), 1–14.

Hall, G. S. (1924a). *Adolescence: Its psychology and its relation to physiology, anthropology, sociology, sex, crime, religion, and education* (Vol. 1). New York: Appleton.

Halverson, R. (2004). Accessing, documenting, and communicating practical wisdom: The *phronesis* of school leadership practice. *American Journal of Education, 111*(1), 90–121.

Hamilton, D. (1989). *Towards a theory of schooling.* London: Falmer Press.

Hamilton, D. (1999). The pedagogic paradox (or why no didactics in England?). *Pedagogy, Culture, and Society, 7*(1), 135–152.

Hammerness, K., Darling-Hammond, L., with Grossman, P., Rust, F., & Shulman, L. (2005). The design of teacher education programs. In L. Darling-Hammond, J. Bransford, P. LePage, K. Hammerness & H. Duffy (Eds.), *Preparing teachers for a changing world: What teachers should learn and be able to do* (pp. 390–441). San Francisco: Jossey-Bass.

Hargreaves, A. (2003). *Teaching in the knowledge society: Education in the age of insecurity.* Maindenhead, UK: Open University Press.

Harvey, D. (2000). Cosmopolitanism and the banality of geographical evils. *Public Culture 12*(2), 529–564.

Hayhoe, R. (2000). Redeeming modernity. *Comparative Education Review, 44*(4), 423–439.

Heideking, J. (2000). Implications of the rise of "Confucian" East Asia. *Daedalus, 129*(1), 195–218.

Heilbron, J., Magnusson, L., & Wittrock, B. (Eds.). (1998). *The rise of the social sciences and the formation of modernity: Conceptual change in context, 1750–1805.* Dordrecht, The Netherlands: Kluwer Academic.

Hennon, L. (2000). The construction of discursive space as patterns of inclusion/ exclusion: Governmentality and urbanism in the U.S.A. In T. Popkewitz (Ed.), *Educational knowledge: Changing relationships between the state, civil society, and the educational community* (pp. 243–264). Albany: State University of New York Press.

Hershkowitz, R. & Schwarz, B. (1999). The emergent perspective in rich learning environments: Some roles of tools and activities in the construction of sociomathematical norms. *Educational Studies in Mathematics, 39,* 149–166.

Hidalgo, N., Siu, S., Bright, J., Swap, S., & Epstein, J. (1995). Research on families, schools, and communities: A multicultural perspective. In J. Banks (Ed.), *Handbook of research on multicultural education* (pp. 498–524). New York: Macmillan.

Hirst, P. (1994). The evolution of consciousness: Identity and personality in historical perspective. *Economy and Society, 23*(1), 47–65.

Hofstadter, R. (1955). *The age of reform from Bryan to F.D.R.* New York: Vintage.

Holmes Group, The. (1990). *Tomorrow's schools.* East Lansing, MI: Author.

Hultqvist, K. (2006). The future is already here—as it always has been: The new teacher subject, the pupil, and the technologies of the soul. In T. Popkewitz, K. Petersson, U. Olsson, & J. Kowalczyk (Eds.), *"The future is not what it appears to be": Pedagogy, geneaology and political epistemology, in honor and in memory of Kenneth Hultqvist* (pp. 20–61). Stockholm: Stockholm Institute of Education Press.

Hunt, J. (2003). Forward. National Commission on Teaching and America's Future (2003). *No dream denied: A pledge to America's children* (p. 3). Washington, DC: Author.

Hunter, I. (1988). *Culture and government: The emergence of literary education.* Basingstoke, UK: Macmillan.

Hunter, I. (1994). *Rethinking the school: Subjectivity, bureaucracy, criticism.* New York: St. Martin's Press.

Jack, M. (1989). *Corruption and progress: The eighteenth-century debate.* New York: AMS Press.

Jaguaribe, B. (2001). Modernist ruins: National narratives and architectural forms. In D. P. Gaonkar (Ed.), *Alternative modernities* (pp. 327–349). Durham, NC: Duke University Press.

Jehlen, M. (1986). *American incarnation: The individual, the nation, and the continent.* Cambridge, MA: Harvard University Press.

Joncich, G. M. (1962). Science: Touchstone for a new age in education. In G. M. Joncich (Ed.), *Psychology and the science of education: Selected writings of Edward L. Thorndike* (pp. 1–26). New York: Teachers College Press.

Joncich, G. M. (1968). *The sane positivist: A biography of Edward L. Thorndike.* Middletown, CT: Wesleyan University Press.

Kaestle, C., Damon-Moore, H., Stedman, L. C., & Tinsley, K. (1991). *Literacy in the United States: Readers and reading since 1880.* New Haven, CT: Yale University Press.

Kant, I. (1939). *Perpetual peace* (N. Butler, introduction). New York: Columbia University Press (Original work published 1796).

Kant, I. (1970). Idea for a universal history with a cosmopolitan purpose (H. B. Nisbet, Trans.). In H. Reiss (Ed.), *Kant's political writing* (pp. 41–53). Cambridge, UK: Cambridge University Press (Original work published 1784).

Kazamias, A. (2006). *The Turkish Sisyphus: Atatürk, Islam and the quest for European modernity.* Athens, Greece: Centre of Comparative Education, International Education Policy and Communication.

Kelly, A. (2003). Research as design. *Educational Researcher, 32*(1), 3–4.

Kliebard, H. (1986). *Struggle for the American Curriculum.* London: Routledge and Kegan Paul.

Koselleck, R. (1985). *Futures past: On the semantics of historical time* (K. Tribe, Trans.). Cambridge, MA: MIT Press.

Kowalczyk, J. & Popkewitz, T. S. (2005). Multiculturalism, recognition, and abjection: (Re)-mapping Italian identity. *Policy Futures in Education, 3*(4), 432–435.

Kristeva, J. (1982). *Powers of horror: An essay on abjection* (L. Roudiez, Trans.). New York: Columbia University Press.

Krug, E. (1964). *The shaping of the American high school, 1880–1920.* Madison: University of Wisconsin Press.

Krug, E. (1972). *The shaping of the American high school, 1920–1941* (Vol. 2). Madison: University of Wisconsin Press.

Kuklick, B. (1985). *Churchmen and philosophers: From Jonathan Edwards to John Dewey.* New Haven, CT: Yale University Press.

Kvale, S. (2003). The church, the factory, and the market: Scenarios for psychology in a postmodern age. *Theory and Psychology, 13*(5), 579–603.

Labaree, D. (2004). *The trouble with ED schools.* New Haven, CT: Yale University Press.

Lagemann, E. C. (2000). *An elusive science: The troubling history of education research.* Chicago: University of Chicago Press.

Lampert, M. (1990). When the problem is not the question and the solution is not the answer: Mathematical knowing and teaching. *American Educational Research Journal, 27*(1), 29–63.

Lather, P. (2007). *Getting lost.* Albany: State University of New York Press.

Lawn, M. (2001). Borderless education: Imagining a European education space in a time of brains and networks. *Discourse: Studies in the Cultural Politics of Education, 22*(2), 173–184.

Lesko, N. (2001). *Act your age: A cultural construction of adolescence.* New York: Routledge.

Lindblad, S. & Popkewitz, T. S. (Eds.). (2004). *Educational restructuring: International perspectives on traveling policies.* New York: Information Age.

Lindner, R. (1996). *The reportage of urban culture: Robert Park and the Chicago School* (A. Morris, J. Gaines, & M. Chalmers, Trans.). Cambridge, UK: Cambridge University Press.

Low, V. (1982). *The unimpressible race: A century of educational struggle by the Chinese in San Francisco.* San Francisco: East/West.

Lybarger, M. (1987). Need as ideology: Social workers, social settlements and the social studies. In T. Popkewitz (Ed.), *The formation of the school subjects: The struggle for creating an American institution* (pp. 176–189). New York: Falmer Press.

Maeroff, G. (2003). *A classroom of one: How online learning is changing our schools and colleges.* New York: Palgrave Macmillan.

Mann, H. (1867a). *Lectures and annual reports on education.* Cambridge, MA: Fuller.

Mann, H. (1867b). *Life and works of Horace Mann* (Vol. II). Cambridge, MA: George C. Rand & Avery.

Martin, G. H. (1895). *New standards of patriotic citizenship.* Paper presented at the 34th annual meeting of the National Educational Association, St. Paul, MN.

Marx, A. (2003). *Faith in nation: Exclusionary origins of nationalism.* New York: Oxford University Press.

Mattingly, P. (1977). *The classless profession: American schoolmen in the nineteenth century.* New York: New York University Press.

Mauss, M. (1979). *Sociology and psychology: Essays.* London: Routledge & Kegan Paul (Original work published 1938).

McCalman, I. (2003). *The last alchemist: Count Cagliostro, master of magic in the age of reason.* New York: HarperCollins.

McEneaney, E. (2003). Elements of a contemporary primary school science. In G. S. Drori, J. W. Meyer, F. O. Ramirez, & E. Schofer (Eds.), *Science in the modern world polity: Institutionalization and globalization* (pp. 136–154). Stanford, CA: Stanford University Press.

McKnight, D. (2003). *Schooling: The Puritan imperative and the molding of an American national identity: Education's "errand into the wilderness."* Mahwah, NJ: Lawrence Erlbaum.

McMahan, D. M. (2001). *Enemies of the enlightenment: The French counterenlightenment and the making of modernity.* Oxford, UK: Oxford University Press.

McMahon, D. M. (2006). *Happiness: A history.* New York: Atlantic Monthly Press.

Mead, G. H. (1934). *Mind, self, and society from the standpoint of a social behaviorist.* Chicago: University of Chicago Press.

Mehta, P. B. (2000). Cosmopolitanism and the circle of reason. *Political Theory, 28*(5), 619–639.

Mehta, U. S. (1997). Liberal strategies of exclusion. In F. Cooper & A. Stoler (Eds.), *Tensions of empire: Colonial cultures in a bourgeois world.* Berkeley: University of California Press.

Menand, L. (2001). *The metaphysical club.* New York: Farrar, Straus & Giroux.

Meyer, J. W. (1986). Myths of socialization and of personality. In M. S. Thomas, C. Heller, & D. Wellbery (Eds.), *Reconstructing individualism: Autonomy, individuality, and the self in Western thought* (pp. 208–221). Stanford, CA: Stanford University Press.

Meyer, J. W., Boli, J., Thomas, G., & Ramirez, F. (1997). World society and the nation-state. *American Journal of Sociology, 103*(1), 144–181.

Meyer, J. W. & Jepperson, R. (2000). The "actors" of modern society: The cultural construction of social agency. *Sociological Theory, 18*(1), 100–120.

Meyer, J. W., Kamens, D. H., Benavot, A., Cha, Y.-K., & Wong, S.-Y. (1992). *School knowledge for the masses and national primary curriculum categories in the twentieth century.* Washington, DC: Falmer Press.

Mincu, M. (2006). *Patterns of citizenship and education in post-communist settings: The role of myths, rhetoric, and ideologies.* Paper presented at the BAIC Conference on Diversity and Inclusion, Belfast, Ireland.

Mirzoeff, N. (2005). *Watching Babylon: The war in Iraq and global visual culture.* New York: Routledge.

Monaghan, J. & Saul, W. (1987). The reader, the scribe, the thinker: A critical look at reading and writing instruction. In T. Popkewitz (Ed.), *The formation of the school subjects: The struggle for creating an American institution* (pp. 85–122). New York: Falmer Press.

Moran, B. (2005). *Distilling knowledge: Alchemy, chemistry, and the scientific revolution.* Cambridge, MA: Harvard University Press.

Morrison, T. (1992). *Playing in the dark: Whiteness and the literary imagination.* Cambridge, MA: Harvard University Press.

Murphy, M. (1990). *Blackboard unions: The AFT and the NEA 1900–1980*. Ithaca, NY: Cornell University Press.

National Board for Professional Teaching Standards. (2001). *Adolescence and young adulthood mathematics standards: For teachers of students ages 14–18+* (2nd ed.). Stanford, CA: Author.

National Commission on Excellence in Education (1984). *A nation at risk: The full account*. Cambridge, MA: USA Research.

National Commission on Teaching and America's Future. (1996). *What matters most: Teaching for America's future*. Washington, DC: Author.

National Commission on Teaching and America's Future. (2003). *No dream denied: A pledge to America's children*. Washington, DC: Author.

National Council of Teachers of Mathematics (NCTM). (1989). *Curriculum and evaluation standards for school mathematics*. Reston, VA: Author.

National Council of Teachers of Mathematics (NCTM). (2000). *Principles and standards for school mathematics*. Reston, VA: Author.

National Research Council. (2002). *Scientific research in education*. Washington, DC: Center for Education, Division of Behavioral and Social Sciences and Education, Committee on Scientific Principles for Education Research, National Research Council.

Nelson, B. S., Warfield, J., & Wood, T. (2001). Introduction. In T. Wood, B. S. Nelson, & J. Warfield (Eds.), *Beyond classical pedagogy: Teaching elementary school mathematics* (pp. 5–9). Mahwah, NJ: Lawrence Erlbaum.

Nisbet, R. (1979). *History of the idea of progress*. New York: Basic Books.

No Child Left Behind Act of 2001, 20 U.S.C. §6301. (2002). Public Law 107–110.

Nussbaum, M. (1996). Patriotism and cosmopolitanism: Martha Nussbaum with respondents. In M. Nussbaum & J. Cohen (Eds.), *For the love of country: Debating the limits of patriotism* (pp. 3–17). Boston, MA: Beacon Press.

Nye, D. (1999). *American technological sublime*. Cambridge, MA: MIT Press.

Nye, D. (2003). *America as second creation: Technology and narratives of new beginnings*. Cambridge, MA: MIT Press.

O'Donnell, J. (1985). *The origins of behaviorism: American psychology, 1876–1920*. New York: New York University Press.

Ohanian, S. (1999, May). *One size fits few: The folly of educational standards*. Portsmouth, NH: Heinemann.

Oshinsky, D. (2000, August 26). The Humpty Dumpty of scholarship: American history has broken in pieces: Can it be put together again? *New York Times*, A17, A19.

Pagden, A. (2000). Stoicism, cosmopolitanism, and the legacy of European imperialism. *Constellations, 7*(1), 3–22.

Passavant, P. (2000). The governmentality of discussion. In J. Dean (Ed.), *Cultural studies & political theory* (pp. 115–131). Ithaca, NY: Cornell University Press.

Pocock, J. G. A. (2003). *Machiavellian moment: Florentine political thought and the Atlantic republican tradition*. Princeton, NJ: Princeton University Press.

Pollock, A. (2006, January 17). Custom-made microbes, at your service. *New York Times*, D1, D4.

Popkewitz, T. (1984). *Paradigm and ideology in educational research: The social functions of the intellectual*. London: Falmer Press.

Popkewitz, T. (Ed.). (1987). *The formation of school subjects: The struggle for creating an American institution.* London: Falmer Press.

Popkewitz, T. (1991). *A political sociology of educational reform: Power/knowledge in teaching, teacher education, and research.* New York: Teachers College Press.

Popkewitz, T. (1997). A changing terrain of knowledge and power: A social epistemology of educational research. *Educational Researcher, 26*(9), 5–17.

Popkewitz, T. (1998a). Dewey, Vygotsky, and the social administration of the individual: Constructivist pedagogy as systems of ideas in historical spaces. *American Educational Research Journal, 35*(4), 535–570.

Popkewitz, T. (1998b). *Struggling for the soul: The politics of education and the construction of the teacher.* New York: Teachers College Press.

Popkewitz, T. (2001). Rethinking the political: Reconstituting national imaginaries and producing difference in the practices of schooling. *International Journal of Inclusion, 5*(2–3), 179–207.

Popkewitz, T. (2004a). The alchemy of the mathematics curriculum: Inscriptions and the fabrication of the child. *American Educational Journal, 41*(4), 3–34.

Popkewitz, T. (2004b). Is the National Research Council committee's report on scientific research in education scientific? On trusting the manifesto. *Qualitative Inquiry, 10*(1), 62–78.

Popkewitz, T. (2004c). The reason of reason: Cosmopolitanism and the governing of schooling. In B. Baker & K. Heyning (Eds.), *Dangerous coagulations: The uses of Foucault in the study of education* (pp. 189–224). New York: Peter Lang.

Popkewitz, T. (2004d). Standards and making the citizen legible. *Journal of Learning Sciences, 13*(2), 243–256.

Popkewitz, T. (Ed.). (2005). *Inventing the modern self and John Dewey: Modernities and the traveling of pragmatism in education.* New York: Palgrave Macmillan.

Popkewitz, T. (2006). Education between psychology and religion. In E. Birgitte, K. Nielsen, & M. Nissen (Eds.), *Pædagogisk psykologi—positioner og perspektiver* (pp. 211–240). Frederiksberg, Denmark: Roskilde Universitetsforlag.

Popkewitz, T. & Bloch, M. N. (2001). Administering freedom: A history of the present—Rescuing the parent to rescue the child for society. In K. Hultqvist & G. Dahlberg (Eds.), *Governing the child in the new millennium* (pp. 85–118). New York: Routledge Falmer.

Popkewitz, T. & Brennan, M. (Eds.). (1998). *Foucault's challenge: Discourse, knowledge and power in education.* New York: Teachers College Press.

Popkewitz, T., Franklin, B., & Pereyra, M. (Eds.). (2001). *Cultural history and critical studies of education: Critical essays on knowledge and schooling.* New York: Routledge.

Popkewitz, T. & Gustafson, R. (2002). The alchemy of pedagogy and social inclusion/exclusion. *Philosophy of Music Education Review, 10*(2), 80–91.

Popkewitz, T. & Lindblad, S. (2000). Educational governance and social inclusion and exclusion: Some conceptual difficulties and problematics in policy and research. *Discourse, 21*(1), 5–54.

Popkewitz, T. & Lindblad, S. (2004). Historicizing the future: Educational reform, systems of reason, and the making of children who are the future citizens. *Journal of Educational Change, 5*(3), 229–247.

Porter, A. & Smithson, J. (2001). Are content standards being implemented in the classroom? A methodology and some tentative answers. In S. H. Fuhrman (Ed.), *From the capitol to the classroom: Standards-based reform in the States* (One Hundredth Yearbook of the National Society for the Study of Education, pp. 60–80). Chicago: The University of Chicago Press.

Porter, D. (1991). *Haunted journeys: Desire and transgression in European travel writing.* Princeton, NJ: Princeton University Press.

Porter, T. (1995). *Trust in numbers: The pursuit of objectivity in science and public life.* Princeton, NJ: Princeton University Press.

Qi, J. (2005). A history of the present on Chinese intellectuals: Confucianism and pragmatism. In T. S. Popkewitz (Ed.), *Modernities, inventing the modern self, and education: The traveling of pragmatism and John Dewey* (pp. 255–278). New York: Palgrave Macmillan.

Rabinow, P. (Ed.). (1984). *The Foucault reader.* New York: Pantheon Books.

Rabinow, P. (1999). *French DNA: Trouble in purgatory.* Chicago: University of Chicago Press.

Rajchman, J. (1997). *Constructions.* Cambridge, MA: MIT Press.

Rancière, J. (2004a). *The flesh of words. The politics of writing* (C. Mandell, Trans.). Stanford, CA: Stanford University Press.

Rancière, J. (2004b). *The philosopher and his poor* (J. Drury, C. Oster, & A. Parker, Trans.). Durham, NC: Duke University (Original work published 1983).

Rancière, J. (2004c). *The politics of aesthetics.* Retrieved 01-05-2007 from http://theater.kein.org/node/99

Rancière, J. (2006). *Hatred of democracy* (S. Cororan, Trans.). London: Verso.

Ravitch, D. (Ed.). (1995, October). *Debating the future of American education: Do we need national standards and assessments?* Brookings Dialogues on Public Policy. Washington, DC: Brookings Institute.

Ravitch, D. (1996). *National standards in American education: A citizen's guide.* Washington, DC: Brookings Institute.

Reed, E. (1997). *From soul to mind. The emergence of psychology from Erasmus Darwin to William James.* New Haven, CT: Yale University Press.

Reese, W. (1995). *The origins of the American high school.* New Haven, CT: Yale University Press.

Restivo, S. (1993). The promethean task of bringing mathematics to earth. In S. Restivo, J. P. V. Bendegem, & R. Fischer (Eds.), *Math worlds: Philosophical and social studies of mathematics and mathematics education* (pp. 3–17). Albany: State University of New York Press.

Reuben, J. (1996). *The making of the modern university: Intellectual transformations and the marginalization of morality.* Chicago: University of Chicago Press.

Rockefeller, S. (1991). *John Dewey: Religious faith and democratic humanism.* New York: Columbia University Press.

Rodgers, D. T. (1998). *Atlantic crossings: Social politics in a progressive age.* Cambridge, MA: Belknap Press of Harvard University Press.

Rose, N. (1999). *Powers of freedom: Reframing political thought.* Cambridge, UK: Cambridge University Press.

Rose, N. (2001). Biopolitics in the twenty-first century: Notes for a research agenda. *Distinktion, 3,* 25–44.

Ross, D. (1972). *G. Stanley Hall: The psychologist as prophet.* Chicago: University of Chicago Press.

Ross, D. (1991). *The origins of American social science.* New York: Cambridge University Press.

Ross, E. A. (1920). *Principles of sociology.* New York: Century.

Russell, S. J. (1999). Mathematical reasoning in the elementary grades. In L. Stiff & F. Curcio (Eds.), *Developing mathematical reasoning in grades K–12: 1999 yearbook* (pp. 1–12). Reston, VA: National Council of Teachers of Mathematics.

Schlereth, T. J. (1977). *The cosmopolitan idea in enlightenment thought, its form and function in the ideas of Franklin, Hume, and Voltaire, 1694–1790.* South Bend, IN: University of Notre Dame Press.

Scott, J. (1991). The evidence of experience. *Critical Inquiry, 17,* 773–797.

Scott, J. C. (1998). *Seeing like a state: How certain schemes to improve the human condition have failed.* New Haven, CT: Yale University.

Shapiro, M. (1992). *Reading the postmodern polity: Political theory as textual practice.* Minneapolis: University of Minnesota Press.

Shapiro, M. (1999). *Cinematic political thought: Narrating race, nation and gender.* New York: New York University.

Shapiro, M. (2001). *For moral ambiguity: National culture and the politics of the family.* Minneapolis: University of Minnesota Press.

Shavelson, R., Philips, D., Towne, L., & Feuer, M. (2003). On the science of education design studies. *Educational Researcher, 32*(1), 25–28.

Shibata, M. (2005). *Japan and Germany under the U.S. occupation: A comparative analysis of the post-war education reform.* Lanham, MD: Lexington Books.

Shimakawa, K., (2002). *National abjection: The Asian American body onstage.* Durham, NC: Duke University.

Simon, M. (1995). Reconstructing mathematics pedagogy from a constructivist perspective. *Journal for Research in Mathematics Education, 26*(2), 114–145.

Simon, M. & Masschelein, J. (2006, February 8–10). *The governmentalization of learning and the assemblage of a learning apparatus.* Paper presented at the Foucault and Adult Education/Adult Learning Conference. Linköping, Sweden: Linköping University.

Sklansky, J. (2002). *The soul's economy: Market society and selfhood in American thought, 1820–1920.* Chapel Hill: University of North Carolina Press.

Small, A. W. (1896). *Demands of sociology upon pedagogy.* Paper presented at the 35th annual meeting of the National Educational Association, St. Paul, MN.

Smith, M. & O'Day, J. (1990). Systemic school reform. In *Politics of Education Association Yearbook* (pp. 233–267). New York: Falmer Press.

Sobe, N. (2006). Slavic emotion and vernacular cosmopolitanism: Yugoslav travels to Czechoslovakia in the 1920s and 1930s. In A. Gorsuch & D. Koenker (Eds.), *Turizm: The Russian and East European tourist under capitalism and socialism* (pp. 82–96). Ithaca, NY: Cornell University Press.

Soja, E. (1989). *Postmodern geographies: The reassertion of space in critical social theory.* London: Verso.

Spadafora, D. (1990). *The idea of progress in eighteenth-century Britain.* New Haven, CT: Yale University Press.

Stanic, G. (1987). Mathematics education in the United States at the beginning of the twentieth century. In T. Popkewitz (Ed.), *The formation of the school subjects: The struggle for creating an American institution* (pp. 145–175). New York: Falmer Press.

Steedman, C. (1995). *Strange dislocations: Childhood and the idea of human interiority, 1780–1930.* Cambridge, MA: Harvard University Press.

Steffe, L. & Kieren, T. (1994). Radical constructivism and mathematics education. *Journal for Research in Mathematics Education, 25*(6), 711–734.

Steffe, L. & Kieren, T. (1995). Toward a working model of constructivist teaching: A reaction to Simon. *Journal for Research in Mathematics Education, 26*(2), 146–159.

Steiner-Khamsi, G. (Ed.). (2004). *The global politics of educational borrowing and lending.* New York: Teachers College Press.

Steiner-Khamsi, G. & Stolpe, I. (2006). *Educational import: Local encounters with global forces in Mongolia.* New York: Palgrave Macmillan.

Sutherland, R. & Balacheff, N. (1999). Didactical complexity of computational environments for the learning of mathematics. *International Journal of Computers for Mathematical Learning, 4*, 1–26.

Taguchi, H. (2006). Reconceptualizing early childhood education: Challenging taken-for-granted ideas. In J. Einarsdottir & J. T. Wagner (Eds.), *Nordic childhoods and early education: Philosophy, research, policy, and practice in Denmark, Finland, Iceland, Norway, and Sweden* (pp. 257–287). Charlotte, NC: Information Age.

Taylor, C. (1989) *Sources of the self: The making of modern identity.* Cambridge, MA: Harvard University Press.

Thorndike, E. L. (1921). The psychology of drill in arithmetic: The amount of practice. *Journal of Educational Psychology, 12*(4), 183–194.

Thorndike, E. L. (1923a). *Educational psychology. Volume I: The original nature of man.* New York: Teachers College, Columbia University.

Thorndike, E. L. (1923b). *Educational psychology. Volume II: The psychology of learning.* New York: Teachers College, Columbia University.

Thorndike, E. L. (1935). *The psychology of wants, interests, and attitudes.* New York: Appleton-Century Crofts.

Thorndike, E. L. (1962a). Darwin's contribution to psychology. In G. M. Joncich (Ed.), *Psychology and the science of education: Selected writings of Edward L. Thorndike* (pp. 37–47). New York: Bureau of Publications, Teachers College, Columbia University (Original work published 1909).

Thorndike, E. L. (1962b). Education: A first book. In G. M. Joncich (Ed.), *Psychology and the science of education: Selected writings of Edward L. Thorndike* (pp. 69–83; 141–147). New York: Bureau of Publications, Teachers College, Columbia University (Original work published 1912).

Thorndike, E. L. (1962c). Principles of teaching. In G. M. Joncich (Ed.), *Psychology and the science of education: Selected writings of Edward L. Thorndike* (pp. 55–69). New York: Bureau of Publications, Teachers college, Columbia University (Original work published 1906).

Thorndike, E. L. (1962d). The psychology of arithmetic. In G. M. Joncich (Ed.), *Psychology and the science of education: Selected writings of Edward L. Thorndike* (pp. 83–91). New York: Bureau of Publications, Teachers College, Columbia University (Original work published 1922).

Thorndike, E. L., Cobb, M. V., Orleans, J. S., Symonds, P. M., Wald, E., & Woodyard, E. (1923). *The psychology of algebra.* New York: Macmillan.

Thorndike, E. L. & Woodworth, R. S. (1962). Education as science. In G. M. Joncich (Ed.), *Psychology and the science of education: Selected writings of Edward L. Thorndike* (pp. 48–69). New York: Bureau of Publications, Teachers College, Columbia University (Original work published 1901).

Todorov, T. (1984). *The conquest of America: The question of the other*. Norman: University of Oklahoma Press.

Tönnies, F. (1957). *Community & society [Gemeinschaft und Gesellschaft]* (E. Charles P. Loomis, Trans.). East Lansing: Michigan State University (Original work published 1887).

Tough, P. (2006, November 26). What it takes to make a student. *New York Times Magazine*, Section 6, 44–51, 69–72, 77.

Toulmin, S. (1990). *Cosmopolis: The hidden agenda of modernity*. New York: Free Press.

Tröhler, D. (2000). The global community, religion, and education: The modernity of Dewey's social philosophy. *Studies in Philosophy and Education, 19*, 156–96.

Tröhler, D. (2006). *Max Weber and the Protestant ethic in America*. Unpublished paper, Switzerland Pestalozzianum Research Institute for the History of Education, University of Zurich.

Turner, F. J. (1994). The significance of the frontier in American history. In J. M. Faragher (Ed.), *Rereading Frederick Jackson Turner* (pp. 31–60) New Haven, CT: Yale University Press (Original work published 1893).

U. S. Department of Education (2003). No Child Left Behind. Washington, DC. Retrieved July 16, 2007 from http://www.ed.gov/nclb

U.S. Government Printing Office. (1874). *A statement of the theory of education in the United States of America as approved by many leading educators*. Washington, DC: Author.

Valenzuela, A. (Ed.). (2005). *Leaving children behind: How "Texas-style" accountability fails Latino youth*. Albany: State University of New York Press.

Valero, P. (2003). *Reform, democracy, and mathematics education*. Unpublished doctoral dissertation, Danish University of Education, Copenhagen.

Varela, J. (2000). On the contributions of the genealogical method in the analysis of educational institutions. In T. Popkewitz, B. Franklin, & M. Pereyra (Eds.), *Cultural history and education: Critical studies on knowledge and schooling* (pp. 107–124). New York: Routledge.

Venn, C. (2002). Altered states: Post-enlightenment cosmopolitanism and transmodern socialities. *Theory, Culture and Society, 19*(1–2), 65–80.

Wagner, P. (2001a). *A history and theory of the social sciences*. London: Sage.

Wagner, P. (2001b). *Theorising modernity: Inescapability and attainability in social theory*. London: Sage.

Wald, P. (1995). *Constituting Americans: Cultural anxiety and narrative form*. Durham, NC: Duke University.

Ward, L. F. (1883). *Dynamic sociology, or applied social science, as based upon statistical sociology and the less complex sciences*. New York: D. Appleton.

Warfield, J. (2001). Where mathematics content knowledge matters: Learning about and building on children's mathematical thinking. In T. Wood, B. S. Nelson, & J. Warfield (Eds.), *Beyond classical pedagogy: Teaching elementary school mathematics* (pp. 135–155). Mahwah, NJ: Lawrence Erlbaum.

Weber, M. (1958). *The Protestant ethic and the spirit of capitalism* (T. Parsons, Trans.). New York: Charles Scribner and Sons (Original work published 1904–1905).

Weiss, C. (1993). Shared decision making about what? A comparison of schools with and without teacher participation. *Teachers College Record, 95*(1), 67–92.

Welch, H. G., Woloshin, S., & Schwartz, L. (2007). How two studies on cancer screening led to two results. *New York Times,* March 15. D5.

Westbrook, R. (1991). *John Dewey and American democracy.* Ithaca, NY: Cornell University Press.

Wiebe, R. (1995). *Self-rule: A cultural history of American democracy.* Chicago: University of Chicago.

Wiggins, G. & McTighe, J. (2005). *Understanding by design* (Exp. 2nd ed.). Alexandria, VA: Association for Supervision and Curriculum Development.

Wilford, J. (2006, August 1). Transforming the alchemists [Electronic version]. *New York Times.*

Wisconsin Department of Public Instruction. (2005). *Music and educational reform.* Madison, WI: Author.

Wittgenstein, L. (1966). *The philosophical investigations: A collection of critical essays* (2nd ed.). Notre Dame, IN: University of Notre Dame Press (Original work published 1953).

Wittrock, B. (2000). Modernity: One, none, or many? European origins and modernity as a global condition. *Daedalus, 29*(1), 31–60.

Wong, S. & Chang, S. (Eds.). (1998). *Claiming America: Constructing Chinese American identities during the exclusion era.* Philadelphia: Temple University Press.

Wood, G. (1991). *The radicalism of the American Revolution.* New York: Vintage Books.

Wood, G. (1999, October 7). The American love boat. *New York Review of Books 56*(15), 40–42.

Zeichner, K. (1996). Teachers as reflective practitioners and the democratization of school reform. In K. Zeichner, S. Melnick, & M. Gomez (Eds.), *Currents of reform in preservice teacher education* (pp. 199–214). New York: Teachers College Press.

Author Index

Subject Index